MILLER'S

COLLECTING MODERN
BOOKS

COLLECTING MODERN
BOOKS

CATHERINE PORTER

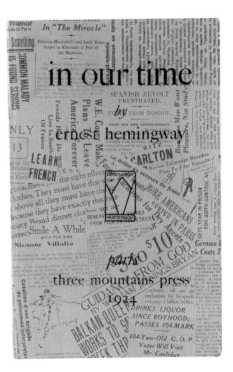

Miller's Collecting Modern Books

Catherine Porter

First published in Great Britain in 2003 by Miller's,
a division of Mitchell Beazley,
imprints of Octopus Publishing Group Ltd,
2–4 Heron Quays, London E14 4JP

Miller's is a registered trademark of Octopus Publishing Group Ltd

Commissioning editor: Anna Sanderson
Executive art editor: Rhonda Fisher
Project editor: Peter Taylor
Design: Jester Designs
Editor: Catherine Blake
Proofreader: Kim Richardson
Indexer: Sue Farr
Picture research: Emma O'Neill
Production: Sarah Rogers
Special photography: Ken Adlard

The publishers will be grateful for any information that will assist them in keeping future
editions up to date. While every care has been taken in the preparation of this book, neither the
author nor the publisher can accept any liability for any consequence arising from the use thereof,
or the information contained therein. Values shown should be used as a guide only,
as prices vary according to geographical location and demand.

ISBN 1 84000 723 0
A CIP catalogue record for this book is available from the British Library
Set in Minion and Trade Gothic
produced by toppan printing co., (hk) ltd
printed and bound in china

Contents

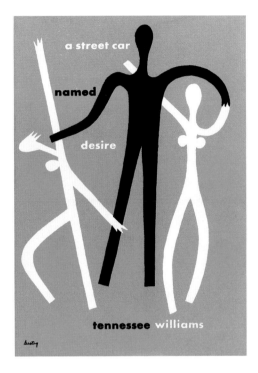

1

Foreword

I would never advise anyone to collect books – or anything else for that matter – purely for investment. But I recently asked a friend and book collector in North America how he had managed to acquire such beautiful copies of first editions of the modern authors he was collecting. "Look at me," he cried. "Twenty years ago I was the toast of the town. Today? I'm broke. I never believed in all that flash-money, so I spent it on getting the best possible copies of my favourite books…" His star in the entertainment world had waned, and meanwhile he had spent his money two ways: half on the stock market, and half on his first love, book collecting. As others might spend on extending their house, on holidays, or motor cars, so my friend had derived enormous pleasure from buying books. Now he had been almost "wiped out", he said, in the decline of the stock market at the turn of the millennium. He was of course far from being truly broke. Nevertheless, with the fall in share prices, the library he has accumulated embodies not just his life's greatest pleasure but also his best investment.

To enjoy collecting, your chosen field has to get under your skin. Modern literary first editions and manuscripts are doubly attractive to many of us in the English-speaking world because they represent one of the few remaining fields where there is still a reasonable abundance of supply (unlike, for instance, early 16th- or 17th-century works) and we have a natural affinity with the key authors and works. As time progresses, perhaps fewer of us will have actually read all the books, but we will probably have seen the film, the stage-play or the TV adaptation. This very accessibility fuels interest and sharp price-increases in certain areas (the first editions of Jane Austen or the Brontë sisters, for instance), which brings its own problems for the novice collector. But at the same time there are less fashionable areas that might be fertile territory for a passionate collector with half an eye to a good long-term bet.

Why people collect and why it is important

There are many obvious reasons why it is important that first editions and manuscripts are kept safe in some form, often by institutions. On one level, they are cultural objects we must preserve in order for us to understand our past, and on another they are often the

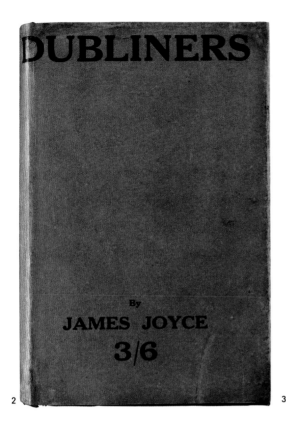

A BOY'S WILL

BY
ROBERT FROST
AUTHOR OF "NORTH OF BOSTON"

NEW YORK
HENRY HOLT AND COMPANY
1915

2   3

only existing texts of some of the greatest writings ever produced.

Remarkably, very important discoveries of texts still occur, although few believed they could have survived. For instance, in the course of less than 18 months between the end of 2000 and the middle of 2002 three separate major discoveries of papers relating to James Joyce's *Ulysses* were made. All were sold either at auction or by private treaty. The status of the previously available drafts of this text, perhaps the greatest novel of the 20th century, had been the subject of intense critical debate for decades. The last fragment of the text to have appeared was in the early 1960s. Now these new discoveries suddenly produced at least 19 further separate drafts of various chapters, which will overturn most accounts of the novel written in the last 40 years, and occupy scholars for decades to come. Aside from their textual importance these manuscripts, with their overlapping layers of drafts with revisions and annotations, were all extraordinarily beautiful objects to look at, vividly capturing the creative process. Two individual chapters of *Ulysses* were sold at auction for more than £750,000

1 James Joyce. *Chamber Music.* 1907. The first issue, inscribed by Joyce in the month of publication to his best friend and (later) betrayer and "Judas" Vincent Cosgrave. **£25,000–35,000/$40,000–56,000**. The first printing comprised 509 copies, with fewer than 50 in the first binding, of which about 15 remain known today.

2 James Joyce. *Dubliners.* 1914. In the very scarce dust-jacket, this copy inscribed by Joyce to his publisher Crosby Gaige **£100,000–150,000/$160,000–240,000**. Ordinary copy in red cloth, £3,000–5,000/$4,800–8,000.

3 Robert Frost. *A Boy's Will.* New York, 1915. First American edition of the author's first book, inscribed to Frederick B. Adams Jnr, **£1,000–1,500/$1,600–2,400**

($1,125,000) each; the other archive, with at least 17 further chapters and additional material – discovered beneath a pile of worthless papers in an old box in a storehouse – was sold for £8,000,000 ($12,000,000) to the National Library of Ireland.

But even when texts have been widely disseminated, and no new discoveries of early manuscript drafts are ever likely to be made again, the earliest version or edition of a work has a unique allure. But what is this allure? Perhaps it lies in our desire to engage with the original text as it was at the moment (in its printed form, at least) of its first worldly manifestation. There is also a sensory pleasure – the touch and smell of a historic literary object. Book-collecting may be unique in this respect, since the simple physical process of handling a book, turning its pages, even reading it (though not too much) is a form of total interaction that can rarely be repeated with other collected objects.

Getting involved

There is perhaps no better advice than that proffered by the American collector Frederick B. Adams, Jnr, who started acquiring books in 1928 (his first book was the signed limited edition of Virginia Woolf's *Orlando*) and who was still assiduously cultivating his collection at his death in January 2001. When he was interviewed by a newspaper in the 1950s he simply said, "Collect from the heart." You don't need lofty motives, you just need an author, a period, a subject, an illustrator or some other interest that has touched you in some way to give you a way in and your first purchase. You may have a friend who has introduced you to an area, you may have an abiding passion for a subject that recalls your childhood, or you may have developed an interest in a particular country or culture, perhaps

having travelled there. It may just be an extension of your professional interest arising from your occupation (a number of medics collect medical books, for instance). Whatever it is, use it as your primary motivation rather than an urge for financial reward, or a desire to invest.

Fred Adams became passionate about a select group of English and American writers, some with little in common apart from his love of their work: they included the Shropshire novelist Mary Webb, Ernest Hemingway, Virginia Woolf, the American mid-West writer Willa Cather and poets Robert Frost and A.E. Housman. He sought to collect each author as extensively as possible, including the first book edition, the first publication in periodicals, special inscribed (or "association" copies) and then – the brave leap so often baulked at by more timid collectors – letters and autograph manuscripts. To explore

4 Graham Greene. *Brighton Rock*. 1938. First English edition, in dust-jacket (this copy with some restoration) **£20,000–25,000/ $32,000–40,000**. The first edition, published one month earlier in New York, in dust jacket, £800–1,200/$1,280–1,920. First English edition without dust jacket, £300–500/$480–800.

5 Graham Greene. *After Two Years*. Anacapri, 1949. One of 25 privately printed copies, inscribed by Greene to his mistress's sister. **£20,000–25,000/$32,000–40,000**

4

5

his subjects in such depth made, he felt, for a particularly rich collection. As is so often the case, this also made for a substantial long-term investment: when the library was sold at auction at Sotheby's London in November 2001 it made over £2 million.

An early lesson learnt by Fred Adams might be summarized as "buying the real thing", and is the straight-forward ability to differentiate between a book inscribed after the event by an author compared with one executed, as it were, genuinely and in the heat of the moment. After a reading by the American poet Robert Frost at Yale in the 1920s Adams summoned courage to ask the writer to inscribe a copy of his first book, *A Boy's Will*. But it immediately became the last time, as he explained, "that he ever inscribed to me an edition published before the beginning of our friendship, since I feel a certain disdain for artificial or post-facto inscriptions, and have never attended an autographing party in a bookshop". All of the presentation copies he acquired from this point were either to close friends of the authors, members of their family, or other writers.

Highspot collecting

There is another, increasingly popular method of collecting, which is to concentrate not on single authors but on highlights or, as they are known in the US, "highspots". Collectors seek one key book by an author rather than all of his or her works: examples are Aldous Huxley's *Brave New World* and Joseph Heller's influential novel *Catch-22*, the title of which became a defining post-war American catch-phrase. Available for less than £300/$450 at the beginning of the 1990s, it now inhabits a space with other post-war classics, such as J.D. Salinger's *The Catcher in the Rye* or Jack Kerouac's *On the Road*, and would normally fetch £3,000–4,000/$4,500–6,000 at auction. Heller's own densely annotated copy for a possible stage adaptation made $88,000 (£58,700) in New York in October 2002, and is an interesting example of a first edition with unique authorial association.

Highspot collecting is often based around a "canon" established by an authority in the field, normally a printed work listing those works that aspire to the compiler's standards. Examples of such authorities are Cyril Connolly's *One Hundred Books from the Modern Movement* and Carmen Callil and Colm Toibin's *The Modern Library: the 200 best novels in English since 1950*. Another similar approach would be to collect prize-winning novels: Booker Prize winners, or winners of other prizes like the Guardian Fiction or Orange Prize.

6

7

6 and **7** Vladimir Nabokov. *Lolita*. Paris, 1955. Two volumes in the original wrappers, inscribed by Nabokov to Graham Greene **£120,000–160,000/$192,000–256,000.** Ordinary copy, £2,000–3,000/$3,200–4,800.

Such authoritative lists can be very useful starting points for a collector, but it is perhaps even more rewarding if you develop your own interests and establish your own personal canon.

Determinants of value

There are some key factors that affect value and should be borne in mind before you buy:

1) **Is the book complete?** This is less of a problem with modern books, but it does occasionally happen that half-titles are missing from modern first editions, or end-papers have been replaced. Such preliminary or supplementary leaves are considered integral to the book's completeness by collectors. With illustrated and moving picture books, it is important to ensure that all illustrations are present.

2) **Condition.** It is very important to keep an eye out for tears or "chips" on dust-jackets, and any restoration. Repairs to its jacket can significantly enhance a book's appearance, but they should be acknowledged by the vendor. It is sometimes advisable to take jackets out of their protective plastic covers when they are on view in an auction, or in a bookshop, to look for signs of restoration. The loss of part of the original jacket will lower the value (slightly or more considerably, depending on the extent), but at the same time a copy in a jacket with just a little restoration is far preferable to one in a heavily torn or chipped jacket.

3) **Issue points.** Be aware that sometimes seemingly identical copies can have what are termed "issue points" that can decrease or increase value. For example, the first edition of Ian Fleming's *Live and Let Die* comes with a dust-jacket on the inner flap of which there is sometimes a note about the cover design, and sometimes there is not. Without the note (adjudged the earlier state), it can fetch £3,000–5,000/$4,500–7,500; but with the note, it is very much the poor relation, fetching often only a few hundred pounds. With any issue points, do not be afraid to check with an expert.

4) **The special association or presentation copy.** This can have a truly transformative effect on what is otherwise quite an ordinary copy of a first edition. For instance, any book by Graham Greene bearing an inscription, allusion to or connection with his mistress Catherine Walston (his anguished affair with her was the basis for his novel *The End of the Affair*) commands a significant premium. A related example is the uncorrected proof copy of the same novel, which Greene sent to his friend Evelyn Waugh for review, annotated by his comments. The strength of the market in this area is demonstrated by the price this book

fetched at auction in London in 1996 (£18,000 [$27,000]); healthy enough, but comfortably surpassed in New York in 2002 ($45,000 [£30,000]).

More dramatically, there is the case of the first (Paris) edition of Vladimir Nabokov's (in)famous novel *Lolita*, inscribed by the author to Greene in the year it was finally published in England and the US, after Greene himself had very much championed and defended the work. Available in the book trade in the early 1990s for under £20,000 ($30,000), it was subsequently sold in New York in October 2002 for $240,000 (£160,000). Or, finally, James Joyce's first regularly published book *Chamber Music*, inscribed in the month of publication to his friend but later betrayer "Judas" Vincent Cosgrave, sold in London in 1994 for £11,000 ($16,500) but then fetched $50,000 (£33,300), also in New York in 2002. All these examples were part of a collection of mainly unique inscribed, presentation or association items assembled by the American collector Roger Rechler, sold at Christie's New York in October 2002. This collection was assembled in the space of just a few years, but the quality of the copies and their associations ensured that the sale still exceeded expectations by fetching over $6 million.

It still occasionally happens that inscriptions or associations are missed by booksellers or auction experts. So opportunities do sometimes arise to pick up a fabulous association copy for a bargain.

5) **Provenance.** This is simply the previous history and ownership of a particular book or manuscript, and it can have a substantial effect on price. Many collectors seek out copies once owned by famous collectors.

6) **Binding.** For collectors of modern books, the chief requirement is simply to acquire books in their original cloth bindings. Modern books that have been rebound in fancy leather have usually been poor copies in damaged cloth or with torn dust-jackets. Of course, there are sometimes specially sanctioned limited editions of regularly published books bound in special bindings by the publishers, which have a steadily increasing value. An example would be the only limited edition "James Bond" book, *On Her Majesty's Secret Service*, limited to 250 copies in quarter vellum and signed by Ian Fleming (worth £2,000–3,000/$3,600–4,800).

7) Finally, **illustration,** to be borne in mind for children's and illustrated books in particular. The artist may be more sought-after than the author, or a later edition of a classic text may be collectable because of the illustrations.

Any of these key determinants combine with the degree of rarity of a particular copy to supply its market value. Be aware that rarity alone is not a sufficient guarantor of worth. For instance, there is a number of extremely limited editions of works by now forgotten poets from the first half of the 20th century (one of ten copies, one of 20 copies, etc.), and these, although apparently rare, are no longer desired by serious collectors.

Trends and developments

One of the enjoyable aspects of collecting contemporary books is trying to catch a future "classic" work or "master" author at an early stage, when their books are still relatively cheap. If you had bought Virginia Woolf's *Mrs Dalloway* on publication day on 14 May 1925, for instance, it would have cost you 7s. 6d.; a copy was sold at auction in London on 6 November 2001 for £12,000 (with the all-important dust-jacket). A contemporary reader could have picked up the first edition of T.S. Eliot's *The Waste Land*, published in New York in December 1922, at $1.50; a copy was sold in an American auction in February 2001 for $20,000 (£13,300). However, for every Eliot and Woolf there has been an author such as John Galsworthy, whose works (the success of *The Forsyte Saga* notwithstanding) fetch little more than they did in the 1920s. How can one predict who among the current crop of authors will be seen as masters of their art in years to come?

Recently, something unprecedented has happened: the market has not waited for the dust to settle before attributing to a work or author classic or semi-legendary status. Traditionally the collecting market has remained somewhat isolated from the huge media hype that often now accompanies publication. Yet within three years of the first appearance of *Harry Potter and the Philosopher's Stone*, in 1997, the collecting interest in this book had exploded to such an extent that astonishing prices were being paid for good copies: $14,000 (£9,330) in the spring of 2000, on an international auction site, and £11,000 ($16,500) in July 2001 (together with the three subsequent volumes published so far in the series). The print-

8

9

10

11

From satin cases poured in rich profusion;
In vials of ivory and coloured glass
Unstoppered, lurked her strange synthetic perfumes,
Unguent, powdered, or liquid—troubled, confused
And drowned the sense in odours; stirred by the air
That freshened from the window, these ascended
In fattening the prolonged candle-flames,
Flung their smoke into the laquearia,
Stirring the pattern on the coffered ceiling.
Huge sea-wood fed with copper
Burned green and orange, framed by the coloured stone,
In which sad light a ~~coloured~~ dolphin swam.
Carver
9

8 and **9** T.S. Eliot. *The Waste Land.* Hogarth Press, 1923. First English edition, inscribed by Eliot to the poet and novelist Richard Aldington; with autograph corrections **£70,000–100,000/ $112,000–160,000**. Ordinary copy, £1,500–2,000/$2,400–3,200. The first edition, New York, 1922, has various issue points to check. A first issue, £1,200–1,600/$1,920–2,560.

10 Virginia Woolf. *Night and Day.* 1919. In the rare dust-jacket **£25,000–35,000/$40,000–56,000**. Ordinary copy, £300–500/$480–800.

11 Hart Crane. *The Bridge.* Paris, 1930. One of 50 copies on Japanese vellum signed by Crane **£12,000–16,000/ $19,200–25,600**. Ordinary edition of 200 copies, £600–800/$960–1,280.

runs for the first edition of volumes 2–4 have been 10,000, 15,000 and (extraordinarily) 1 million copies respectively. The rarity value is therefore entirely compressed in the first title.

The lesson for the budding collector in this new age of "instant classics" is difficult to assess. Authors of the Modernist period (roughly 1880 to the present day) have acquired their reputation by critical and popular consensus over time, gradually emerging as the most heavily collected and therefore most highly valued. There is, then, a mixture of "high Modernism" and popular, more "accessible" classics in the list of first edition highlights or highspots sought by most collectors. On the one hand, the defining works of writers such as Virginia Woolf, T.S. Eliot, James Joyce and even Gertrude Stein command great attention. Some of Stein's works, by no means universally popular and often esoteric, remain very desirable amongst collectors: her experimental second book *Portrait of Mabel Dodge*, for instance, achieved $15,000 (£22,500) at auction in New York in October 2002. On the other hand – although often in a slightly lower price bracket – there are popular or cult novels such as Harper Lee's *To Kill a Mockingbird* and Anthony Burgess' *A Clockwork Orange*, or established children's classics by authors such as Beatrix Potter and A.A. Milne.

Some works, F. Scott Fitzgerald's *The Great Gatsby*, for instance, transcend both categories and consequently achieve among the very highest prices for a regular first edition in a dust-jacket ($140,000 [£93,300] in New York in autumn 2002). If you add to all this notoriety a movie tie-in (Vladimir Nabokov's *Lolita*, for example) you can expect a further surge of demand and interest.

An area that seems to have been relatively neglected in recent years is modern poetry, T.S. Eliot and a few other Olympians excepted. Interestingly, the increased appetite amongst collectors for "difficult" works such as Joyce's *Finnegans Wake* seems to have been accompanied by a levelling-off of interest in the poetry of masters such as Basil Bunting, Wallace Stevens, Robert Lowell, or John Ashbery. These are poets who are perhaps perceived as lacking a strong central narrative (epic or otherwise) that would make them more memorable. A re-evaluation over time might bring some of these neglected writers to the fore again.

Fruitful ground for collectors might lie in such a direction. Collectors have not necessarily had to compete at high price levels to assemble a world-beating collection. Some, without possessing huge resources, but always possessed of a passion for their field and a tenaciousness in pursuing their bibliophilic interests, have quietly and steadily amassed concentrated or wide-ranging collections. Sometimes these collections have subsequently been sold at auction for remarkably large sums, and I can personally recall the astonishment of widows or former partners at the prices fetched, when they had previously seen their loved one pursue their hobbies diligently but with no real thought of their investment potential.

Whatever your particular area of interest, the best advice would seem to be to collect with a similar degree of attentiveness and intensity. One thinks again of Frederick Adams' dictum, "collect from the heart". Walter Benjamin also comes to mind, when he wrote, in "Unpacking My Library": "inside [the collector] there are spirits, or at least genii, which have seen to it that for a collector – and I mean a real collector, a collector as he ought to be – ownership is the most intimate relationship one can have to objects. Not that they come alive in him; it is he who lives in them" ("Unpacking My Library", translated by Harry Zohn, collected in *Illuminations*, edited by Hannah Arendt, New York, 1968).

Peter Selley
Sotheby's Book Department

Captions to illustrations

The general style of the captions is to provide the name of the author, followed by the title, place of publication if not London, date and description of illustrations or limitation (if relevant). Books are first editions unless so stated. In Illustrated Books (pages 114–31) the name of the artist precedes the author; in Fine Printing (pages 132–43) the press or typographer precedes the author; and in Binding (pages 144–51) the binder precedes the author. In English and American Literature (pages 26–81) dust-jackets are mentioned when present, but in Children's Books (pages 82–113) and Illustrated Books, although not mentioned, as a general rule they are present on books post-1940.

Note on prices provided in this guide

The figures provided for the books illustrated in this guide are auction sale-room estimates. The estimates can of course be exceeded (sometimes very considerably) for different issues, copies in superlative condition or for those with additional attributes such as authorial inscriptions, special bindings or interesting provenance. For many regular items booksellers' prices as seen in catalogues, at book fairs or on the Internet are often significantly higher, although this price differential is subject to wide variation. For instance, new "benchmark" prices are often established at auction for particularly rare or unique books, exceeding both previous estimates and dealers' asking prices.

The pound/dollar conversion is £1= US$1.6.

How to Buy and Sell Books

The principal ways of buying and selling are through auctions, booksellers (operating from a shop or by appointment from home), book fairs and through the Internet (see page 19). There are organizations such as the Antiquarian Booksellers' Association (ABA) and Provincial Booksellers' Fairs Association (PBFA) in the UK and the Antiquarian Booksellers' Association of America (ABAA), through which dealers and book fair dates and venues can be located (see Useful Addresses on page 156 for details). All three organizations publish handbooks listing members, specializations, and glossaries.

Auction houses range from major international companies such as Sotheby's and Christie's with large specialist book departments in London and New York, to smaller specialist auction houses, such as Bloomsbury Book Auctions in London and Swann Galleries in New York, who sell mainly books and related material. The larger auction houses have specialist departments with several sales a year run by experts who concentrate on one area alone, and therefore know their field, but the books are costlier. The smaller houses tend to be run by staff with a wider general knowledge and will offer books at lower price levels. These auction houses act as agent between seller and buyer, taking commission from the former and premium from the latter. Commission is usually between 6 per cent and 15 per cent (although this is negotiable on a larger consignment) and premium ranges from 10 per cent to 20 per cent. This premium should always be taken into account when bidding in an auction: the price at which the hammer falls is not the final price. Auctions provide an element of competition, which can push the final price way beyond a pre-sale estimate if two parties are determined to battle over a book on the day.

Buying at auction need not be a daunting prospect. Informative catalogues are available well in advance, the experts will provide condition reports, viewing usually lasts several days, during which the books can be carefully inspected, and there is a short period after the sale in which they can be returned if found faulty. Read the small print in the catalogue to understand your rights and the process of buying. Auction houses request proof of identification and bank references prior to registration for bidding. A paddle will be supplied with a number which should be raised clearly when bidding, and then lowered. Collectors often instruct dealers to bid on their behalf at auction, paying an additional commission to the dealer (usually of 10 per cent). If bidding on your own behalf it is wise to set an upper limit and be prepared to walk away if this is exceeded – although if a book is really scarce, in exceptional condition or with important associations, you may have to be flexible.

The majority of collectors acquire their books through book dealers, either directly from their shop or through the Internet. Booksellers during the 18th and 19th centuries would have sold old and new books, published titles themselves and sold prints, games and stationery. Specialization occurred at the beginning of the 20th century as the number of books published escalated. There are still a few large general second-hand or antiquarian bookshops, some of which also sell new books, but the majority of dealers now specialize, or work from home with viewing by appointment or through the Internet. With catalogues and Internet access one can build up a rapport with a dealer and find a teacher, confidant, and friend – maybe one who will offer early viewing of new stock. By asking a dealer to act for you at auction you can benefit from their knowledge and expertise, and from their access to relevant reference books for checking issue points and other pertinent bibliographical information. Many dealers are happy to share their knowledge and love of books with someone eager to learn, but there will always be a few who prefer to keep some of their expertise to themselves – it is their business, they will reason.

For the collector the growing number of book fairs will provide an unparalleled opportunity for viewing a huge choice of books, a choice not even rivalled yet by the Internet. At fairs, books can be picked up, handled and checked in minute detail.

1 Cecil Court, just off the Charing Cross Road in London, is home to many antiquarian and second-hand bookshops, print and map shops.

Catalogue Entries

A typical auction catalogue entry:

781 TOLKIEN, J.R.R. The Hobbit. *George Allen & Unwin, 1937*

8vo, FIRST EDITION, FIRST ISSUE, ("Dodgeson" corrected in ink on inside lower flap of dust-jacket), PRESENTATION COPY INSCRIBED BY THE AUTHOR, 10 illustrations and pictorial endpapers by the author, 2 pages advertisements, original pictorial green cloth, original pictorial dust-jacket, *adhesive tape marks to endpapers, fore-edge slightly spotted, dust-jacket frayed at head and foot of spine* References: Hammond and Anderson A3

£25,000–35,000

Author's (or artist's) surname listed first followed by initials or forename and title where relevant. If the name is only present in the book as initials or as a pseudonym then the full name or real name will be given either in square brackets or inverted commas.

The **title of the book** is followed by details of place of publication, publisher, and date. English books are usually assumed to have been published in London. If the date is not printed in the book and is known only from bibliographical reference it will be added in square brackets.

Size and edition statement is then provided with limitation if relevant. Often the **issue points** are clarified here.

Special features such as presentation inscriptions, signature or inserted manuscript material will then be noted.

Illustrations are listed and described.

Binding is described. For modern books such as this, "original" is the keyword, and the dust-jacket is listed here.

Condition is described, with internal followed by external. More detailed condition reports can be obtained.

Price: auction houses will suggest a price band based on previous copies sold at auction. This is a guide and may be exceeded or not reached. At auction a reserve is usually agreed with the vendor and if the bidding does not reach this level the book will remain unsold.

References: bibliographical information referred to.

A bookseller's catalogue entry:

15 BROOKE, Leslie (illustrator). Robert H. Charles (author) A Roundabout Turn. *London, Frederick Warne And Co. Ltd. 1930*

Square 8vo. Original burnt-orange cloth, pictorially decorated in brown with a design of a toad to the upper board, lettered in gilt at spine and upper cover, decorated endpapers; preserved and protected by the original dust-wrappers, repeating the same design; pp. [48]; with 4 fine full-colour plates and 25 glorious black-and-white illustrations; a very fine copy in a similar wrapper; exceedingly scarce.

First edition. A limited edition of only 65 numbered copies, signed by Leslie Brooke, of which this is example number 51. The story, cleverly written in verse, tells the tale of a toad who visits the fair.

£398.00

Booksellers' catalogue descriptions can be more subjective with the description of both the book itself and its condition given in more detail. Some booksellers provide the bare minimum of information necessary to list the books for sale, others supply informative description and personal footnotes on the importance of the book.

The Book

The size or format of a book is expressed by the number of times a single sheet of paper is folded into the sections which, when gathered and sewn, make up the finished volume. The sizes of a sheet will vary but never the number of folds (generally the size of sheets has increased over the years), and once you have mastered the terminology, it will be easier to understand the physical description of a book in a catalogue. There are other sizes in use, but these are becoming increasingly uncommon, and usually indicate a variation within one size (royal 8vo, crown 8vo). Sometimes books will be measured in inches or millimetres, especially if extra large or small, to provide a more accurate description.

Folio   1 fold 2 leaves   Fo. or 2o

Quarto   2 folds 4 leaves   4to

Octavo   3 folds 8 leaves   8vo

Duodecimo "twelvemo"   4 folds 12 leaves   12mo

Sextodecimo "sixteenmo"   5 folds 16 leaves   16mo

Vicesimo-quarto "twentyfourmo"   6 folds 24 leaves   24mo

Tricesimo-secundo "thirtytwomo"   7 folds 32 leaves   32mo

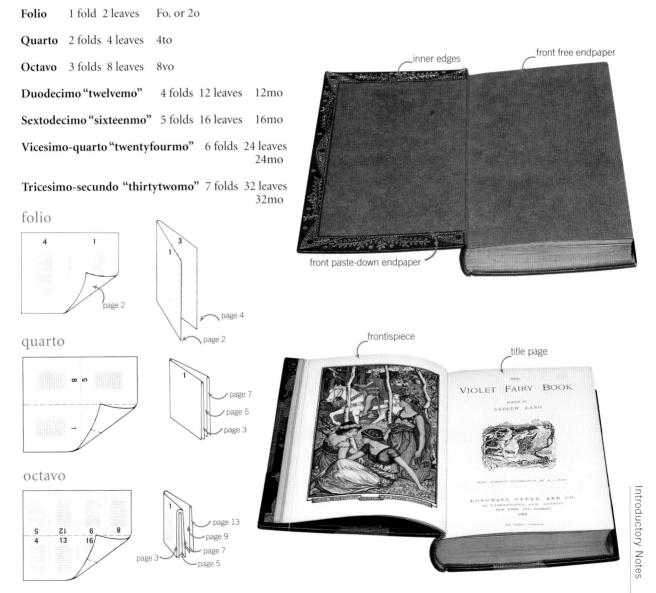

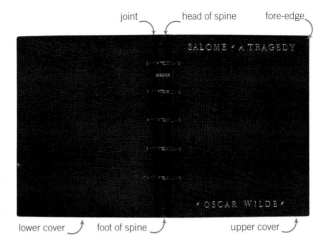

Original Illustration Processes

Today the majority of books are illustrated through photo-mechanical means of reproduction, with original processes being used in small print-runs only. The earliest form of illustration in the printed book was the simple woodcut. Over the centuries, engraving on wood matured and developed into a highly effective form of illustration. Engraving on metal was first used in the 16th century but the technique was not fully utilized until the 17th century. Lithography was invented at the end of the 19th century although another 30 years passed before the autolithograph was fully appreciated in the 1930s. Colour was initially added to illustrations by hand, with great advances being made in the printing of colour at the end of the 19th century. The four-colour printing process revolutionized illustration in the early part of the 20th century and by the 1920s the French process of pochoir, adding colour by hand through stencils, had been adopted by the Curwen Press (see pages 124–127). The major illustration processes in use during the 20th century are explained and demonstrated below. There are three principal types: relief, intaglio, and planographic.

RELIEF PROCESSES are those techniques in which the area to be inked is raised above that which is to remain white. They include the woodcut and wood-engraving.

Woodcut

Initially a drawing is made on a smooth block of soft wood, such as pear, sycamore, cherry or beech, which is cut lengthwise along the grain. The lines of the design are left untouched and the wood is cut away on either side with a knife or a chisel for larger areas, leaving a raised image that will retain the ink. The block is then inked, the paper laid over the design and pressure applied either by hand or with a printing press. Woodcuts were the earliest form of illustration to be used in Europe, appearing at the end of the 14th century. The technique had become less popular by the end of the 16th century but was revived at the end of the 19th century by William Morris for the borders of his Kelmscott Press books and was later used by artists such as Paul Gauguin, Edvard Munch, and the German Expressionists.

Wood-engraving

Similar to a woodcut, but the drawing is usually made on a block of hard wood such as box, which is cut across the grain and less likely to splinter. The design is cut with a burin (a steel rod with a sharpened tip) rather than a knife, so that a greater degree of delicacy in outline and

shading can be achieved. The fine lines are lower than the surface that carries the ink and they print white. As the engraver works, white chalk will often be rubbed into the lines to clarify the design. The first artist to explore this technique fully was Thomas Bewick in the late 18th century, and it has been used ever since. Wood-engravings were printed in colour by using separate blocks for each colour or by adding one colour at a time, the lightest first. Edmund Evans perfected this process with his toy books for children in the late 19th century. During the 19th century commercial wood-engravers would translate an artist's drawing on to the wood; this was a successful technique, but one that artists ultimately found unsatisfactory. Wood-engraving as an original form of illustration was revived in 1910 by Noel Rooke and Eric Gill, and it became the most successful and widely used illustration process for the limited edition private press books of the 20th century (see pages 121–3).

In the INTAGLIO PROCESS, the surface to be inked is lower than the areas remaining blank. The surface is usually of metal, copper or steel, although linoleum, celluloid or wood can be used. Copper came into general use around 1520, but does not wear well; in the 1820s, with larger print-runs required, steel was chosen for its more durable printing surface. However, steel is hard to engrave, and today copper is more often used, being faced with steel after the surface has been engraved. The ink is applied with a roller and forced into the grooves. The surface of the plates is wiped clean and plate and paper pressed together, forcing the paper into the grooves to receive the ink.

Engraving

A burin is used to cut a design on the metal plate, and the rough edges are removed with a scraper. The technique was first used for printing on paper in the second quarter of the 15th century in Germany and Italy, remaining predominantly a method of reproducing original work until the 20th century. With the advances of photo-mechanical reproduction artists turned afresh to the medium, and as with original wood-engraving, it was used in limited edition books, successfully adopted by artists such as David Jones and David Hockney.

Etching

Grooves and hollows are formed by the corrosive action of acid (biting), rather than by cutting with a tool. The plate is coated with a waxy substance (the ground) impervious to acid, and the design is made through this with a needle,

1 Ornamental woodcut border and initial for a page of William Morris' *A Dream of John Ball*, Kelmscott Press, 1892.

2 Wood-engraved illustration by Sir Edward Burne-Jones within woodcut border for *A Dream of John Ball*, Kelmscott Press, 1892.

3 Enlarged detail showing the difference between the woodcut border and the finer lines of the wood-engraved illustration.

4 Engraved illustration for John Goodman's *American Natural History*, Philadelphia, 1831.

5 Enlarged detail showing the fine lines typical of an engraving.

laying bare the metal. The back and edges of the plate are protected with varnish and the plate dipped in acid. The bare metal corrodes in stages according to the areas of light and dark required; each area is coated in varnish as it is completed. The ground and varnish are finally removed and the plate is inked. The result is softer than an engraving, because of the uneven effect of the acid on the metal. This process has been used throughout the 20th century, especially by French artists and by contemporary artists such as Tom Phillips and Jim Dine.

PLANOGRAPHIC processes are those in which the printing surface is at the same level as that to remain blank. This is achieved by exploiting the simple phenomenon that grease and water do not mix. The area to be printed is impregnated with grease and the blank areas are moistened. When the greasy ink is applied it adheres to the greased area only.

Lithograph

The image is drawn directly on to the surface, traditionally stone but now usually a metal plate, which will absorb grease and water equally. Lithographic chalk (a mixture of wax or soap, lampblack, and shellac) or ink (the chalk dissolved in water) is used to draw the image. The design is protected with a solution of gum arabic and acid before the remaining areas are moistened. A heavy ink is rolled over the surface, and the paper and plate are then pressed together. Lithography was invented in 1798 by Aloys Senefelder and was frequently used to reproduce scenic views. Calligraphic text is often lithographed alongside the illustration. It was primarily employed as a reproductive medium by firms of commercial lithographers, but in the 1920s Harold Curwen encouraged artists to use the lithograph as an original medium (autolithograph). Artists thereby learnt to employ the technique themselves, and their work can be found in some of the most interesting illustrated books of the 20th century, especially those by Paul Nash, Barnett Freedman, and E. McKnight Kauffer (see page 104).

Offset lithography is when the image on the lithographic plate is first printed on to an intermediate rubber "blanket" roller, and from this on to the paper.

6 Etched illustration by Tsougouharu Foujita in Michel Vaucaire's *Barres paralleles*, Paris, 1927.

7 Enlarged detail showing the softer finish caused by the acid.

8 Lithographed illustration by Kathleen Hale for her story *"Henrietta" the Faithful Hen*, 1943.

9 Enlarged detail showing the soft colours.

The Internet

The Internet has transformed book-collecting. Once the second-hand book world was the preserve of the dusty shop, books piled high, the occasional catalogue and certainly very few computers, but today most dealers and collectors have embraced the new technology. With a click of the mouse books can be located in California or Canterbury, and the most expensive or the cheapest copy of a particular book can be found. Copies can be compared around the world. Leg-work, telephone calls and wants lists have been replaced by search engines and keywords. The Internet provides the collector with direct access to book dealers through their own web-sites and catalogues online, with search engines such as www.google.com, useful for background information, and with important sites such as www.abebooks.com and www.worldbookdealers.com.

It is perhaps these two that have most altered the book world in that dealers register with each site and list their books for sale. The collector then enters directly into a transaction and may in future choose to communicate through the dealer's own web-site. Many of the books listed are accompanied by photographs, but it is always important to check the condition carefully. There are also useful articles and bibliographical tools available on both sites; www.worldbookdealers.com allows various degrees of access according to subscription level. The general site www.ebay.com worked for a while in partnership with the auction house Sotheby's. There are several specialist book sections including "Antiques and Collectibles" that are worth browsing through. Books can be purchased immediately or during the online auction, and are usually accompanied by a photograph.

The major auction houses list their catalogues online about three weeks prior to an auction, at which point individual entries and photographs can be accessed, and results of sales are also easily available. www.icollector.com hosts information from several smaller and foreign auction houses. The Internet has enabled many small dealers to expand their business, no longer having to rely on the endless round of book fairs; others have moved into the country or abroad, safe in the knowledge their business will flourish with Internet access. Ironically, far from destroying the world of the printed book, the tools of technology have ensured a wider audience and greater accessibility for what was once a rarefied world.

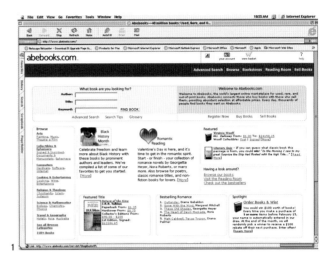

1

2

1 The home page for www.abebooks.com.

2 The home page for www.worldbookdealers.com.

Dust-jackets

Early dust-jackets are exceptionally scarce and those pre-1910 almost always comprise plain wrappers with simple lettering and perhaps a small design. The earliest often had panels cut to allow the author and title to be read from the spine.

It is unclear when the first dust-jacket appeared but a copy of Lewis Carroll's *The Hunting of the Snark* (1876) is known in a dust-jacket. Conan Doyle's *The Adventures of Sherlock Holmes* (1892) and Rudyard Kipling's *The Second Jungle Book* (1895) were both issued in a blue pictorial jacket; it appears that the first volume of *The Jungle Book* had either a simple glassine wrapper or no dust-jacket at all. All three of these books are exceptionally rare in this state, but perhaps the two most sought-after jackets, of which there are to date only two or three known copies of each book in the dust-jacket, are *The Wind in the Willows* (1908) and *The Hound of the Baskervilles* (1902).

From World War I on, with increasing competition in the book world, the jacket was employed by publishers as a marketing tool and its design became more important. Fragile and usually taken off by the purchaser and either discarded or placed in a drawer and subsequently lost, pre-1940 jackets remain uncommon. The presence of the original glassine jacket on a copy of Ernest Hemingway's *Three Stories & Ten Poems* (1923) in the Rechler sale at Christie's New York in 2002 ensured a price of $119,500 (£85,900). There is a sizable premium to be paid for books in dust-jackets, and condition plays a large part in the price. A sought-after book such as *The Hobbit* (1937) can be £1,500–2,000/$2,400–3,200 in the original cloth, £4,000–6,000/$6,400–12,00 in a torn dust-jacket and £20,000–30,000/$30,000–45,000 in a fine dust-jacket at auction.

One should usually insist on the presence of the jacket for books published after World War II, but the acquisition of books with jackets from these early years will depend entirely on how much one is prepared to pay. Fashion is the dictator here: in earlier times collectors had no time for the jackets, but today's collectors demand jackets in the best possible condition.

Dust jackets are of particular interest if they are designed by notable artists: Rex Whistler and John Piper were both prolific designers of dust jackets. Artists such as E. Mcknight Kauffer and Barnett Freedman worked with new techniques of colour printing to produce striking pictorial jackets during the Thirties. New styles of typography and art, such as Surrealism and Cubism, influenced jackets during the Twenties and Thirties, as did the lighting of early cinema. Vanessa Bell produced a wonderful series of jackets for her sister, Virginia Woolf. Publishers such as Victor Gollancz created instantly identifiable books in printed yellow jackets, designed by Stanley Morison, while others used striking typography to make an impression. Jackets can also contain pertinent bibliographical information such as price or edition, or interesting autobiographical material. The collector needs to be aware of issue points on jackets, such as price (the rare first-issue jacket of *The Wind in the Willows* is priced at 6/- and the second issue at 7/6); or mistakes corrected ("Dodgeson" is misspelt on the inside lower flap of the first issue of *The Hobbit* and is corrected by hand in ink).

One should check for the presence of later titles or printings on a dust-jacket, a sure indication of a later issue: *When We Were Very Young* and *Winnie the Pooh* both have points such as this to check. John Grisham's *The Firm* comes in a jacket in two issues, the second mentioning books published at a later date. The second-issue dust-jacket for John Fowles' *The Collector* lists several book reviews on the inside flap. The second-issue jackets for Ian Fleming's *Casino Royale* and *Live and Let Die* also have have blurb on the inside flap not found on the first issues, relating to the design and execution of the jackets. Beatrix Potter's books were issued in glassine wrapper with printed price and information relating to titles already published. Wrappers were printed for the two books issued each year with no identifying title and one needs to check the list of books already published to make sure that the correct wrapper for the year is present.

It is important to check the condition carefully, for some rare early jackets can be heavily restored and it is wise to be aware of this. With sophisticated technology clever forgeries of rare jackets have appeared on the market. The only way of telling the difference is in the tone and quality of the paper used. If a jacket is rare, adopt a cautious approach and seek the advice of an expert.

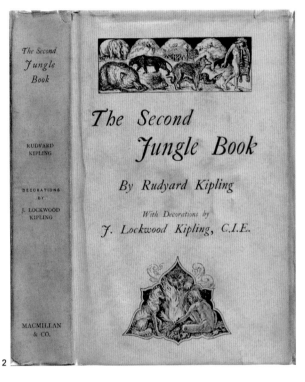

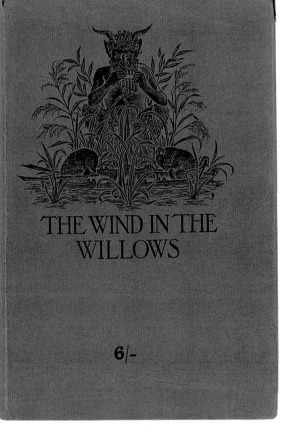

1 Arthur Conan Doyle. *The Hound of the Baskervilles*. 1902.
Exceptionally rare in the dust-jacket, of which only two copies are
known. **£80,000–100,000/$128,000–160,000**

2 Rudyard Kipling. *The Second Jungle Book*. 1895. Scarce in the
dust-jacket. **£6,000–8,000/$9,600–12,800**

3 Kenneth Grahame. *The Wind in the Willows*. 1908. Exceptionally
rare in the first-issue dust-jacket priced 6/-, of which only a few
copies are thought to exist. **£60,000–80,000/$96,000–128,000**

Manuscripts and Original Artwork

For many collectors, the logical progression from owning an ordinary copy of a book is to acquire an association copy (one signed, inscribed or presented by the artist/author/publisher) or an original letter or manuscript by a particular author.

Original manuscript material retains the closest connection with the author, especially if the manuscript contains annotations or corrections in the author's own hand. Individual letters are not that uncommon but it is the content and provenance of letters as well as manuscripts that will always determine the value. A letter by Winston Churchill passing the time of day with a friend may only be worth a few hundred pounds, but when an exceptional series of letters to his brother, Jack, his closest personal confidant, discussing the important Dardanelles campaign, his strategy and his personal worries, came onto the market in 1997, competition was intense, and they greatly exceeded the estimates, the most expensive reaching £45,000 ($67,000). Many 20th-century authors have donated their archives to institutions, and others have been sold upon their death to British or American libraries, so complete manuscripts or even typescripts are rare. Ian Fleming's manuscripts, for instance, are in the Lily Library in Indiana, but it is thought that possibly two remain in private hands. These would be highly sought-after, even more so because the current market for Fleming is particularly strong. Commercially popular he may be, but he is not widely regarded as one of the greatest authors of the century. Authors such as Jack Kerouac, on the other hand, combine popular acclaim and iconic status with literary standing, and this combination also guarantees high sale-room prices. When the manuscript scroll of Jack Kerouac's *On the Road* and the "Eumaeus" episode of James Joyce's *Ulysses* came on to the market in 2001, they each fetched over $1million.

Beatrix Potter's quintessential picture letters to children may command four-figure sums, but when one is the forerunner of a story, such as the 1893 letter to Noel Moore about a rabbit called Peter, or that to his brother Eric about a frog, then the value will run into six figures.

In contrast an ordinary letter by her can be priced at just a few hundred pounds. Enid Blyton, who was an extraordinarily prolific letter-writer, could pen several hundred letters a day, and hence these have very little commercial value, except for the 1949 letter to the artist Harmsen Van der Beek in which she set out her ideas about Noddy, accompanied by sketches of the toy characters, which realized £30,000 ($45,000) at auction in 1998.

The illustrated book flourished in the 20th century and the range of styles available to the collector is huge. For many interested in the illustrations, the ultimate goal is to obtain the original artwork. During the first half of the century artists such as Arthur Rackham and Edmund Dulac held regular sales of the original paintings for their gift books, timed to coincide with the date of publication. Other artists left their work to languish in the dusty archives of publishers, for until fairly recently artwork was usually deemed to be the property of the publisher. Publishers changed hands, and pictures were lost or given away, as they were often unappreciated. Artists now have the same rights of copyright and ownership as authors and original artwork is collected today in much the same way as manuscripts.

Tastes change and fashions dictate values, but the "big names" such as Arthur Rackham, Edmund Dulac, Kay Nielsen, Beatrix Potter, and E.H. Shepard will always

command large sums. However, for each of these artists there is a wide price range. Arthur Rackham's paintings for *Peter Pan*, *A Midsummer Night's Dream*, *Rip van Winkle* or *Alice's Adventures in Wonderland* will be more expensive than those for Wagner or his early black-and-white work. Edmund Dulac's early "Blue Period" paintings command far greater sums than his later Persian-style work. Beatrix Potter's most valuable pictures will always contain rabbits and E.H. Shepard drawings have to be of Winnie the Pooh or one of his friends to be expensive. It is useful to look at the body of work by E.H. Shepard, for whereas an ink drawing of Winnie the Pooh can easily command a high five-figure sum, an ink drawing for *Tom Brown's Schooldays* will only fetch a few hundred pounds. Drawings for *Wind in the Willows* have recently begun to climb as Winnie the Pooh drawings become prohibitively expensive for the average collector. Subject-matter is very important in determining price. Fairies and fantasy are particularly in vogue at the moment and a Margaret Tarrant painting of fairies will command more than a straightforward picture of children.

There are many fakes or copies on the market, some contemporary with the artists, such as those of Kate Greenaway, popular in her day and hence worth faking at the time, and others being churned out more recently by unscrupulous artists and dealers. It is always worth enlisting the help of an expert, perhaps a dealer, scholar or auction house, to authenticate work. Artists whose work is known to have been forged include Arthur Rackham, Louis Wain, William Heath Robinson, Mabel Lucie Attwell, and Beatrix Potter. Generally, an artist has to be well-established and their books to have a pedigree of steady high prices for the paintings to have great value.

There are many fine contemporary artists working on children's and illustrated books, and this could make a good area for a new collector to start, as the pictures are generally very reasonably priced. The one exception to this has been Thomas Taylor's watercolour for the upper cover of *Harry Potter and the Philosopher's Stone*. This was sold at auction in 2001 for an exceptional price as a result of the huge media interest and publicity surrounding the books and the release of the film. Watercolours for the later books failed to reach the high expectations placed on them in subsequent sales, highlighting the need for caution and careful balancing when looking at artwork for later or less important works.

1 Ian Fleming. The author's complete typescript of *Chitty-Chitty-Bang-Bang*, with autograph corrections by the author, 119 leaves. c.1964. **£15,000–20,000/$24,000–32,600**

2 Thomas Taylor. Original watercolour drawing for the front cover of J.K. Rowling's *Harry Potter and the Philosopher's Stone*. 1997. **£70,000–80,000/$112,000–128,000**

2

Timeline

Turn of the Century

1880 *The Trumpet Major*, Thomas Hardy

1883
Treasure Island, R.L. Stevenson

1895
The Time Machine, H.G. Wells

1896
The Kelmscott Chaucer

1900
Lord Jim, Joseph Conrad

1900 *The Wonderful Wizard of Oz*, L. Frank Baum

1901
The Tale of Peter Rabbit,
Beatrix Potter
The Doves Press founded
Sangorski & Sutcliffe Bindery opens

1905
Doves Press Bible completed

1908
The Hole Book, Peter Newell

Modernism

1910
Howard's End, E.M. Forster
Post-Impressionists exhibition
Revival of wood-engraving

1915
The Good Soldier, Ford Madox Ford
Voyage Out, Virginia Woolf
The Rainbow, D.H. Lawrence
Devil's Devices, Eric Gill

1920
Poems, Wilfred Owen
The Story of Dr. Dolittle, Hugh Lofting
Society of Wood-Engravers formed

1922 *The Waste Land*, T.S. Eliot

1922
Ulysses, James Joyce
The Velveteen Rabbit, William Nicholson

1924
Gregynog Press opens
When We Were Very Young, A.A. Milne

1925
Mrs Dalloway, Virginia Woolf
Golden Cockerel *Troilus and Criseyde*

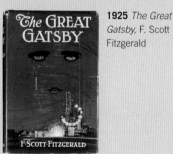

1925 *The Great Gatsby*, F. Scott Fitzgerald

The 1930s

1930
Poems, W.H. Auden
Swallows and Amazons, Arthur Ransome
Gulliver's Travels, Rex Whistler
Rampant Lions Press formed

1930 Golden Cockerel *Canterbury Tales*

1932
Adventures of the Black Girl in Search of God, John Farleigh
Urne Buriall, Paul Nash
Ecclesiasticus, Ashendene Press

1937
And To Think I Saw It On Mulberry Street, Dr Seuss

1938
Murphy, Samuel Beckett

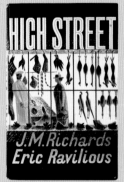

1938 *High Street*, Eric Ravilious

1939
Brighton Aquatints, John Piper

Angry Young Men

1949

Treasure Island, Mervyn Peake
Noddy in Toyland, Enid Blyton
Edgar Mansfield teaches binding at
    Central School of Arts and Crafts

1954 *Lord of
the Flies,*
William Golding

1954

Lucky Jim, Kingsley Amis
The Fellowship of the Ring, part 1 of
    Lord of the Rings, J.R.R. Tolkien

1955

Waiting for Godot performed
    in England

1956

Long Day's Journey Into Night,
    Eugene O'Neill

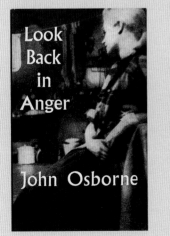

1956 *Look Back in Anger*, John Osborne

1957

Hawk in the Rain, Ted Hughes

Postmodernism

1960 Trial of *Lady
Chatterley's Lover*

1963

The Collector, John Fowles
Where the Wild Things Are,
    Maurice Sendak

1967

Alice's Adventures in Wonderland,
    Ralph Steadman
Index Book, Andy Warhol

1969

First Booker Prizewinner, P.H. Newby,
    Something to Answer For

1975

No Man's Land, Harold Pinter

1981 *Midnight's Children*, Salman Rushdie

1981

Rocket Press founded

1987

Engraving Then and Now,
    Retrospective 50th Exhibition
    of Society of Wood-Engravers

Contemporary

1989

The third "Great Omar" Sangorski &
Sutcliffe jewelled binding completed

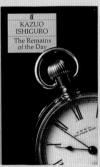

1989 *The Remains
of the Day,*
Kazuo Ishiguro
wins Booker Prize

1993

Birdsong, Sebastian Faulkes
A Suitable Boy, Vikram Seth
Trainspotting, Irvine Welsh

1995

Northern Lights, Philip Pullman
Seamus Heaney wins Nobel Prize
    for Literature

1995–2000 "His Dark Materials" trilogy,
Philip Pullman

1997

*Harry Potter and the
    Philosopher's Stone*, J.K. Rowling
Cold Mountain, Charles Frazier

1999

Quentin Blake first Children's
    Poet Laureate

2001

The Amber Spyglass, Philip Pullman,
    wins Whitbread Book of the Year

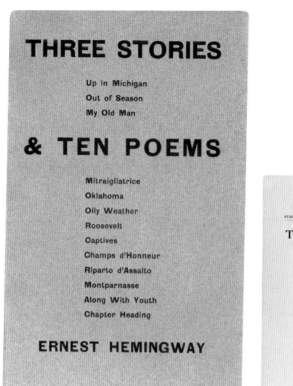

1

2

3

English and American Literature

The first printings of English and American literature from roughly the late 1880s to the present day are often referred to colloquially as "modern first editions". This useful catch-phrase summarizes the field of interest but throws up important associated terms that the collector must grasp. What is an "edition", or an "issue", a "printing" or a "state"? In strict bibliographical terms an "edition" comprises all the copies of a book printed from one substantial setting of type. An "impression" or "issue" are subsets of the edition and can often be printed several months or years later. Hence one should refer more accurately to the "first impression" or "first printing", but "first edition" is the term that is generally used. There can be variant "states" of each impression caused by alteration to type during the printing process. Alterations made later are "re-issues". (See the Glossary, pages 152–3, for more detailed explanations of these terms, but note also that many book dealers use them incorrectly.) The aim is to obtain the earliest form of the text, and where two or more states or issues exist, the first is preferable and prices will reflect this. These variants may exist because of errors of text or illustration discovered during printing (such as the incorrect name use of "Joanne Rowling" on the copyright page of *Harry Potter and the Prisoner of Azkaban*); text altered because of libel or someone's dissatisfaction (Siegfried Sassoon's poem was removed in the second issue of Robert Graves' *Goodbye to all That*); or illustrations altered on aesthetic or moral grounds (the plates were altered in *The Wonderful Wizard of Oz*).

Most contemporary books contain a publisher's number sequence identifying the impression, and the lower numbers are removed as later impressions are printed. As already mentioned on pages 20–1 dust-jackets can also exist in various issues. American first editions used to be harder to identify correctly, although many state "first printing", but most contemporary books contain the number sequence today. Bibliographies exist for many of these authors, price

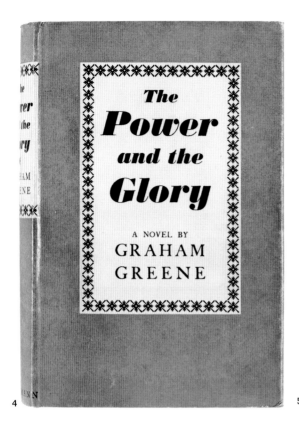

The Power and the Glory

A NOVEL BY GRAHAM GREENE

4

J.K. Rowling

Harry Potter and the Philosopher's Stone

BLOOMSBURY

5

guides and booksellers and auction catalogues often list relevant points, and care should be taken to check these before acquisition. Sometimes an English author can be published initially in the US, so that the true first edition will have an American imprint: the true first edition of Agatha Christie's earliest book, *The Mysterious Affair at Styles*, is the American John Lane imprint of 1921, and the American edition of Graham Greene's *Brighton Rock* precedes the English edition. Sometimes titles are changed for the American market: *Harry Potter and the Philosopher's Stone* was changed to *Harry Potter and the Sorcerer's Stone* and Graham Greene's *The Power and the Glory* was published under the title *The Labyrinthine Ways*.

It follows that if the collector is looking for the earliest state of the text, then advance proof copies will be of interest. Proofs exist in various different forms, but the most relevant are the "galley proofs" sent to the author and other interested parties for correction and proof-reading. There will only be a few copies of these and they will sometimes have substantial alterations to the final printed text or contain manuscript annotations, and as such can command high prices. However, since the 1970s, publishers have issued proof copies as

1 Ernest Hemingway. *Three Stories & Ten Poems*. Paris. 1923. One of 300 copies, the author's first book. **£15,000–25,000/ $24,000–40,000**

2 and **3** Virginia Woolf. *Two Stories*. The Hogarth Press. 1915. The first book published by the Hogarth Press. One of 150 copies. **£10,000–15,000/$16,000–24,000**.

4 Graham Greene. *The Power and the Glory*. 1940. In the dust-jacket. **£4,000–7,000/$6,400–11,200**

5 J.K. Rowling. *Harry Potter and the Philosopher's Stone*. Proof copy in wrappers with author incorrectly given as "J.A. Rowling" on title page. **£1,000–1,500/$1,600–2,400**

a means of gaining advance publicity and reviews, and these rarely, if ever, contain textual variations. This has led to the current market in proof copies being rather depressed, unless there are textual alterations, manuscript annotations, presentation inscriptions or other points of interest. The third "Harry Potter" title, *Harry Potter and the Prisoner of Azkaban*, was the last to be issued in proof form, and was done so in small numbers, creating a scarcity factor and corresponding higher value.

The Turn of the Century

Towards the end of the 19th century and the start of the 20th century changes began to appear in the literary world. Victorian literature – moral, realist and popular – a product of its age of imperialism, staunch family values and accepted politics, began to die. In its place came a literature that was more complex and quite different, which spread throughout Europe and then, more slowly, to the US. Society was evolving with the growth of urban populations, the acceleration of technological change, improved education and literacy, revolutionary changes in the perception of sexuality and in the world of science as expounded by Charles Darwin, the rise of social sciences such as psychology and sociology, and shifting attitudes towards the role of women. All these combined to create a changing environment in which the writer could flourish, questioning and creating something new, even re-examining the novel itself, its role and format. The typical Victorian three-decker novel, often preceded by monthly or weekly publication in parts, designed for libraries or subscription, gave place to shorter single volumes, designed to be purchased quite cheaply and read by individuals. The novel began to take the place of poetry and drama as the dominant literary medium.

Towards the end of 1899, Henry James announced a new "self-consciousness" in fiction: "It can do simply everything, and that is its strength and its life." The writers who started to break free from Victorian tradition and led the way for others to follow were Thomas Hardy, Sir Arthur Conan Doyle, Robert Louis Stevenson and Rudyard Kipling. Henry James, H.G. Wells, Oscar Wilde,

and W.B. Yeats cemented the break and formed the start of the Modern movement. Conan Doyle, Stevenson, and Kipling wrote many books, but today only a few of their works command high prices among collectors: it is the important transitional works that collectors seek, and their other work can be acquired for a few pounds. Conan Doyle wrote historical fiction but is best known for his detective novels, while Stevenson and Kipling found fame for their children's books (and in Stevenson's case also for his supernatural work, *The Strange Case of Dr Jekyll and Mr Hyde*, 1886). Their adventure and historical novels are today less widely read. H.G. Wells wrote many books, but is best remembered for his science-fiction works. W.B. Yeats was the founding-father of the modern Irish movement.

Henry James, born in New York in 1843, settled in England in 1876 in the search for stimulus for his writing. His body of work progressed in distinct stages as it developed from the influences of the Victorian tradition

1 Oscar Wilde. *A House of Pomegranates*. 1891. In the pictorial cloth decorated by Charles Ricketts. **£1,000–1,500/ $1,600–2,400**

2 Evelyn Waugh. *Brideshead Revisited*. 1945. One of 50 copies printed for friends of the author, normally inscribed by Waugh. **£10,000–20,000/$16,000–32,000**

3 Walt Whitman. *Leaves of Grass*. Philadelphia, 1891. The ninth separate edition, the "death-bed" edition, the last supervised and approved by the author. Second issue in grey wrappers. **£2,000–3,000/$3,200–4,800**

THOMAS HARDY

Thomas Hardy had a long and extremely distinguished career: his first book, *Desperate Remedies*, was published in 1871 and his final work, *Winter Words*, after his death in 1928. Hardy's fictional world is a place of change and unrest; the Church is seen as intrusive and irrelevant to the complexities of the modern world, and its place taken by a sense of fate. *Tess of the D'Urbervilles* (1891) and *Jude the Obscure* (1895) deal with characters wrenched from their roots and thrown into a strange tumultuous world, who progress towards a new awareness through suffering, emotion or education. His discussion of sexuality outraged his contemporaries. His female characters, while not completely emancipated, are stronger and more interesting than his male protagonists. For D.H. Lawrence, he marked the passing of fiction from Victorian to Modernist and had a great impact on his important work *The Rainbow* (1915).

Little work by Thomas Hardy had come on to the market for many years until the fine collection put together by the American bibliophile Frederick B. Adams appeared for sale in 2001 at Sotheby's. This exceptional collection of 19th- and 20th-century English and American literature included over 320 lots of presentation copies, fine copies in the original cloth and letters by Thomas Hardy. The resulting high prices confirmed his importance in modern literature, but by studying the catalogue and prices realized carefully, interesting points

are thrown up. A fine copy of his first book, *Desperate Remedies*, in the original cloth made £32,450 ($48,675) whereas another copy in a variant but rarer binding, in poor condition, fetched only £9,988 ($14,982). A better-known work, *Under the Greenwood Tree* (1872), his second book, also in original cloth but with some wear, made £17,500 ($28,000), whereas another copy in a trial binding made £9,400 ($14,100). Probably the only known presentation copy of what was perhaps his first "modern" novel, *Far from the Madding Crowd* (1874), made £29,000 ($43,500). Interestingly, his greatest works and those for which he is best known, *The Return of the Native* (1878), *The Mayor of Casterbridge* (1886), *Tess of the D'Urbervilles* (1891), and *Jude the Obscure* (1895), made less. The latter two are easier to find as they were printed in larger editions of about 1,000 copies, whereas the earlier books appeared in editions of only about 500 or 700 copies. In his later years he turned to poetry, and his *Wessex Poems* (1898) can be seen as one of the most important early collections of modern poetry.

1 Thomas Hardy. *The Trumpet Major*. 3 volumes, 1880. One of 1,000 copies. In the original pictorial cloth. **£20,000–30,000/ $32,000–48,000**

2 Thomas Hardy. *Tess of the D'Urbevilles*. 3 volumes, 1892. The second impression, original cloth. **£600–800/$960–1,280**

1

2

to highly complex and modern pieces such as the ghost story *The Turn of the Screw* (1898) and *The Wings of a Dove* (1902). As his work changed and progressed, he lost popular readership during the 1880s but gained critical appreciation as a succession of writers realized his importance, such as his contemporaries Joseph Conrad and Ford Madox Ford and those of the new generation, Virginia Woolf and Gertrude Stein. His most sought-after book today, however, is his first great popular novel, *The Portrait of a Lady* (1881), which first introduced a key theme of American expatriate bohemians, not his later great Modernist works. This was first published in three volumes in an edition of 150 copies, and is today rare in good condition. Although several of his works were first published in the US, it is generally the first English editions that collectors seek. His first novel, *Roderick Hudson*, although dated 1876, was actually published in 1875 and did not appear in England until 1880. There are various issue points for his works, notably binding variants for the English edition of *What Maisie Knew* (1897).

Decadence and sexuality are themes that are generally associated with the 1890s, and it is perhaps the tales of Oscar Wilde that most epitomize these. They are slim works, but controversial: *The Portrait of Dorian Gray* (1890); *Salome*, written in French in 1893 and translated in 1894, which was refused a licence; and *The Ballad of Reading Gaol* (1898), written while Wilde was in prison for the crime of homosexuality. His comic plays, quite different in style, satirize the society of the time, the best known being *The Importance of Being Earnest* (1895). His work was generally issued in many different formats, including numbered, signed copies, mostly published by John Lane and Elkin Mathews or Leonard Smithers.

Leonard Smithers set up in business on his own in 1894 as a publisher and antiquarian bookseller, and after Wilde's trial took over from John Lane as the principal publisher of the "Decadent School" of the 1890s, putting out Wilde and Beardsley when no-one else would touch them. He supported W.B. Yeats and Ernest Dowson, and published *The Savoy Magazine*, which took over from *The Yellow Book* as the representative magazine of the movement, but went bankrupt in 1899. From then until his death, he made a living by issuing pirated editions of Wilde and Beardsley through a bookdealer in Fulham. Smithers' works could make a fascinating collection and an invaluable reference tool would be the 1996 Phillips London auction catalogue "Leonard Smithers and the 1890s. The Booth Collection of Books Published by Leonard Smithers".

4 Oscar Wilde. *The Picture of Dorian Gray*. 1891. One of 250 copies signed by Wilde, this a presentation copy inscribed by the author in November 1894. **£6,000–8,000/$9,600–12,800**

5 Henry James. *The Portrait of a Lady*. Boston, 1892. First US edition. **£200–300/$320–480**. First edition, 1881, £6,000–8,000/ $9,600–12,800.

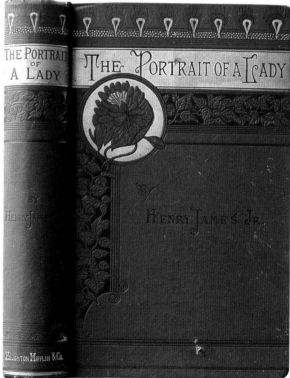

EDWARDIAN ERA: JOSEPH CONRAD

The death of Queen Victoria in 1901 ushered in the Edwardian era, whose authors have generally been overshadowed by the next decade's great Modernist writers. There developed two distinct strands of literature: the complex and experimental "avant-garde", and the widely read "contemporary" realist literature. Much of the work published during this time was populist, fairly conservative and traditional in style, although often questioning of society. G.K. Chesterton's "Father Brown" tales were wildly successful, while Arnold Bennett, Walter de la Mare, Hugh Walpole, Hilaire Belloc, and the Poet Laureate John Masefield sold well. All today can be acquired for very reasonable sums and their work provides a fine representative body of an often-neglected era.

Joseph Conrad, a Polish émigré born in 1857, became a naturalized British subject in 1888, but his life and work reflected the disorders of Europe. His stories, even when set in the Congo, usually mirror the world of London and dying colonialism, a world of disorder and disjointed time, in which his protagonists undergo arduous quests, physical or psychological. He was concerned about effects rather than mere narrative. He wrote his first book, *Almayer's Folly*, in 1895. The first state omits an "e" from "generosity" and the word "of" at the foot of page 110, and is worth a great deal more than the second corrected state.

His first important book, which initiated his experiments with novelistic form, is *The Nigger of Narcissus* (1898). This was initially published in 1897 in the US as *The Children of the Sea*. The first British edition can be found in various impressions: the copyright edition, of which only a handful of copies in wrappers are known to exist and as such is highly sought-after; and three different impressions of the ordinary edition, which can be identified by size differences in the publisher's imprint on the spine and number of advertisement pages.

The majority of his books exist in various states and bibliographical help is required to check these. The only bibliography of Conrad, however, is by Cagle and exists solely on microfilm, so the collector may need to seek expert advice or peruse previous catalogues for issue points. In 1902 Conrad published the preface to *The Nigger of Narcissus*, and this is now sought-after in its own right as one of the key manifestos of modern literature; only 100 copies were printed, bound in wrappers. His major collection of short stories, comprising "Youth", "Heart of Darkness", and "The End of the Tether", all of which had appeared in the *Edinburgh Magazine*, was *Youth: A Narrative and other Stories* (1902). The first issue has the advertisements dated "10/02". It is an important book and still very affordable today. The work that first gave him popular success and acceptance was *Chance* (1913). This work has a complex bibliographical history to check relating to its title page, binding imprint and advertisements. The book was actually published in 1914 and copies exist with various states of the title page dated 1913 and 1914. Copies in the dust-jacket can fetch significant sums.

1 Joseph Conrad. *Chance*. 1913. Second issue, in the dust-jacket. **£10,000–15,000/$16,000–24,000**

2 Joseph Conrad. *Youth*. Edinburgh and London, 1902. Includes the author's celebrated story "Heart of Darkness". **£600–900/ $960–1,440**

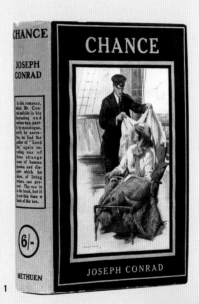

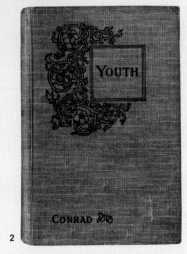

The Great War: Goodbye to All That

The 1914–18 war was the catalyst for a great deal of literary output. For the first time writers challenged the accepted sentimental view of war, and many of those who served did not live to see their works published. Novels, fictional or partly autobiographical, and poetry, some written during the War and others many years afterwards, were powerful and usually disillusioned. The poet Rupert Brooke, known to generations for his famous poem "The Soldier" ("If I should die...") died at the age of 28 and his war verse was published posthumously to great acclaim as *1914 and Other Poems* (1915). His poetry echoed the accepted sentimental and heroic view of young men going to fight. Despite the fact that it is his war verse for which he is best remembered, his early privately printed compilations are most desired by collectors, the first being *The Pyramids* (1904).

The later poets became rapidly disillusioned as the harsh reality of war set in, and their poetry is far bleaker. It is probably Wilfred Owen whose work sums this up best. His important book *Poems*, containing "Dulce et Decorum est", was first published in 1920 and exists in two issues. Other poets one could look for include Isaac Rosenberg, killed in action in 1918, whose *Youth* was printed privately in an edition of about 100 copies in 1915, and Charles Hamilton Sorley, killed at Loos in 1915, who is perhaps less well known and more affordable; his *Marlborough and Other Poems* was published in 1916. However, for many it is the great novels, mostly published during the 1920s and 1930s and pacifist in sentiment, that best represent the War. Siegfried Sassoon's important trilogy, *Memoirs of a Fox-Hunting Man* (1928), *Memoirs of an Infantry Officer* (1930) and *Sherston's Progress* (1936), was published in various different editions, the most expensive being the numbered, signed and illustrated edition. Sassoon's anger and frustration at the futility of war is also plain in his verse, which emphasizes the chasm between those who decide and those who fight. He published many volumes of verse, but it is only really the first, *Poems* (1906), that commands a high price.

Other important novels to look for are Ford Madox Ford's *The Good Soldier* (1915), Robert Graves' *Goodbye to All That* (1929, the first issue containing an unauthorized poem by Siegfried Sassoon on pages 341–3), Richard Aldington's *Death of a Hero* (1929; the first unexpurgated edition was not printed until 1930 in an edition of 300 copies), R.C. Sheriff's *Journey's End* (1928), Erich Maria Remarques' *All Quiet on the Western Front* (1929) and Ernest Hemingway's *A Farewell to Arms* (1929).

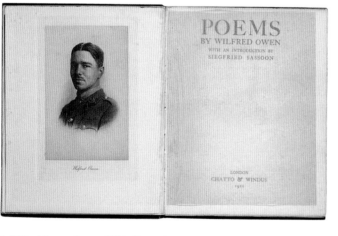

1 Wilfred Owen. *Poems*. 1931. "Second impression" with additional poems and introduction by Sassoon. **£30–50/$48–80**

2 Robert Graves. *Poems (1926–1930)*. 1931. **£80–100/$128–160**

English and American Literature

32

MODERNISM: VIRGINIA WOOLF AND BLOOMSBURY

The years 1908–14 were a period of experimentalism throughout Europe. New ideas and movements were springing up, from art to typography, and naturally these came to influence literature in a major way. Virginia Woolf wrote: "On or about December 1910 human nature changed... all human relations shifted... and when human relations change there is at the same time a change in religion, conduct, politics and literature" ("Mr Bennet and Mrs Brown", 1924). She pinpoints this shift to the month of the first French Post-Impressionist and Cubist exhibition, organized by her friend Roger Fry. Its effects spread, and many of the greatest Modernist writers published works in 1910–15: E.M. Forster's *Howard's End* appeared in 1910, D.H. Lawrence's *The White Peacock* in 1911, James Joyce's *Dubliners* in 1914, and Virginia Woolf's *The Voyage Out* in 1915.

The fragmentation of Europe, in particular Russia, and its heady artistic experimentation, much of it brought to Paris and London through dance and the stage, had a profound influence on the new generation of writers, none more so than the Bloomsbury Group. It was never a formal group but more a gathering of friends – writers, intellectuals, critics, and painters – whose most famous members included Virginia Woolf, her sister Vanessa Bell, their husbands Leonard Woolf and Clive Bell, the economist John Maynard Keynes, Roger Fry, Duncan Grant, and E.M. Forster. They were united by their taste for discussion and their contempt for the traditional and conventional, and many of their books were issued by Leonard and Virginia Woolf's Hogarth Press. Lytton Strachey's *The Eminent Victorians* (1918), in which Victorian beliefs are damned, was one of their key texts. This and other important texts, such as Roger Fry's *Vision and Design* (1920), could make an interesting collection should one's budget not stretch to the major creative works. Virginia Woolf was heavily influenced by Roger Fry, who curated the influential "Manet and the Post-Impressionists" exhibition. Her stream-of-consciousness style of writing echoed the fragmentary outlook of the avant-garde painters and typographers working out of Europe. She wished to free the novel from commonly received conventions such as time, plot, and identity. Her earliest work, *The Voyage Out* (1915), and in particular the experimental *Mrs Dalloway* (1925) and *To the Lighthouse* (1927), are her most sought-after books and fine copies in their distinctive dust-jackets designed by Vanessa Bell are now rare. Her later works are not nearly as expensive and are relatively common.

1 Virginia Woolf. *To the Lighthouse*. The Hogarth Press, 1927. In the dust-jacket. **£1,000–1,500/$1,600–2,400**

2 Virginia Woolf. *Kew Gardens*. The Hogarth Press, 1919. One of 150 copies. **£7,000–9,000/$11,200–14,400**

3 Virginia Woolf. *Monday or Tuesday*. The Hogarth Press, 1921. Pictorial boards. **£800–1,200/$1,280–1,920**

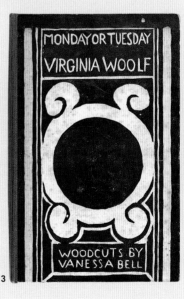

E.M. FORSTER AND D.H. LAWRENCE

E.M. Forster said of himself that he came at "the fag-end of Victorian liberalism", but with his later work he was closely associated with the Bloomsbury Group. He published six novels, upon which his fame rests, many short stories, books of verse and critical works. His three early works, *Where Angels Fear to Tread* (1905), *The Longest Journey* (1907), and *A Room with a View* (1908), deal with repressed sexuality. In 1910 he published *Howard's End*, a complex novel that acknowledged that society was changing. *A Passage to India* (1924) was perhaps his most questioning and widely acclaimed novel. It was also his last, for he claimed that the world of his fiction had gone. His work and its belief in liberalism had a huge influence on many successive writers. There are issue points to watch for when collecting his work, usually in the form of the advertisements, and while his six novels are expensive, the remainder of his large body of work is not.

D.H. Lawrence was a great friend of E.M. Forster, and both passionately believed in seeking new social and emotional unity. Lawrence was completely persuaded that his mission as a novelist and critic was to usher in new forms of thought and content. He believed the role of the novelist was to deal with human life as a whole and influence by example. He in turn was much affected by the new theories propounded by Freud. His body of work is vast and much of it was dogged by controversy. It took his contemporaries a long time to come to terms with his difficult, deeply poetic, sensual, and individualized work. Initially he was lionized by the Bloomsbury Group and then discarded; in retaliation, Lawrence described them as upper-middle-class "black beetles".

Lawrence's first work, *The White Peacock*, was initially published in the US in 1911, and is present in two issues, the first with integral title page and copyright date of 1910, the second with tipped-in title page and copyright date of 1911. The first English edition was published by Heinemann in 1911 and is also present in two issues, the first with the publisher's windmill device on the lower cover.

Exiling himself abroad in 1912 with his German wife, Frieda, Lawrence secured his reputation with the publication of *Sons and Lovers* in 1913 (the first issue without dated title page or with dated title page tipped-in), *The Rainbow* in 1915 (first issue in blue-green cloth) and *Women in Love* in 1921 (the true first edition was printed in an edition of 1,250 copies in the US). His later work was that of an exile, much of it political or psychological, although for his most controversial book, *Lady Chatterley's Lover* (1928), he returned to his Nottingham countryside. It was privately printed in Florence in an edition of 1,000 copies that are rare and expensive for the collector, but there are numerous other printings of this book to look for, including pirated and unauthorized editions. It was not published in England until 1932 when some of the text was removed. In 1960 Penguin fought a legal battle to publish an unexpurgated edition.

1 D.H. Lawrence. *Lady Chatterley's Lover*. Florence, 1928. One of 1,000 copies. **£2,000–3,000/$3,200–4,800**

2 D.H. Lawrence. *Lady Chatterley's Lover*. Penguin, 1960. First unexpurgated edition published in UK. **£10–20/$16–32**

3 E.M. Forster. *A Passage to India*. 1924. In the dust-jacket. **£2,500–3,500/$4,000–5,600**

JAMES JOYCE

The great Irish writer James Joyce, often given the accolade "father of Modernism", also had difficulty being accepted by publishers and censors. Both Lawrence and Joyce exemplified one of the themes running through much modern literature: exile and the rebellious, fractured journey into the unknown. Both spent much of their lives actually in exile, echoing the modern image of the artist as an outsider in a mythical and spiritual sense. In 1904, having left Ireland, Joyce began to draft the majority of his later published pieces, and it was to this year that much of his later work referred.

His first work, *Dubliners*, completed in 1905, was rejected by numerous London publishers until it was taken up by a Dublin firm, but then postponed and not published until 1914 by Grant Richards. By that time his first collection of verse, *Chamber Music*, had been published in 1907 by Elkin Mathews (the first edition is present in three variant issues). *A Portrait of the Artist as a Young Man* was published in the US in 1916 and in the UK by the Egoist Ltd, and *Ulysses* was written in three different cities, but published in Paris privately in 1922 in a limited edition. Confiscated on the grounds of obscenity in Britain and the US, it was not made legally available for many years. There are hence numerous different editions of this complex work for the collector to look for: the prohibitively expensive 100 copies, on handmade paper, of the Shakespeare and Company 1922 edition; the 150 copies on large paper and 750 ordinary copies of the 1922 edition (all bound in fragile blue paper wrappers); the 2,000 copies of the 1922 Egoist Press edition; the 1934 New York Random House edition; the 1936 Bodley Head limited edition; and the first trade edition of 1937. Ulysses was initially conceived as one of the short stories for *Dubliners*, but grew to have a life of its own. Formed from a series of "episodes", the events of one day, 16 June 1904, it often stretches fictional realism to a point of absurdity and yet it observes character and detail intimately and precisely. His use of stream-of-consciousness, parody and variations of language combined to form a style all of his own. His later *Finnegans Wake* (1939), also published in several formats, was even more complex and, for many, unreadable.

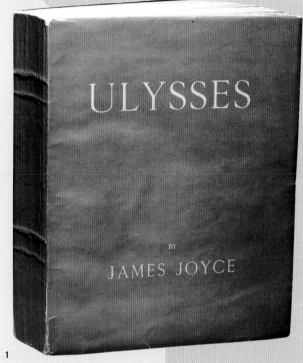

1

2

1 James Joyce. *Ulysses*, Paris: Shakespeare & Company, 1922. Three issues, all in original blue wrappers: 1/100 signed by Joyce. **£70,000–100,000/$112,000–160,000**. 1/150 on large paper. £25,000–35,000/$40,000–56,000. 1/750 on handmade paper. £12,000–18,000/$19,200–28,800

2 James Joyce. *Pomes Penyeach*. Paris, 1927. Original boards. **£200–300/$320–480**

The Twenties: The Bright Young Things

The 1920s were a period of enjoyment and hope, filled with colour and exuberance, with French avant-garde painting, German typography, Russian ballet and stage design, and the new music: jazz. Society enjoyed itself, but always with the memory of the War in the background. It seemed as though the aristocracy had never had it so good, but towards the end of the decade this changed and the suicide rate rose as debt and the Depression set in. P.G. Wodehouse, Evelyn Waugh, and Aldous Huxley are three notable writers who brilliantly charted this period.

The eccentricities and fashions of these inter-war years were superbly captured by Wodehouse. Between 1902 and his death in 1975 he published over 120 volumes of novels and short stories, and he is still avidly read and collected today. *The Pothunters* (1902) was his first book but his famous characters Bertie Wooster and his valet Jeeves appeared years later, in the short story "Extricating Young Gussie" in the *Strand* (January 1916), and in book form in the collection *The Man with Two Left Feet and Other Stories* (1917). *My Man Jeeves* (1919), comprised eight short stories, four about Jeeves, and was issued in two dust-jackets, dated 1919 and 1920. The first separate "Jeeves" story was *Thank You, Jeeves* (1934). The first "Blandings Castle" book was *Something Fresh* (1915). The "PSmith" series first began with *Mike* (1909) and the second part of this book was later reissued in 1935 as *Enter PSmith*.

All the pre-1915 titles are scarce and not generally known in the dust-jacket. Publications from the mid-1920s can generally be found in the dust jackets, which today are a wonderful pictorial record of the era. His books without dust-jackets from the late 1920s and 1930s can be found easily for modest sums, but if the jackets are present, the prices increase sharply. Titles from the 1940s on become far more affordable and easily obtainable in jackets. There are issue points to the majority of his novels: the earliest binding of *The Pothunters*, for instance, has a silver loving-cup stamped on the upper cover and spine, whereas the second binding has the frontispiece illustration reproduced on the upper cover. Prices can be up to five times greater for the earliest binding.

Evelyn Waugh also dealt with light-hearted aristocratic society of the time, but his early satirical novels have a far greater depth and contain a brittleness and menace that fully captures the fragility and cynicism he perceived all around him. His first two novels, *Decline and Fall* (1928) and *Vile Bodies* (1930) are now rare in the original dust jackets and hence command high prices. *A Handful of Dust* (1934) was a brilliant commentary on the collapse of a rural feudalism faced with the new metropolitan and cynical lifestyle of the "bright young things". His most popular novel, *Brideshead Revisited* (1945), explored the same themes but with more nostalgia for the continuation and tradition of accepted beliefs and values, and with the first glimmers of his later religious convictions. The first edition was printed for the author privately in 1944 and issued in 1945 in an edition of only 50 copies bound in wrappers, and is worth considerably more than the normal edition issued by Chapman and Hall in 1945.

Waugh also wrote verse and travel books, and one of his more unusual and sought-after works is his adolescent volume of verse, *The World to Come: A Poem in Three Cantos*, privately printed in 1916. His first adult published work was *PRB: An Essay on the Pre-Raphaelite Brotherhood*, privately printed in 1926. It is generally only the most well-known and early novels that command sums in excess of £500/$750 and his later work can be picked up for relatively little. Many of the books were also issued in limited editions signed by Waugh. Prices for his books rose considerably with the interest generated by the televising of *Brideshead Revisited*, but recently have remained fairly static.

Aldous Huxley's early work was similar in style in that it portrayed and explored the self-conscious pursuit of modernity; his later work, however, was full of despair. *Crome Yellow* (1921) was also a satirical country-house novel which ensured his reputation as a brilliant and cynical novelist. Many of his later works were from exile and portrayed his friends in similar exile, notably D.H. Lawrence. His most popular work, *Brave New World* (1932), was a futuristic novel about social stability and the new religious, scientific, and technological beliefs that tested accepted norms such as the family unit. A limited edition of 324 signed copies was issued in the same year.

---

1 P.G. Wodehouse. Collection of eight first editions. As a group: **£3,000–3,500/$4,800–5,600**.

2 P.G. Wodehouse. *The Clicking of Cuthbert*. 1922. In dust-jacket. **£1,000–1,500/$1,600–2,400**

3 Evelyn Waugh. *Scoop*. 1938. In dust-jacket. **£600–900/ $960–1,440**

4 Evelyn Waugh. *Vile Bodies*. 1930. In dust-jacket. **£3,000–5,000/ $4,800–8,000**

5 Aldous Huxley. *Brave New World*. 1932. In dust-jacket. **£2,500–3,500/$4,000–5,600**

The Lost Generation

American literature had taken longer to shake off the traditions of the past, and authors such as Mark Twain, Henry David Thoreau, Washington Irving, Herman Melville, Edgar Allan Poe, and Nathaniel Hawthorne retained their influence long after their death. American writing embraced the new and "modern" initially when in exile. Whole generations of writers left the US in the 20th century to embrace the stimulus and change of Europe, following in the footsteps of Henry James. One of the first was Stephen Crane, whose impressionist novel *The Red Badge of Courage* was published in 1893. Friends with and neighbours of, Henry James and H.G. Wells, all three encouraged each other in their experiments with new techniques and themes.

It was in the aftermath of the War in the 1920s and from deep within the influence of Paris that the greatest "modern" American writers surfaced, often gathered around Sylvia Beach's second-hand bookshop, Shakespeare and Company. It was Sylvia Beach who supported James Joyce and published the first edition of *Ulysses*. It began to be deemed essential for a writer to break free from the stultifying traditions of American literature and to come to Europe in order to develop.

American writers living in Paris in the early years of the 1920s were described as "the lost generation" by Gertrude Stein when discussing his contemporaries with Ernest Hemingway. The term stuck and the mystique surrounding these writers continues to attract collectors today. The best-known were Ernest Hemingway, F. Scott Fitzgerald, and John Dos Passos, and other names to look for could include Sherwood Anderson and Hart Crane.

The phrase suggests the sense of alienation and philosophical uncertainty characterized by much of their writing and also the awareness at the time that they formed a circle distinct from their predecessors. Traditionally middle-class and viewing art as a means of escape through a bohemian and radical way of life, they were initially hostile to the society they saw around them in the 1920s, but by the 1930s some of the writers had become committed politically or socially in response to the demoralization, fragmentation, and militarization they found in Europe. The strongly experimental atmosphere created literary salons and small printing presses, and encouraged feverish literary activity, much of it proving to be the greatest of the century. London, too, was host to some of the most important American writers of the century, such as T.S. Eliot and Ezra Pound. Women became significant contributors to the avant-garde, in particular Gertrude Stein and Kay Boyle in Paris and Amy Lowell in London.

1 Stephen Crane (as "Johnston Smith"). *Maggie, a Girl of the Streets.* New York, 1893. Original wrappers. Author's first book. **£3,000–5,000/$4,800–8,000.** One of a few copies printed privately for the author.

2 Theodore Dreiser. *Sister Carrie.* New York, 1900. Author's first book. **£3,000–4,000/$4,800–6,400**

3 Edgar Allan Poe. *Murders in the Rue Morgue.* Philadelphia, 1843. First edition of the first detective story, one of approximately 15 surviving copies, in original wrappers. **£50,000–70,000/$80,000–112,000**

ERNEST HEMINGWAY

Ernest Hemingway and F. Scott Fitzgerald perhaps best sum up this period, but their early works are expensive and beyond the reach of the average collector. Ernest Hemingway was born in Illinois in 1899 and as a boy developed a passion for the outdoor pursuits that so marked his novels. After a short period as a journalist he enlisted in an ambulance unit and was severely wounded at the close of the War. This affected him deeply, forcing him to confront death and annihilation, themes recurrent throughout his books and often thrown into contrast with the extreme pleasures and physical attributes available in life. Sent as a newspaper correspondent to Paris, he began to write under the instruction of Gertrude Stein and Ezra Pound. He emerged as the most gifted of the "Lost Generation" and is still widely read and avidly collected today.

His earliest books are exceptionally hard to find in fine condition and command vast prices. His first two books were privately printed in editions of 300 and 170 copies: *Three Stories and Ten Poems* (Paris, 1923), and *In Our Time* (Paris, 1924). The first was bound in wrappers and the second in boards, and both are notoriously fragile. *In Our Time*, a series of short stories about the expatriate American, was published in a trade edition in the US in 1925 and in the UK in 1926 and there are numerous textual differences between the two.

His first major success was *The Sun Also Rises* (New York, 1926), in which two expatriates are forced to confront the hollowness of their lives against the passionate background of the bullfighting and drinking of the fiesta at Pamplona in Spain. There are issue points to watch for in this expensive work, notably "stoppped" misspelt on page 181. The first UK edition of 1927 was titled *Fiesta*.

The novel for which Hemingway is best remembered today is *A Farewell to Arms* (New York, 1929), and this too can be found in a limited edition of 510 copies, an ordinary copy with no disclaimer on page [x], the later issue with the disclaimer added, and two issues of the first UK edition of 1929. His work from 1930 on, which tends to rework earlier themes, with the exception of *For Whom the Bell Tolls* (New York, 1940), can be found relatively easily.

Living in Cuba in the latter part of his life after serving in World War II, and frustrated with his increasing inability to continue with his active life, Hemingway shot himself in 1961. Cyril Connolly, in his important book *100 Key Books of the Modern Movement from England, France and America 1880–1950*, describes him thus: "No other writer here recorded stepped so suddenly into fame, or destroyed with such insouciance so many other writers or ways of writing or became such an immediate symbol of an age."

1 Ernest Hemingway. *In Our Time*. Paris, 1924. One of 170 copies. Pictorial boards. **£15,000–25,000/$24,000–40,000**

2 Ernest Hemingway. *A Farewell to Arms*. New York, 1929. In the dust-jacket. First issue with no disclaimer on p.[x]. **£1,000–1,500/ $1,600–2,400**

3 Ernest Hemingway. *For Whom the Bell Tolls*. New York, 1940. In the dust-jacket. **£800–1,200/$1,280–1,920**

F. SCOTT FITZGERALD

The best exponent of the American "bright young things" led a deeply disillusioned and troubled life. Born in Minnesota in 1896, he was educated as a Catholic, and his first story, a piece of detective fiction, appeared in his school magazine when he was 13. After studying at Princeton, he wrote his first novel, the semi-autobiographical *This Side of Paradise* (New York, 1920), while serving in the army. This youthful work of failed dreams, coupled with his message of waste and the need for responsibility, suited his generation and became a best-seller, making him rich. Marrying Zelda a week after its publication, he embarked on an extravagant lifestyle and for many he defined the age of jazz and the 1920s, but instinctively he felt the balance was flawed. In his next major work, *The Beautiful and the Damned* (New York, 1922), he continued to chronicle this hollow world of parties and money, but the public did not like the gloomy satire of this work and those which followed. The dust-jacket for this book is found in two issues: the first has the title in white outlined in black.

His greatest novels, *The Great Gatsby* (New York, 1925) and *Tender is the Night* (New York, 1934), although finding critical acclaim from T.S. Eliot and others, had little popular or commercial success. The first issue of *The Great Gatsby* has various issue points to check, and the first-issue dust-jacket for *Tender is the Night* has no printed reviews.

It is later generations who have appreciated and recognized his work for what it is and the importance of his themes of "responsibility", the interior exhaustion and decline of leadership at all levels of society, and his insights into the American class system. In many ways his novels chart the breakdown of the American dream itself during the inter-war years.

Fitzgerald died in 1940, exhausted and having written only five novels and a few volumes of short stories, but his small body of work has become highly sought-after and correspondingly expensive. His reputation began to be revived during the 1950s, and by the 1960s he was regarded, along with Ernest Hemingway, as one of the great US writers.

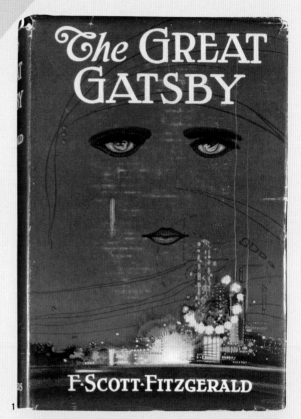

1 F. Scott Fitzgerald. *The Great Gatsby*. New York, 1925. In the first-state dust-jacket with "jay Gatsby" on lower cover. **£70,000–100,000/$112,000–160,000**

2 F. Scott Fitzgerald. *Tender is the Night*. New York, 1934. In a repaired first-state dust-jacket, without reviews. **£5,000–8,000/$8,000–12,800**

The Great Depression

The 1930s was for many a period of transition, for others it brought the prophecy of another war. It was a decade that seemed to spell little hope: 1929 and the Wall Street Crash, the Great Depression and the huge migration of the rural workforce of Middle America. Encroaching cynicism and nihilism led to the rise of the American gangster novel and the exploration of the underworld and its corruption, while other writers turned to the heart of America and its people, and how they too were losing their innocence.

William Faulkner spent the majority of his life in the state of Mississippi. His first book was a collection of verse, *The Marble Faun* (Boston, 1925), his first novel, *A Soldier's Pay* (New York, 1926). Both are exceedingly rare, and although it was intended that 1,000 copies of *The Marble Faun* be printed, in fact only 500 were, of which about 300 were destroyed. There are issue points to check for the majority of his works, in particular for his best-known book, *The Sound and the Fury* (New York, 1929): the first-issue dust-jacket is unpriced and has "Humanity Uprooted" priced at $3.00 on the lower cover.

Although his works spring from and are about the people of Mississippi, they transcend the regional, defining an imaginative vision of human existence through myth. Although often brutal in its realism and employing Modernist techniques and devices, he does affirm the good part of human values, while recognizing that through external events these often fail. A prolific writer, Faulkner was awarded the Nobel Prize for Literature in 1950. His books are generally expensive, the earliest ones exceptionally so, although those post-1940 become more readily available.

John Steinbeck was also awarded the Nobel Prize in 1962. It is his work *The Grapes of Wrath* (New York, 1939) that for many best evokes the Great Depression and the rural migration of 1930s middle America. His first book was *Cup of Gold* (New York, 1929), present in two issues, the first with the top edge stained blue and "First published August, 1929" on the copyright page. His work is not as expensive as those authors previously mentioned, many finding it too objective, and even his best-known books, *The Grapes of Wrath*, *Of Mice and Men* (New York, 1937), and *Tortilla Flat* (New York, 1935), are not too expensive. The majority of his work has issue points to check. As with Faulkner, most of his work is related to one place: the California of his childhood, or of the 1930s.

Other writers of the 1930s to look for could include Sinclair Lewis, whose best-known work is *Main Street* (New York, 1920), and Thomas Wolfe, whose greatest novel was his first, *Look Homeward, Angel* (New York, 1929).

1 William Faulkner. *The Sound and the Fury*. New York, 1929. In the first-issue dust-jacket with advertisement for *Humanity Uprooted* on lower cover priced at $3.00. **£4,000–5,000/$6,400–8,000**

2 John Steinbeck. *The Grapes of Wrath*. New York, 1939. In the dust-jacket. **£2,000–3,000/$3,200–4,800**

3 Thomas Wolfe. *Look Homeward, Angel*. New York, 1929. Author's first book, in dust-jacket. **£1,500–2,500/$2,400–4,000**

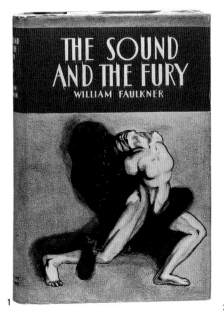

The Political Thirties

The 1930s were shaped by battle: the memory of the Great War (for many, the exorcizing of its horrors, for others, guilt at not being part of it); the spectre of Stalinist Russia and the march of Communism; the rise of the Fascists in Spain and Germany; and the ever-looming presence of another Great War. No longer could the artist write in splendid, experimental isolation: external politics and society became inextricably linked with the role of the writer. What had appeared avant-garde in the 1920s was now accepted and institutionalized, and writers who had only been published privately or by small presses were now embraced by mainstream firms. Whereas in the 1920s everything had seemed possible, and hope and experiment seemed the key, in the 1930s destruction and bitterness, guilt, anger, and frustration held sway. There was an intense desire to change society and many writers temporarily joined the Communist party or went to Spain to fight for the Republican Party against General Franco. By the close of the decade, most of these had become disillusioned and returned to models they were familiar with. One group of writers came to be known as the "Auden Generation", sharing a political ideology and, often homosexual tendencies; they were W.H. Auden, Christopher Isherwood, Stephen Spender, Cecil Day-Lewis, and Louis MacNeice.

The poet W.H. Auden's rise to fame had been swift. Recognized by his contemporaries at Oxford, his public acclaim came with publication of "Paid on Both Sides" in T.S. Eliot's influential periodical *The Criterion* in January 1930, followed in September by the Faber publication *Poems*. This compilation of verse had initially been printed privately in 1928 by Stephen Spender in an edition of 45 copies bound in orange wrappers. This is one of the legendary rarities of 20th-century literature, and although its limitation statement claims 45 copies were printed, the true number was closer to 30, of which about 11 copies are known today. He was a prolific poet and although considered one of the greatest of the century, his work, apart from the 1928 edition of *Poems*, can mostly be acquired for under £200/$300. Although poetry was hugely influential at the time and widely read, many collectors today have veered away from it, not reading it themselves. Apart from a few sought-after classics such as Hart Crane's *The Bridge* and T.S. Eliot's *The Waste Land*, poetry remains an undervalued area of collecting, and may be ripe for reassessment. A pivotal literary figure, W.H. Auden collaborated with his friends and contemporaries. With Christopher Isherwood he wrote several plays, including *The Dog Beneath the Skin* (1935), and with Louis MacNeice volumes of prose such as *Letters from Iceland*

(1937) about their trek across Iceland. In 1937, after a brief spell in Spain against Franco, he wrote a poem titled *Spain*, the royalties from which went to Medical Aid for Spain. All these works were published by Faber, whose editor at the time was T.S. Eliot. This was the beginning of their important list of critically acclaimed writers, a tradition which continues today. The publications of Faber could make a good starting-point for a collector. The books have always had an individual feel, with distinctive design and typography, and in 1981 their whole list was overhauled by the Pentagram Design Partnership and strict house rules on design were laid down. They are today some of the most interesting books around from both a literary and a design point of view.

Apart from his collaborations with Auden, Christopher Isherwood is best known by most people for two works of fiction, *Mr Norris Changes Trains* (1935) and *Goodbye to Berlin* (1939). Set in Berlin where he went to teach for four years (sent, he claimed, by W.H. Auden), these books reflect the vibrant and sexually ambiguous life of the city. The sketch "Sally Bowles" from *Goodbye to Berlin* was published separately by the Hogarth Press in 1937 and was subsequently turned into the film and musical *Cabaret*. Both he and Auden left Europe for the US in 1939, Auden for the East Coast and Isherwood for the more liberal West Coast, where he spent some time as a Hollywood script-writer. His first published book was *All the Conspirators* (1928), and it is only this and the two aforementioned novels that command four-figure sums, the remainder of his work being widely available under £100/$150.

Stephen Spender began his career as a poet with the exceptionally rare pamphlet *Nine Experiments by S.H.S.: Being Poems Written at the Age of Eighteen*, hand-printed in an edition of about 18 copies by the author. The track record of this piece at auction over the past 13 years is interesting: it reached $57,000 (£38,000) in the Bradley Martin sale in New York in 1990, later that same year in London it realized £24,000 ($36,000) at auction, but in 1996 at auction it was unsold on an estimate of £7,000–9,000/$10,500–13,500. A salutary lesson for the collector: often the first appearance at auction of such a rare item as this ensures an exceptional price, which may take many years to be repeated. Stephen Spender's next work was the uncommon *Twenty Poems* (1930), published in an edition of 135 copies, of which 75 were signed; however, the remainder of his verse compilations, the last of which was published in 1994, the year before his death, his novels, plays, and numerous critical works can easily be found for under £100/$160. Other political poets of this

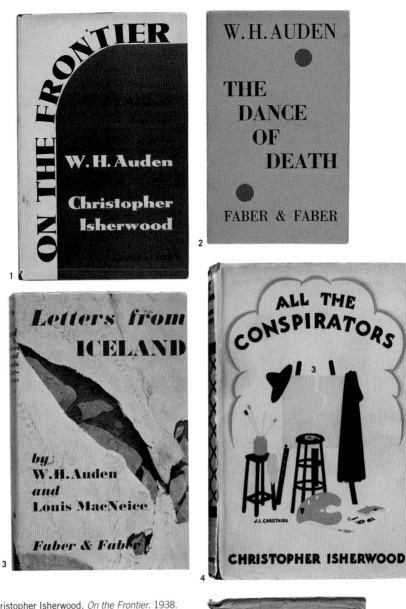

1 W.H. Auden and Christopher Isherwood. *On the Frontier*. 1938. In the dust-jacket. **£200–300/$320–480**

2 W.H. Auden. *The Dance of Death*. 1933. In the dust-jacket. **£200–300$320–480**

3 W.H. Auden and Louis MacNeice. *Letters from Iceland*. 1937. In the dust-jacket. **£100–150/$160–240**

4 Christopher Isherwood. *All the Conspirators*. 1928. In the dust-jacket. **£200–300/$320–480**

5 Stephen Spender. *Nine Experiments*. Hampstead, 1928. One of 30 copies. The author's first book. **£20,000–30,000/ £32,000–48,000**

period worth looking for include the Scottish nationalist poet Hugh MacDiarmid and the Marxist Edward Upward.

George Orwell was a committed socialist and defined himself as a political, but not Communist, writer. His early and most sought-after works, including his first novel, *Burmese Days*, initially published in the US in 1934, and *A Clergyman's Daughter* (1935), took a fictional look at the narrowness of the British abroad, but it was his gritty political journalism that ensured his reputation, as well as works such as *Down and Out in Paris and London* (1933), for which he drew on his own experiences. He too left to fight in Spain from where he returned politically disillusioned. His best-known works, although not his most valuable, are the two anti-totalitarian fables, *Animal Farm* (1945) and *Nineteen Eighty-Four* (1949), the latter present in two colours of dust-jackets, red being the earlier.

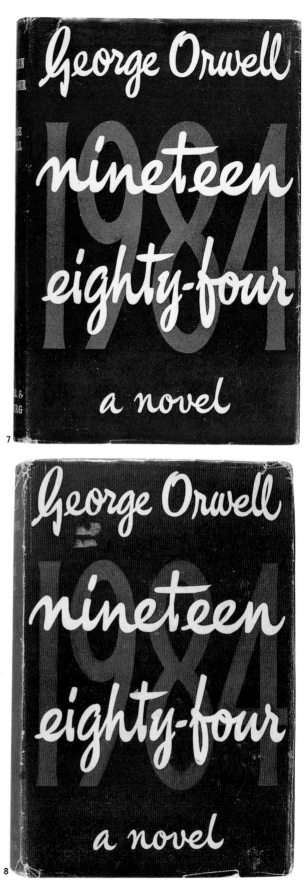

6 George Orwell. *Animal Farm*. 1945. In the dust-jacket.
£2,000–3,000/$3,200–4,800

7 George Orwell. *Nineteen Eighty-Four*. 1949. In green dust-jacket.
£1,400–1,800/$2,240–2,880

8 George Orwell. *Nineteen Eighty-Four*. 1949. In red dust-jacket.
£700–900/$1,120–1,440

GRAHAM GREENE

Graham Greene was described by his biographer Norman Sherry as "the chronicler of our age, a tormented man, a great Catholic... He was that curious hybrid, a popular writer, but never insubstantial and light. He was a genuine writer, a near genius." Cyril Connolly wrote: "Graham Greene is one of the few Catholic writers who is also a modernist."

Greene's writing career spans the entire 20th century, his first published work, *Babbling April*, appearing in 1925, his last, *A World of My Own* (1992), after his death in April 1991. Widely read and critically respected in his day, at home and abroad, he remains so today and has become one of the most collected authors of the century. His major themes were nurtured while at boarding school where his father was headmaster: betrayal, the struggles of the underdog, and a criticism of authority, whether secular or religious. Many of his 26 novels were set abroad and a battle with Catholicism runs throughout many of them. The phrase "whisky priest", now a part of our vocabulary, came from Greene.

Collecting Graham Greene is a relatively straightforward affair, for fine copies of his later novels from 1948 on can be acquired for a few hundred pounds, including important titles such as *The End of the Affair* (1951), *The Third Man* (1950), and *The Heart of the Matter* (1948). Most of his earlier works, although more expensive, can be found regularly in the low thousands. It is worth waiting for the best copies available, and to be aware of issue points for titles such as *Stamboul Train* (1932): the advanced state of the text known in proof form was suppressed and although it is assumed a published version of this may exist, none has to date been located. *The Name of*

Action (1930) has the jacket priced at 7/6 and contains reviews of his first novel, *The Man Within* (1929). *The Power and the Glory* (1940) was issued in the US in the same year as *Labyrinthine Ways*. However, there are two legendary rarities: *Rumour at Nightfall* (1931) and *Brighton Rock* (1938). The first was suppressed by the author and later by his estate, and is relatively unknown, and the second, although issued in a large print-run of 8,000 copies, is simply exceedingly scarce in the jacket. The rare issue is the first English edition, for the American edition preceded the English by one month. Works inscribed by Greene are not uncommon, but when the inscription is to his wife, Vivien, or to his mistress, Catherine Walston, the prices will become very high.

If one is interested in collecting Graham Greene, the 16 December 1996 Sotheby's London catalogue of the collection of Clinton Ives Smullyan would be worth acquiring. In that sale Greene's own annotated proof copy of *The End of the Affair* (1951), sent to Evelyn Waugh for his comments and annotated by him, realized £18,000 ($27,000), and a first edition of the book inscribed to Dorothy Glover fetched £6,000 ($9,000). In the Rechler sale in New York in 2002 the exact same pair realized $45,000 (£30,000).

1 Graham Greene. *The Confidential Agent.* 1939. In the dust-jacket.
£3,000–5,000/$4,800–8,000

2 Graham Greene. *Travels with my Aunt.* 1969. In the dust-jacket.
£100–150/$160–240

3 Graham Greene. *The Third Man.* 1950. In the dust-jacket.
£200–300/$320–480

The Post-war British Novel

Throughout the 1940s and 1950s critics announced that the novel was dead, that there were no longer any great writers. The influential writer and critic Harold Nicholson wrote in *The Observer* in 1954, "I do not see, therefore, that the conditions which render fiction a relevant form of expression exist in the current generation." This was, however, precisely the period during which the careers of some of the greatest post-war writers began: Angus Wilson, Doris Lessing, Anthony Burgess, Muriel Spark, Iris Murdoch, William Golding, and Kingsley Amis. In fact, 1954 is generally thought now to be the key year for the emergence of this post-war fiction, the year in which two major first novels were published, William Golding's highly sought-after *Lord of the Flies* and Kingsley Amis' *Lucky Jim*. It was also the year in which J.R.R. Tolkien published the first volume in his trilogy *The Lord of the Rings*, *The Fellowship of the Ring*, which has shot up in value due to the film release.

Books from this period were generally published in larger print-runs, no longer had their dust-jackets discarded and tend to be more readily available in good condition to the new collector on a smaller budget. There is a wealth of names to choose from according to one's own taste or interest, but there are some trends worth looking at and some key names to be noted that are generally regarded as the best of the generation. Novelists of this period are some of the most accessible writers for the new collector to acquire, both from content and price. It is essential that the dust-jacket is present, and condition should be of the best for all books from this date.

For various reasons, several important authors produced long series of novels over a period of years, and these often proved to be astute social and historical commentaries on their age. It is usually only the first publication of each author that will command a price in three figures. Perhaps the best known and most collected is Anthony Powell's 12-volume "A Dance to the Music of Time" (1951–75), *A Question of Upbringing* (1951), being the first. Henry Williamson wrote a 15-volume saga "A Chronicle of Ancient Sunlight" between 1951 and 1969. C.P. Snow wrote the 11-volume series "Strangers and Brothers" between 1940 and 1970, which charted the arrival and development of the welfare state and the nuclear age, and Joyce Cary wrote two trilogies, the first including *The Horse's Mouth* (1944), the second *Not Honour More* (1955).

In 1956 the "kitchen sink" painters, a group of left-wing realists whose depiction of everyday reality provided them with their label, exhibited at the Venice Biennale. Their influence was as far-reaching as the Post-Impressionists who exhibited in London in 1910. In the same year John Osborne's *Look Back in Anger* was performed at the Royal Court Theatre, and the term "angry young men" was also coined. A whole group of novelists began to emerge who charted everyday life (mostly working-class), unified by the desire to escape up and out of its restrictions. Alan Sillitoe's *Saturday Night, Sunday Morning* (1958) and *The Loneliness of the Long-Distance Runner* (1959), winner of the Hawthornden Prize, Colin MacInnes' *Absolute Beginners* (1957), Nell Dunn's *Up the Junction* (1963), John Braine's *Life at the Top* (1964), and Bill Naughton's *Alfie* (1966) are some of the best-known and collected works. Often it was the accompanying film or dramatization that guaranteed the survival of these works. For several of these writers it was their first work that ensured their fame and reputation and is still the work most widely read and sought-after today, but rarely fetching more than £200/$300, with later works perhaps being overlooked and readily available for under £50/$75.

Kingsley Amis achieved fame with his first novel, *Lucky Jim* (1954), although he had previously published two volumes of poetry, in 1947 *Bright November*, and in 1953 *A Frame of Mind*. The hero of his novel, Jim Dixon, was subsequently hailed as one of the first of the "angry young men". His later work often became increasingly conservative and hostile to contemporary life, although full of satirical comedy. Apart from his first novel and volume of verse, which will reach four figures, the remainder of his work can be found easily under £50/$75. The early yellow Gollancz dust-jackets are notoriously fragile,

1 John Fowles. *The Collector*. 1963. In first issue dust-jacket. **£250–350/$400–560**

2 Inner flap of first-issue dust-jacket of *The Collector*, without reviews.

3 Lawrence Durrell. *Justine*. 1957. In the dust-jacket. **£100–150/$160–240**

4 Malcolm Bradbury. *The History Man*. 1975. In the dust-jacket. **£80–100/$128–160**

5 Kingsley Amis. *Lucky Jim*. 1953. In the dust-jacket. **£2,500–3,500/$4,000–5,600**

6 William Golding. *Lord of the Flies*. 1954. In the dust-jacket. **£3,500–4,500/$5,600–7,200**

7 Anthony Powell. "A Dance to the Music of Time". 1951–75. Twelve volumes, dust-jackets. **£1,500–2,000/$2,400–3,200**

1

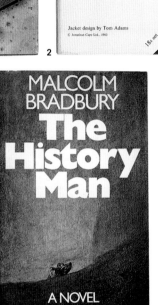

2

THE COLLECTOR

As stark as a police report, this novel opens with the confession of a young suburban clerk who has kidnapped an art student from outside her home in Hampstead. In his own colourless, yet curiously expressive words, Frederick Clegg tells how he held her prisoner in a remote house in the country, which he had bought for the purpose with money won in the football pools. Leaving nothing to chance, he is as meticulous over the details of his complicated plan as he is with the layout of his butterfly collection. At every turn he justifies his actions—'I only wanted to do the best for her, make her happy and love me a bit'—until the outcome seems horrifyingly inevitable.

The girl, thoughtful, yet impetuous and eager for life, and to him a creature from a different world, surreptitiously records Clegg's feelings of inferiority and his pathetic attempts to make her understand him. Desperately she tries to persuade him to release her.

A remarkable feat of imagination, The Collector is a novel of suspense and disquieting perception whose cumulative effect is all too memorable.

Jacket design by Tom Adams
© Jonathan Cape Ltd., 1963

18s net

3

JUSTINE

a novel by Lawrence Durrell

4

MALCOLM BRADBURY
The History Man

A NOVEL

5

LUCKY JIM

C. P. SNOW WRITES:
"It is humorous, self-mocking, hopeful endearing. For promise & achievement combined, it is the best first novel I've read in the last two years"

KINGSLEY AMIS

6

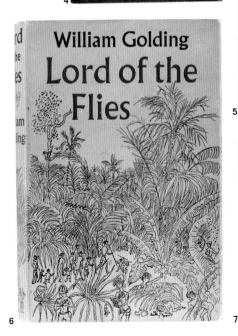

William Golding
Lord of the Flies

7

8

9

10

11

12

13

English and American Literature

though and are often to be found on *Lucky Jim* browned and chipped.

Other major authors to look for from this period include William Golding, Lawrence Durrell, Angus Wilson, John Fowles, and Anthony Burgess.

One of the most radical and innovative novelists of this period was the Irishman Samuel Beckett who published a trilogy in London in 1959: *Molloy, Malone Dies*, and *The Unnamable*. Friend of Joyce, poet, dramatist, novelist, and critic, his work, usually initially published in French, can be looked at best in the context of Irish literature (see pages 70–1). However, the majority of fiction during the 1950s was not radical or experimental, being avowedly popular or realist.

One author who did respond to "modern" fiction, and embraced the concept, being influenced in particular by D.H. Lawrence and Henry Miller, was Lawrence Durrell. His work was also received enthusiastically by the public. Born in India in 1912, and briefly living a bohemian life in England in the 1930s, he ultimately settled in the Mediterranean, first in Corfu then Egypt. His earliest work was verse, *Quaint Fragments* (1931), found in two issues of red boards and blue wrappers, but it was his "Alexandria Quartet", *Justine* (1957), *Balthazar* (1958), *Mountolive* (1958), and *Clea* (1960), that ensured his reputation and remains today the best known of his books. *Justine* was issued in a small print-run initially and was reprinted twice in 1957 and twice in 1958. His most expensive works are the rare early volumes of verse and fiction from the 1930s, including *Panic Spring*, rare in either the 1937 US or UK edition in dust jacket, whereas most of his other books can be acquired for under £50/$75. There was a deluxe one-volume edition of the "Alexandria Quartet" published in 1962, which was limited to 500 copies signed by the author.

William Golding's first and most popular novel was the controversial *Lord of the Flies* (1954). This, and his rare first book, *Poems*, published in 1934, remain today those most sought-after by collectors. *Lord of the Flies* is an important work and has become extremely desirable in the dust-jacket. The majority of his works continued to focus on moral allegory, but the later works became more complex and difficult as he explored the themes of human depravity, free will, and fallen humanity. In 1961 a small pamphlet of his, *The Ladder and the Tree*, was printed by John Randle in an edition of approximately 100 copies. This was Randle's first piece of printing, executed several years before he founded the Whittington Press (see page 142). His most recent stories of the 1980s alternated between land and sea, all dealing with extremity and isolation. *Rites of Passage* was awarded the Booker Prize in 1980 and Golding received the Nobel Prize for Literature in 1983.

Angus Wilson wrote his first novel, *Hemlock and After* (1952), after working at Bletchley Park during the War in code-breaking and signals intelligence. His earliest short stories were published by Cyril Connolly in the important periodical *Horizon* and his first published compilation was *The Wrong Set and Other Stories* (1949). His early work, often biting and cruel, refers constantly to what he perceived as the outdated class system, with his upper-class characters often adrift in the post-war world. His later work continues to look at the anxieties of post-war liberalism, and the role of the writer and the intellectual in this new world. One of his most widely acclaimed novels is the panoramic *Anglo-Saxon Attitudes* (1956), constantly compared to Dickens.

John Fowles' first novel was *The Collector* (1963), which is found in three different issues: a trial binding of black paper-over-boards, top edge plain, the dust-jacket for which has no reviews; rust-coloured boards with similar coloured top edge and jacket with no reviews; and rust boards in jacket with reviews. The first issue is the most expensive, but interestingly, the third issue is rarer and hence more sought-after by collectors than the second issue. His other well-known novels can be found more easily, with various later revised editions and signed limited editions to look for. Fowles' work explores repression and what he sees as its antitheses, sexual energy and freedom. In the absence perhaps of new published work, prices for his books have currently levelled off and in some cases even declined.

Anthony Burgess published his first novel, *Time for a Tiger*, in 1956, but it is the anarchic and experimental novel *A Clockwork Orange* (1962) that remains his best-known and most sought-after work. The first issue dust-jacket is priced at 16/s-, and the first state binding comprises black boards. His first three novels were set in the Far East and later works include the comic trilogy *Inside Mr Enderby* (1963) and its sequels, as well as the long, ambitious, and complex first-person novel *Earthly Powers* (1980).

8 Anthony Burgess. *A Clockwork Orange*. 1962. First issue in black cloth, in the dust-jacket. **£1,000–1,500/$1,600–2,400**

9 Alan Sillitoe. *Saturday Night and Sunday Morning*. 1958. In the dust-jacket. **£80–100/$128–160**

10 Bill Naughton. *Alfie*. 1966. In the dust-jacket. **£100–150 /$160–240**

11 Colin MacInnes. *Absolute Beginners*. 1959. In the dust-jacket. **£100–150/$160–240**

12 David Storey. *Flight into Camden*. 1960. In the dust-jacket. **£100–150/$160–240**

13 John Braine. *Life at the Top*. 1962. In the dust-jacket. **£50–100/$80–160**

American Post-war Writers

The major post-war American writers often tackled more wide-reaching and fundamental issues than their English counterparts, hence their literature often seems more universal and less parochial, and yet often more specific: the role of the US in the international arena and the wars it fought, homosexuality, and the problems of the increasingly vocal black population. Two major American writers working throughout the 1940s and 1950s in fact published their earliest works in the 1920s and 1930s. John Dos Passos wrote his first book, *One Man's Initiation: 1917*, in 1920, and this is to be found in two states of text, both of which were censored, the earliest with broken type on page 35. It was reissued in 1969 with the text complete. *Three Soldiers* (1921) is more complex, with two states of the text and three of the jacket. Perhaps his most famous books are his "U.S.A." trilogy: *The 42nd Parallel* (1930), *1919* (1932), and *The Big Money* (1936), which can also be collected in a limited edition from 1946, signed and numbered by the author and illustrator, Reginald Marsh. Part of the "Lost Generation" of the 1920s, his work covers American social history from a left-wing stance, from which he withdrew during the 1930s. His later work is rather sentimental and nostalgic.

Henry Miller made his name with *Tropic of Cancer* (1934), in which he wrote about the promiscuity of Paris. This and much of his work was repressed by English and American censors. The first edition of this book, as well as of *Tropic of Capricorn* (1939) and his other works were issued privately in Paris, usually by the Obelisk Press, and did not appear in the US until the 1960s. The first issue of *Tropic of Cancer* appeared in green and white wrappers, and the second in plain wrappers but with a pictorial dust-jacket. Both are equally sought-after. All his Parisian imprints are fairly scarce, commanding four-figure sums, but his US imprints are easier to find. His work champions the freedom of the individual, in particular that of the eccentric and the artist, especially in matters of sex, and he repudiates much of the control of modern American society. This and his persistence in using writing as a means of self-development won him a huge following during the 1950s and 1960s.

Norman Mailer and Truman Capote both published their first works in 1948: *The Naked and the Dead*, and *Other Voices, Other Rooms*. Norman Mailer excelled at taking real events and fictionalizing them. Having fought in the War, a recurrent image is that of man on patrol against his enemy in the jungle or city. The fame generated by his first novel dogged him for years and his next few works were not well received by the public. Always politically committed, his works chart the changes in American society throughout the years of McCarthyism, the Vietnam War, Hollywood, and the protest marches of the 1960s. He is an important and easily affordable novelist for the collector who is interested in the role of the US in the modern world. Truman Capote, also a journalist, wrote initially about the South and its decadence. Much of his early writing is rather surreal, but it was with the publication of *Breakfast at Tiffany's* (1958), his most collectable work and subsequently made into a film with a shift of locale to New York, that he achieved fame. His later work was closer to reportage.

Other writers of this period worth looking for include Joseph Heller, whose *Catch-22* (1961), with the first-issue dust-jacket priced at $5.95, was such an instant success. It famously took the author many years to write another. There are also issue points about the first English edition to watch for. Thomas Pynchon's first novel, *V* (1963), was also a success not replicated by his later works. Both these brilliant and important novels are now considerably more expensive than their authors' later works. Another author defined and remembered by his first novel is James Baldwin, whose *Go Tell It on the Mountain* (1953) is a key work, and one of the first in the modern wave of Black American novels. His second novel, *Giovanni's Room* (1956), was eventually published by the Dial Press after fears over censorship of its explicit homosexuality.

1 Joseph Heller. *Catch-22*. New York, 1961. In the dust-jacket. **£1,500–2,000/$2,400–3,200**

2 Henry Miller. *Tropic of Capricorn*. Paris, 1939. **£400–600/ $640–960**

3 John Dos Passos. *The 42nd Parallel*. New York, 1930. In the dust-jacket. **£500–700/$800–1,120**

4 Thomas Pynchon. *The Crying of Lot 49*. Philadelphia, 1966. In the dust-jacket. **£250–350/400–560**

5 Norman Mailer. *Barbary Shore*. New York, 1951. In the dust-jacket. **£200–300/$320–480**

6 Charles Bukowski. *Flower, Fist and Bestial Wail*. Eureka, 1960. Signed on the cover by the author with an ink sketch. **£500–600/$800–960**

7 James Baldwin. *Go Tell it on the Mountain*. New York, 1953. Advance issue in wrappers, with rejected cover design. **£1,000–1,500/$1,600–2,400**

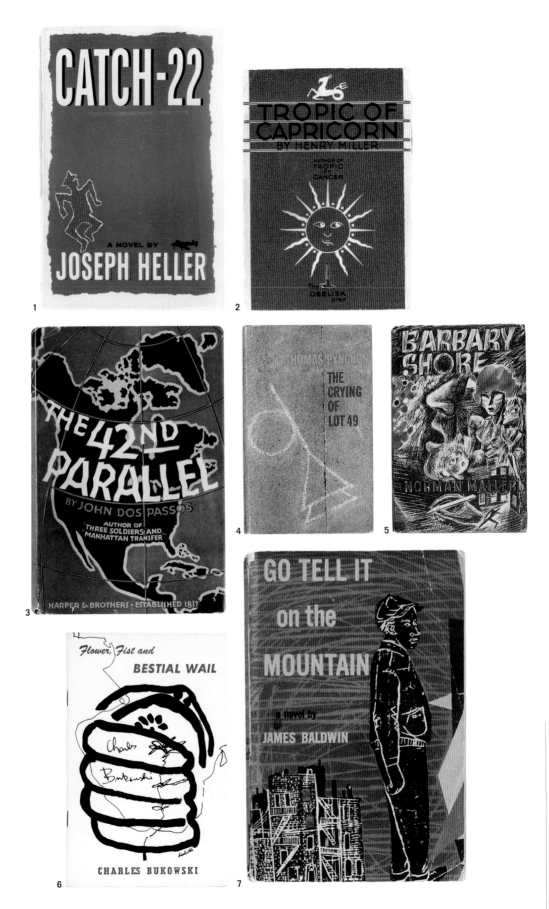

THE BEAT GENERATION

Active in the 1950s was a group of writers who have passed into legend and been accorded cult status: the Beat Generation. The most important of these were William Burroughs, Allen Ginsberg, and Jack Kerouac. Others such as Lawrence Ferlinghetti joined later, but it is the first three whose works are the most sought-after, having defined the thoughts and attitudes of generations of Americans, many of whom are the most influential collectors of today. Jack Kerouac is representative of this generation for most people, and indeed it was he who first coined the term "beat" in 1952, in an article by John Clellon Holmes in *The New Yorker*.

First and foremost the Beat Generation were critical of American complacency under the Ike–Nixon regime, and they investigated new forms of poetry and stretched consciousness. In conjunction with existing bohemian enclaves in New York, San Francisco, and Los Angeles they produced a distinctive style of living and literature. The key works were Allen Ginsberg's poem "Howl", initially censored prior to its final publication in 1955, Jack Kerouac's *On the Road* (1957), William Burrough's *Junkie* (1953) and *Naked Lunch* (1959), as well as Lawrence Ferlinghetti's works issued from his City Lights bookshop in San Francisco. Beat magazines abounded.

On the Road was Kerouac's second novel, following *The Town and the City* (1950), but it is the "Beat" novel collectors aim to acquire, accounting for its high price. The first English edition of 1958 is present in two issues, the first with the author's photo on the rear flap. This seminal novel was written while "on the road" on a continuous scroll of paper which was sold at auction at Christie's New York in 2001 for a sum in excess of $3 million. Presentation copies of his works are notoriously rare. Only five inscribed copies of *On the Road* have been sold at auction in the past 30 years – that to his lover Joyce Johnston was sold at auction at Christie's New York in 2002 for $160,000 (£106,660).

The poet Allen Ginsberg published his first collection of verse, *Howl and other Poems*, in 1956 to huge popular acclaim. Widely regarded today as one of the greatest American poets of the 20th century, he grew from being one of the founding members of the Beat Generation and developed into an intensely political and contemporary poet, whose work touches many. He promoted his friends' work and was largely responsible for their publication. He was awarded many honours, including the National Book Award for *The Fall of America* (1974). His first volume of poems will be beyond the reach of most collectors, but the 1971 signed and limited edition with a new introduction and additional verse is not so expensive, and his subsequent collections are widely available for more modest sums. A fascinating item to acquire for reference would be the catalogue for the 7 October 1999 Sotheby's New York auction "Allen Ginsberg and Friends", which included much literary material, as well as memorabilia from the estates of Kerouac, Burroughs, and Ginsberg.

1 Jack Kerouac. *On the Road*. New York, 1957. In the dust-jacket. **£3,000–4,000/$4,800–6,400**

2 Allen Ginsberg. *Howl and Other Poems*. San Francisco, 1966. Later printing, inscribed by Ginsberg to Ezra Pound. **£4,000–6,000/$6,400–9,600**

American Contemporary Fiction

The market in contemporary fiction is quite unlike any other in that collectors are often choosing to pay a premium for a writer only recently published on a hunch that time will prove their worth, both commercially and from a literary standpoint. Signed first editions do not tend to have the scarcity value they used to, for publishers today demand that their authors regularly attend book-signing sessions. Collecting in this area is often purely a matter of taste, whether one's choice be Tom Clancy, Tom Wolfe, Michael Crichton or John Cheever. It is often the first work of such authors that commands the greatest price, usually being issued in a small print-run: Ken Kesey's great *One Flew Over the Cuckoo's Nest* (1962), for example, has long been a cult novel, with the remainder of his work to date available for very low prices. Authors such as Gore Vidal and John Updike, still prolific, widely read and critically acclaimed, could be worth collecting, but once again it will be their earlier works that are the most valuable. Many avidly collected authors come from within the genres of science fiction, the supernatural or crime and can be best looked at in those contexts.

Once an author has been filmed, such as Tom Clancy (*The Hunt for Red October*, 1984, his first novel) or Michael Crichton (*The Andromeda Strain*, 1969, or *Jurassic Park*, 1990), they will gain a greater audience. Charles Frazier's *Cold Mountain* (1997) is the latest to be assigned film rights with Nicole Kidman as the star, and it is highly likely that the value of the book, already critically acclaimed, will rise as the film is released.

The skill in collecting in this area lies in predicting who the next Ernest Hemingway or Raymond Chandler may be. This will entail being aware of new publications, public and critical opinion, the films that may be in the pipeline, and who the recipients of the various literary awards are, and then taking an educated guess as to their longevity. Authors who have broken boundaries, such as Alice Walker with *The Color Purple* (New York, 1982) or Bret Easton Ellis with *American Psycho* (New York, 1991), will always be worth collecting.

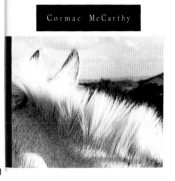

1 Cormac McCarthy. *All the Pretty Horses*. New York, 1992. First volume of the author's "Border" trilogy. In the dust-jacket. **£500–700/$800–1,120**

2 John Grisham. *The Firm*. New York, 1991. In the dust-jacket. **£100–150/$160–240**

3 Hunter S. Thompson. *Hell's Angels*. New York, 1967. In the dust-jacket. Author's first book. **£300–350/$480–560**

British Contemporary Fiction

Andrew Sanders wrote in *The Short Oxford History of English Literature*: "In the 1990s the novel has remained the most accessible, the most discussed, the most promoted, and the most sponsored literary form." There are many contemporary writers for the collector to look for. These may be unashamedly popular such as Dick Francis or Frederick Forsyth, others more complex and avowedly literary, such as A.S. Byatt, or those who have acquired a huge cult following, such as Irving Welsh with *Trainspotting* (1993) or Bruce Chatwin with *On the Black Hill* (1982). As with earlier writers it will probably be the first novel that is the most sought-after, as more often than not, this will be the book that established their reputation and was issued in a small edition. Print-runs increase and later works become more readily available. Martin Amis' first novel, *The Rachel Papers* (1973), is a good example of this. As these contemporary authors become collected, so their publishers seek ways to tap into this and often issue signed limited editions specifically for the market.

So how does one choose which authors to collect? Controversy is often a good pointer: Salman Rushdie's *Midnight's Children* (1981) may be his most sought-after book, but it was his *Satanic Verses* (1988) that drew the world's attention to his work. A film agreement will also boost an author's reputation and usually value: Louis de Bernière's *Captain Corelli's Mandolin* (1994) was his fourth novel but became such a widely read and cult book that when the film rights were assigned his stature as a collectable writer rose. This book is praised in an important work, *The Modern Library: The 200 best novels in English since 1950* by Carmen Callil and Colm Toibin. This, much like Cyril Connolly's earlier book, could give a good indication as to which writers may well be worth collecting for future value and acclaim. Listed in this book are David Lodge, Julian Barnes, and Graham Swift. Others such as Malcolm Bradbury, Tom Sharpe, and Peter Ackroyd are not listed but their works, too, are well worth searching for. Vikram Seth's *A Suitable Boy* (1993) and Sebastian Faulks' *Birdsong* (1993) are two recent works accorded general and critical acclaim that are listed through popular demand in the revised and extended edition of this book. They may no doubt prove in the long term to be valuable additions to a collection of contemporary fiction. A word of caution, however: the hugely popular historical maritime novels of Patrick O'Brian featuring his heroes Jack Aubrey and Stephen Maturin, the first of which is *Master and Commander* (1970), shot up in value during the late 1990s, but recently prices have levelled off.

1 Louis de Bernières. *Captain Corelli's Mandolin*. 1994. In the dust-jacket. First issue in white boards. **£250–350/$400–560**

2 Patrick O'Brian. *Master and Commander*. 1970. In the dust-jacket. The first of the celebrated Jack Aubrey and Stephen Maturin novels. The complete set, in 20 volumes, 1970–99. **£4,000–6,000/$6,400–9,600**

3 Martin Amis. *Dead Babies*. 1975. In the dust-jacket. The author's first book. **£250–350/$400–560**

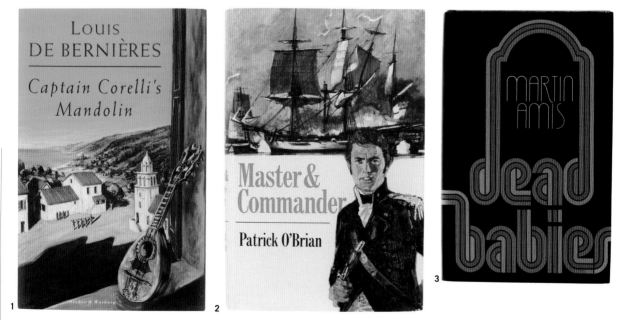

LITERARY AWARDS

The annual literary awards generate feverish activity within the book trade and the book-buying public. The titles listed and, probably more importantly, the winners, could prove to be a good focus for a collection concentrating on contemporary fiction. The awards single out those writers deemed worthy of critical acclaim, which are then usually avidly taken up by the popular readership.

Carmen Callil and Colm Toibin list the major awards and their recipients since 1950 in *The Modern Library*, and these include the Booker Prize, open to citizens of the Commonwealth, Pakistan, and the Republic of Ireland, which was first awarded in 1969 to P.H. Newby for *Something to Answer For*. Subsequent winners have been Iris Murdoch for *The Sea, The Sea* (1978), Salman Rushdie for *Midnight's Children* (1981), Peter Carey for *Oscar and Lucinda* in 1988 and for *The Kelly Gang* (2001), A.S. Byatt for *Possession* (1990), Roddy Doyle for *Paddy Clarke Ha Ha Ha* (1993), and Ian McEwan for *Amsterdam* in 1998.

Joseph Pulitzer was an innovative Hungarian-born American newspaper publisher who, on his death in 1904, left provision for awards for American writers of journalism, letters, and drama, and for education and travelling scholarships. Over the years the board has introduced more awards, now totalling 21 per year. The first Pulitzer Prize was awarded in 1917, and in 2002 it was received by Richard Russo for his novel *Empire Falls*. The selections are occasionally controversial (Ernest Hemingway's earlier work was overlooked, but the Prize was finally awarded to a lesser book, *The Old Man and the Sea*), but Pulitzer-prize-winning authors nevertheless form a roll-call of the best 20th-century American writers, and include Harper Lee, *To Kill a Mockingbird* (1961), Saul Bellow, *Humboldt's Gift* (1976), John Updike, *Rabbit is Rich* (1982), and Philip Roth, *American Pastoral* (1998).

Other prize lists worth considering are the Orange Prize for Fiction by women, the Whitbread Novel Award, and Whitbread First Novel award for British fiction, and for US fiction, the National Book Award. There are also prize awards for Irish, Scottish, Commonwealth, Australian, and New Zealand literature.

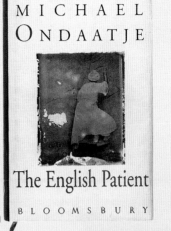

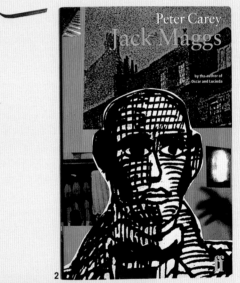

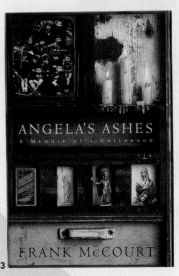

1 Michael Ondaatje. *The English Patient*. 1992. In the dust-jacket. **£350–400/$560–640**

2 Peter Carey. *Jack Maggs*. 1997. In the dust-jacket **£50–80/ $80–128**

3 Frank McCourt. *Angela's Ashes*. 1996. First English edition. In the dust-jacket. **£150–200/$240–320**

Women Writers

Having looked at modern first editions from a chronological perspective, the collector may choose to approach this vast field from a different angle: to concentrate on one particular genre or aspect of literature. Women writers could form a particularly rewarding collection, from the "New Women" of the turn of the century to contemporary writers such as A.S. Byatt, Donna Tartt, and Anne Rice.

The 19th century was a particularly fruitful and important period for women writers, most of whose works are highly sought-after today; they include Jane Austen, the Brontës, George Eliot, and Mary Shelley. The 1880s and 1890s saw the rise of feminist works such as Olive Schreiner's *The Story of an African Farm* (1883). The popular novelist "Ouida" coined the phrase "New Woman" fiction in the 1890s to describe works that looked at the ways in which women began to claim control of their lives. Many of the earliest are now no longer widely read, but could form an interesting selection. Mary Webb's work reflected the Shropshire she loved, its folklore and characters. Widely admired by her contemporaries such as Rebecca West, Thomas Hardy, and John Buchan, it took her death in 1927, the posthumous public acclaim of Stanley Baldwin and the 1952 film of her novel *Gone to Earth* (1917) for her work to be widely recognized.

The American Willa Cather was born in Virginia in 1873 and trained as a journalist before turning to writing full-time. Her work is based on the Mid-West and its people, and has undergone a considerable revival of interest among feminists and literary scholars over the past few years, with corresponding price increases. Her rare first book was a collection of poems entitled *April Twilights* (Boston, 1903); her first prose work was *The Troll Garden* (New York, 1905), present in two issues, the first with the imprint of McClure, Phillips & Co. at the foot of the spine. The majority of her work is found in various issues, including her first novel, *Alexander's Bridge* (New York, 1912).

The 1920s were epitomized by brilliant women writers such as Virginia Woolf, one of the greatest women writers of the century, whose work we have looked at in the context of Bloomsbury and Modernism, but her contemporaries Rebecca West, Vita Sackville-West and Dorothy Richardson could make a fine and less expensive alternative. A feminist and journalist, Rebecca West was greatly influenced by the Pankhursts. Her first novel was *The Return of the Soldier* (New York, 1918), which described the return home of a shell-shocked soldier. She published five further novels during the 1920s and 1930s, and then nothing until *The Fountain Overflows* (1956).

Vita Sackville-West was a close friend of Virginia Woolf, whose work *Orlando* (1928) was inspired by their friendship. Her first published work was verse, *Chatterton*, privately printed in 1909, and her first novel was *Heritage* (1919). She won the Hawthornden Prize and public recognition with the poem *The Land* (1926), and also wrote widely about gardening. Dorothy Richardson was deeply involved in the avant-garde, but the phrase "stream-of-consciousness" had been first adapted for literary usage in an essay on her sequence of novels "Pilgrimage", the first of which was *Pointed Roofs* (1915). As with Willa Cather, interest in her work was revived during the 1960s and 1970s and *Pilgrimage* was re-issued by the Virago Press in 1979.

Also hugely influential were American women writers, many of whom left the US and moved to Paris or London to write. Among the "Lost Generation" of American writers, one of the most influential was a woman. Gertrude Stein set up a literary and artistic salon in Paris, her home from 1903 until her death in 1946, where she supported and encouraged unknown young painters such as Picasso, Braque and Juan Gris. Writers such as F. Scott Fitzgerald sought her out and her relationship with Ernest Hemingway, whose works she undoubtedly influenced, was complex. He helped her type her vast novel, *The Making of Americans*, which had been written 25 years previously, but she felt his much-lauded physical courage was a sham. She experimented with prose writing and for many became the leading avant-garde writer of far-reaching influence. However, she remained unintelligible for much of the popular readership. A prolific writer, much of her work was published in small print-runs in limited signed editions of 90 to 150 copies, which are therefore scarce today. With the revival of interest in feminist literature in the 1960s, her work gained a new following and correspondingly higher prices. Her first work published in France was *A Book Concluding with As a Wife Has a Cow: A Love Story* (1926), which contains four lithographs by Juan Gris and is an important testimony to this relationship. Ten of the 112 copies issued were printed on Japanese vellum and were signed; these are now exceedingly expensive.

Edith Wharton also spent much time in Paris from 1907, and after her divorce settled there, becoming an important figure in the American expatriate community. She was the first woman to win the Pulitzer Prize, for *The Age of Innocence*, in 1920, the first issue of which has the quotation from the burial service instead of the marriage service, "forasmuch as it has pleased Almighty God", at line 7 on page 186, and of course does not mention the

1 Willa Cather. *The Troll Garden*. New York, 1905. The author's first book. First issue with McClure, Phillips imprint. **£600–800/ $960–1,280**

2 Edith Wharton. *The Age of Innocence*. New York, 1920. In the dust-jacket. **£4,000–5,000/$6,400–8,000**

3 Mary Webb. *Gone to Earth*. 1917. In the dust-jacket. **£250–300/ $400–480**

4 Carson McCullers. *The Heart is a Lonely Hunter*. Boston, 1940. Author's first book, in the dust-jacket. **£800–1,200/$1,280–1,920**

5 Eudora Welty. *The Golden Apples*. New York, 1949. In the dust-jacket. **£200–300/$320–480**

award. Unusually, it is this and not her earliest work that collectors seek most keenly. Her first full-length novel was *The Valley of Decision* (1885), and much of her early work is devoted to New York society, the conflict between the old patrician families and the newly rich, and the hostility between the individual and the community. In Paris she renewed her acquaintance with Henry James and, like Gertrude Stein, established a salon near Paris where she entertained and encouraged younger writers. Much of her later work portrays the disintegration of society in the US and Europe. Although she was widely recognized during her lifetime as an important writer, her work underwent a period of neglect. Much of it was revived by the Virago Press during the 1970s and with this came a renewed appreciation by collectors, but most of her books can still be acquired for very modest sums.

Other expatriate women writers living in Paris whose work would be worth looking for include Djuna Barnes and Kay Boyle, both Americans considered important at the time by their peers but perhaps overshadowed by their contemporaries and not as immediately appealing to the public. Djuna Barnes' first book was *The Book of Repulsive Women* (New York, 1915), which was issued with five Art Deco drawings by the author. A writer of short stories and drama, she published only one novel, *Nightwood* (1936). The New York edition of 1937 was issued with an introduction by T.S. Eliot.

There is a wealth of fine women writers working throughout the middle years of the century for the collector to look for, the majority of whom can be acquired fairly inexpensively. The reason for their being overlooked may be that the majority of collectors are male.

Jean Rhys, the daughter of a doctor of Welsh descent but born in the West Indies, also settled in Paris for many years and it is here that much of her early work is set. She was a close friend of Ford Madox Ford who wrote the introduction to her first collection, *The Left Bank* (1927). Much of her work explored the theme of the woman with no identity or roots. Her first novel was *Postures* (1928), and this remains her most sought-after work. After publication of *Good Morning, Midnight* in 1939 she vanished, writing nothing until the extraordinary *Wide Sargasso Sea* in 1966 in which she explored the story of the "mad wife" locked in the garret in *Jane Eyre*. This important work influenced many women writers of the 1960s, but today can still be found under £100/$150.

Ivy Compton Burnett wrote her first work, *Dolores*, in 1911, but it was with the publication of *Pastors and Masters* in 1925 that she started writing seriously. The majority of her novels are set amidst the patriarchal and hierarchical world where landed gentry rule. Her work is composed almost entirely of dialogue and was completely unlike any other style of the time. She continued writing until her death in 1969 and much of her later work, influenced by her breakdown during the War, explored passionate and disruptive forces smouldering beneath the surface of a deceptively calm society. Her work was published initially by William Heinemann and subsequently by Victor Gollancz, with a deluxe edition of 500 sets of her *Collected Works* appearing in 19 volumes in 1972.

The works of Rose Macaulay and Elizabeth Bowen may also make an interesting collection. Rose Macaulay published *Abbots Verney*, her first work, in 1906, but her best-known novels are her last two, *The World My Wilderness* (1950) and *The Tower of Trebizond* (1956), both influenced by and set amidst the devastation of London during World War II. The Anglo-Irish writer Elizabeth Bowen was also hugely influenced by the events of the War. Her first published book was *Encounters: Stories*, 1923, which remains uncommon. Much of her earlier work explored tensions within the landed gentry, but the War provided the background for her best-known work, *The Heat of the Day* (1949), which depicts the life of an Irish woman during the Blitz. This was chosen as a Book Society Choice, and the dust-jacket has a band announcing this.

The 1950s saw the emergence of three great writers who should be central to a collection of women writers: Muriel Spark, Iris Murdoch, and Doris Lessing. The release of the film of her life and the often painful but haunting biography by her husband has re-introduced the name and work of Iris Murdoch to a whole new generation, and it is likely this will result in higher prices for her work. Iris Murdoch's brilliant first novel, *Under the Net* (1954), was a first-person male narrative and was influenced by the work of Samuel Beckett and Jean-Paul Sartre. A cosmopolitan novel, its hero explores the modern nature of art, illusion, fiction, and the novel. An extraordinarily prolific

6 Djuna Barnes. *Ryder*. New York, 1928. 1/3,000 copies. **£70–100/$112–160**

7 Kay Boyle. *Death of a Man*. New York, 1936. In the dust-jacket. **£50–80/$80–128**

8 Gertrude Stein. *Portraits and Prayers*. New York, 1934. Original pictorial boards. **£50–100/$80–160**

9 Iris Murdoch. Collection of 11 novels. In dust-jackets. **£1,200–1,500/$1,920–2,400**

10 Iris Murdoch. *Under the Net*. 1954. Author's first novel. In the dust-jacket. **£600–800/$960–1,280**

11 Muriel Spark. *The Comforters*. 1957. Her first novel, in the dust-jacket. **£100–150/$160–240**

12 Jean Rhys. *The Left Bank*. 1927. In the dust-jacket. Author's first book. **£300–400/$480–640**

writer, she often wrote one novel a year, usually completely different in setting but exploring themes of good and evil, the sacred and taboo, sexuality and the theories of Freud, providing a rich and varied body of work for the collector. It is her first work that remains the most expensive, although perhaps her best-known are *The Bell* (1958), *A Severed Head* (1961), and *The Nice and the Good* (1968, listed in Callil and Toibin). All her work was published by Chatto and Windus and it is generally easy to find with no issue points to check.

Her contemporary, Muriel Spark, was born in Edinburgh into a Jewish family but in 1956 she converted to Catholicism. Initially a biographer and poet, she turned to the novel following her conversion, and her first, *The Comforters* (1957), draws on the work of Evelyn Waugh and Graham Greene and was well received on publication. Her best-known book, highly praised by Callil and Toibin, is *The Prime of Miss Jean Brodie* (1961), an unsettling portrait of an Edinburgh schoolteacher and her group of favoured pupils. Mostly published by Macmillan, her novels tend to be short, often resembling fables or parables which are filled with touches of the bizarre and eccentric. As with the majority of post-war writers her work, apart from the earliest titles, can be found easily for under £50/$75; two of her late novels can be found in limited signed editions. Some of her work, including short stories and children's books, was first published in the US.

Doris Lessing was born in Persia and moved to Southern Rhodesia when she was six, finally settling in London in 1949. In her novel *The Golden Notebook* (1962), described by Callil and Toibin as "one of the most important and influential novels of the late 20th century", she explores the sexual, intellectual, and moral crises of the age. She was the only woman to be grouped together with those "angry young men" of literature during the 1950s. Her first work was *The Grass is Singing* (1950), which examines the obsession of a white woman with her black servant, and was the first of many to probe the workings of the private mind. Always involved with radical politics and the changing destiny of women, and showing a fear of technological disaster, her later novels such as *Briefing for a Descent into Hell* (1971) and *Memoirs of a Survivor* (1975) enter the realm of "inner space fiction" and explore mental breakdown and the equivalent breakdown of society. A series of works written between 1979 and 1983 collectively titled "Canopus in Argus Archives" describe the epic and mythic events of a fictional universe. Although many find her works difficult, they will undoubtedly continue to be collected for a long time.

Moving on to contemporary writers, there are many names to choose from. However, the important factor to remember when collecting all post-war books is that generally print-runs for each title are much larger than for those issued pre-war, hence the scarcity factor, which leads to high four-figure prices, will be absent. Dust jackets are also carefully preserved today and often a collector will purchase two copies of a work, one to read, the other to put aside. This should not deter you from searching for good books, nor from forming your own opinions as to what to collect.

There are many more women writers active today than ever before. These range from the unavowedly popular, such as Helen Fielding (*The Diary of Bridget Jones*, 1999), to the more complex Zadie Smith (*White Teeth*, 2000). Contemporary women writers have excelled at complex, compelling, and psychological crime novels (see pages 79–80) as well as sagas of individual behaviour such as those from the pen of Mary Wesley and Anita Brookner.

Callil and Toibin list 23 works by women, many American, published between 1980 and 1998 in their influential book, including works by Angela Carter, who reinvented the fairy-tale with a macabre twist for the adult reader, Pat Barker, whose three-volumes *Regeneration* (1991), *The Eye in the Door* (1993), and *Ghost Road* (1995) won prizes including the *Guardian* prize and the Booker prize, Donna Tartt, Penelope Fitzgerald, Alice Walker, Anne Rice, Fay Weldon, A.S. Byatt, Toni Morrison, and E. Annie Proulx. Donna Tartt, for instance, published her much-lauded first novel, *The Secret History*, in 1992, and her second, *The Little Friend*, did not appear until 2002, when it was heavily promoted.

Collect what you like, maybe with an eye for what may last and be regarded as fine by generations to come. The shortlisted titles and winners of the Orange Prize for Fiction by women may well be worth keeping an eye on.

13 Doris Lessing. *The Summer before the Dark*. 1973. In the dust-jacket. **£40–80/$64–128**

14 Margaret Atwood. *Alias Grace*. 1996. First English edition. In the dust-jacket. **£25–35/$40–56**

15 Kate Atkinson. *Behind the Scenes at the Museum*. 1995. In the dust-jacket. Author's first novel. **£150–200/$240–320**

16 Mary Wesley. *Jumping the Queue*. 1983. In the dust-jacket. Author's first adult novel. **£20–30/$32–48**

17 Arundhati Roy. *The God of Small Things*. 1997. In the dust-jacket. **£100–150/$160–240**

18 Pat Barker. *The Ghost Road*. 1995. Final volume of her "Regeneration" trilogy. In the dust-jacket. **£150–200/$240–320**

13

14

15

16

17

18

Drama

The stage during the first half of the 20th century was dominated by Irish playwrights Oscar Wilde, W.B. Yeats, J.M. Synge, Sean O'Casey, and Samuel Beckett. Oscar Wilde left Dublin to study at Oxford and was never part of the growing Irish literary movement, but the others were pre-eminent in this circle and can best be looked at in that context (pages 70–71). It is Oscar Wilde's comedies such as *The Importance of Being Earnest* (1895) that have best survived today. His first success was *Lady Windermere's Fan: A Play about a Good Woman* (1892). These plays were all issued in various editions, including signed limited editions, with a few printed on Japanese vellum, providing the collector with various price levels.

Much drama on the stage in London during the 1890s and the opening years of the 20th century came from abroad. Henrik Ibsen was particularly influential, although initially not well received. The best-known British dramatist of this period was George Bernard Shaw. A prolific playwright as well as political novelist, he was awarded the Nobel Prize for Literature in 1925. Perhaps slightly out of fashion at the moment, his work can be readily found for modest sums, the most sought-after being his first published play, *Widowers' Houses* (1893), as well as the privately printed *Pygmalion* (1912), the title page of which reads "Rough Proof-Unpublished". His next play, *Androcles and the Lion* (1913), was issued in the same format in an edition of 50 copies. Both these and *Overruled* were then issued in one volume in 1916. His earliest plays, *The Philanderer* and *Mrs Warren's Profession*, were also written in 1893 but were censored and not performed, even privately, until the early 1900s. The latter play was not performed publicly until the 1920s. He was an imaginative and political writer whose dream was to create a "New Drama" on the stage of the Royal Court in London, which he achieved when several of his plays were produced there between 1904 and 1907.

Shaw dominated the stage for many years, but there were other pre-war dramatists of note, including Arthur Pinero, Robert Sheriff, and Noel Coward. Others, such as John Galsworthy and J.B. Priestley, are completely out of fashion today and their works can be found for not much more than the price at publication.

The plays performed on the London stage during the late 1940s and 1950s were varied and exciting, and included John Osborne's *Look Back in Anger* (1956), which for many marked a watershed in British theatre, T.S. Eliot's *Murder in the Cathedral* (1935) and *The Cocktail Party* (1950), both found in numerous different issues, works by Bertolt Brecht, French dramatists such as Jean Anouilh, and the Irish playwright Samuel Beckett, translated from the French, in particular *Waiting for Godot* (1955). Important plays by American dramatists were also staged, and these included Eugene O'Neill's *The Iceman Cometh* (1946), Arthur Miller's *Death of a Salesman* (1949), and Tennessee Williams' *A Streetcar Named Desire* (1947). These key works are considerably more expensive than those by other dramatists, earlier or later, and most collectors may have to be content with the later works of these playwrights rather than the highspots mentioned here.

In 1962 came the announcement of the creation of a National Theatre in London. Although the company's first performance was in 1963, the theatre itself did not open until 1976. Its rival, the Royal Shakespeare Company, established a reputation for experimental work, and the English Stage Company at the Royal Court Theatre commissioned and presented work by new dramatists. For the collector, work from the late 1960s to the present day provides unparalleled choice and quality. The new generation of playwrights was influenced by their European counterparts: they were provocative, argumentative, often brusque and challenging. Harold Pinter is probably the most original of those who sprang to prominence in the late 1950s, with *The Birthday Party*, *The Caretaker*, and *The Homecoming*. His plays were often written a few years before their performance and publication was timed to coincide with the opening. *The Birthday Party* was first issued in wrappers by Encore Publishing in 1959 and by Methuen in 1960, *The Caretaker* appearing in 1960.

Tom Stoppard is a prolific playwright and one of the most important still writing today. His first play was *Rosencrantz and Guildenstern are Dead*, which was performed by an amateur company at the Edinburgh Festival in 1966 before it moved to London in 1967, when it was published. The majority of his plays are complex and witty comedies, often unresolved and explosive, usually involving characters who are quite out of their depth. Later plays include *Jumpers* (1971), *Travesties* (1975), and *Arcadia* (1993), which was the first by a living playwright to be performed in translation at the prestigious Salle Richelieu at the Comédie Française and issued in a limited edition by the Arion Press in San Francisco in 2001. Stoppard's work is more expensive than that of his contemporaries, which is perhaps indicative of his standing and popularity.

Other notable dramatists of this period include Joe Orton, who wrote five black comedies before his murder in 1967, the first of which was *Entertaining Mr Sloane* (1964), Arnold Wesker, whose *Chips with Everything* was first performed at the Royal Court in 1962, John Arden, who wrote *Serjeant Musgrave's Dance* (1959), Edward Bond, Caryl Churchill, and Alan Ayckbourn.

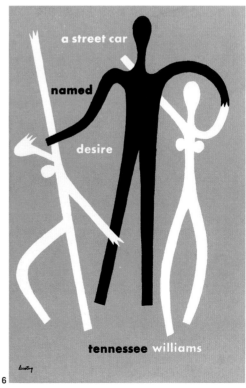

1 John Osborne. *Look Back in Anger*. 1957. In the dust-jacket. **£80–100/$128–160**

2 Harold Pinter. *The Birthday Party and Other Plays*. 1960. In the dust-jacket. **£80–100/$128–160**

3 Eugene O'Neill. *Mourning Becomes Electra*. New York, 1931. In the dust-jacket. **£180–220/$240–352**

4 Terence Rattigan. *The Deep Blue Sea*. 1952. In the dust-jacket. **£20–30/$32–48**

5 Peter Shaffer. *Shrivings*. 1974. In the dust-jacket. **£30–40/$48–64**

6 Tennesse Williams. *A Streetcar Named Desire*. New York, 1947. In the dust-jacket. **£2,000–3,000/$3,200–4,800**

Poetry

Poetry during the 1880s and 1890s was dominated by the last works of Victorian poets, such as Alfred, Lord Tennyson, Algernon Swinburne, and Robert Browning, and by the Symbolist verse of Charles Baudelaire, Paul Verlaine, Arthur Rimbaud, and Stephane Mallarmé being translated from the French. The new verse appearing in Britain during the Edwardian era included patriotic and raucous ballads by Rudyard Kipling. Much of his early verse was issued privately in Lahore, India, and is subsequently rare and expensive. The first was *Schoolboy Lyrics* (1881), a collection of verse not included elsewhere until 1900. *Barrack-Room Ballads and Other Verses* was the first to be published, in England in 1892. Most of his volumes of verse can be found in de-luxe signed editions as well.

Thomas Hardy published his last novel, *The Well-Beloved*, in 1897, and his work from the turn of the century until his death in 1928 was, except for one compilation of short stories, entirely verse. Although several of the poems had been written earlier, his first published book of verse was *Wessex Poems and Other Verses*, issued in 1898 in an edition of only 500 copies, with a few copies in a presentation binding. Hardy's huge expanse of verse reveals a technical mastery and inventiveness, and a wide range of themes including love, nature, and memory. Most of his volumes of poetry were issued in a variety of editions, allowing the collector a wide range of values within which to work.

The highly regarded Shropshire poet A.E. Housman published only six volumes of verse before his death in 1936, of which three were compilations printed privately, although a further 94 poems were published posthu-mously. His first work was *A Shropshire Lad* (1896), the first state of which has "Shopshire" on the label as 33mm wide. There was a second edition of 500 copies in 1898 and an illustrated edition of 1908. His work is often in the form of the tragic ballad, focusing on themes of loss and lost illusions with references to his native county.

Edward Thomas and Edmund Blunden were two poets whose work was shaped by the Great War, although they are not regarded as "war poets" as such. Edward Thomas died during the War in 1917, but his poetry is chiefly about nature and his landscapes are often haunted by ghosts of the past and present. His poems were not widely appreciated for many years, but today his early verse is becoming expensive. His first work, *Six Poems* (1916), was issued under the pseudonym "Edward Eastaway" in an edition of 100 copies. Edmund Blunden is remembered primarily as a war poet, although the majority of his later work was inspired by the county of Kent. His first work, *Poems* (1914), was also issued privately in an edition of 100 copies. A prolific poet, he published numerous volumes up to his death in 1974, many in limited signed or privately printed editions.

1 Thomas Hardy. Page proofs of his poem "The Souls of the Slain", as published in *The Cornhill Magazine*, 1900, with some corrections in the author's hand. **£1,500–2,500/$2,400–4,000**

2 A.E. Housman. *A Shropshire Lad*. 1908. First illustrated edition. **£150–200/$240–320**

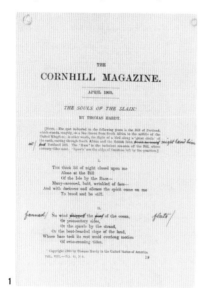

1

2

T.S. ELIOT AND EZRA POUND

Ezra Pound came to England in 1909 and settled there for 11 years. It is these years that can be seen as perhaps the most formative modern poetry, T.S. Eliot claiming Pound was "more responsible for the XXth Century revolution than any other individual". He worked as secretary for W.B. Yeats and stimulated fellow writers but was also highly discriminating of their work. He founded the Imagist school of poets with H.D. (Hilda Doolittle) and Richard Aldington, advocating the use of free rhythms, the concrete, and concise language and imagery. His first work was *A Lume Spento* (Venice, 1908) and his second, *A Quinzaine for this Yule* (1908). Both are exceptionally rare works, being published in editions of 150 and 100 copies. His large body of work is expensive and hard for the collector to acquire, for much of it was published in France in tiny editions by the Ovid Press, Three Mountain Press and Hours Press, including *Hugh Selwyn Mauberley* (Paris, 1920). His most ambitious achievement was the grand multi-cultural *Cantos*, a series of poems published in numerous volumes between 1920 and 1970. Settling in Italy, he broadcast over the radio during the War, which damaged his reputation. This and his extreme political views have perhaps today resulted in his works falling out of favour with collectors, leaving rare and expensive works unsold at a major auction in 2002.

T.S. Eliot, in contrast, was very much at the heart of the literary establishment and was regarded as a figure of great cultural authority. Today he is seen as one of the greatest poets of the century. He was editor of several important literary magazines, director of the publishers Faber, where he built up an impressive poetry list, and recipient of the Nobel Prize for Literature in 1948. Although he was also a dramatist and critic, it is his poetry that is widely regarded as his greatest work. His first published poem was "The Love-Song of J. Alfred Prufrock" which appeared in the periodical *Poetry* in 1917. The majority of his poetry fetches four-figure sums, with works published after 1930 being far more widely available. His greatest and best-known works are *Prufrock and Other Observations* (1917), *The Waste Land* (1922), and *Four Quartets* (New York, 1943, the first issue stating "First American edition", and not published in England until the following year). The great poem *The Waste Land*, about the post-war sense of depression and futility, can be found in three editions: the earliest, published in New York by Boni and Liveright in 1922, is bound in flexible black cloth with "mountain" spelt correctly on page 41; the second was issued by the Hogarth Press in 1923; and in 1962 the Officina Bodoni in Verona printed a signed, numbered edition for publication by Faber. One of his most enduring

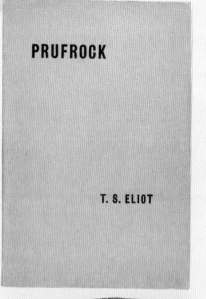

1 T.S. Eliot. *Prufrock and Other Observations*. 1917. One of 500 copies. **£4,000–5,000/$6,400–8,000**

2 Ezra Pound. *A Quinzaine for this Yule*. 1908. The author's second book. Printed wrappers in a blue cloth wrapper hand-lettered by Pound. One of approximately 30 surviving copies. **£20,000–30,000/$32,000–48,000**

works is *Old Possum's Book of Practical Cats* (1939), the inspiration for the musical *Cats*, later issued in an edition with coloured illustrations by Nicholas Bentley.

Poetry in America

Poetry at the turn of the century in the US was dominated by Walt Whitman, whose *Leaves of Grass* (1855), his second published book of verse, had cemented his reputation. However, he was not an immediate success at home, and his importance was only widely recognized when he was taken up by the English poets Dante Gabriel Rossetti and Algernon Swinburne. The book was revised many times with new additions, that of 1860 containing 124 new poems and the fifth edition of 1872 including the Civil War poem "Drum Taps". He received the edition on his deathbed in 1892.

Edwin Arlington Robinson made poetry his career, devoting his life exclusively to writing numerous volumes between 1896 and his death in 1935. The most important poet in the US at the turn of the century, he was one of the earliest American modern poets. His first book, *The Torrent and the Night Before* (Maine, 1896), is scarce, for it is thought that from a print-run of 312 copies only about 60 have survived. This was revised in 1897 as *The Children of the Night* with 50 copies on Japanese vellum. He was awarded the Pulitzer Prize in 1922 (the first year in which it was awarded to a poet), 1925 and 1928, but his works remain very reasonably priced.

Robert Frost was also awarded the Pulitzer Prize, in 1924, for *New Hampshire* (New York, 1923). His first book of verse was *A Boy's Will* (1913), for which he had to come to England for inspiration and recognition. His second book, *North of Boston* (1914), was also initially published in England, but by now his work had been recognized and American publication followed suit the same year. Frost's numerous volumes of poetry exist in many different issues and editions, with limited and illustrated editions of his later work available. His poetry, much of which is about

man's uneasy relationship with land and sky, is far more widely read today than Robinson's and his early work is correspondingly more expensive.

Wallace Stevens is nowadays regarded as one of the greatest of American 20th-century poets. Written in his spare time, much of his poetry was initially published in small magazines between 1910 and 1920. His first volume of verse was *Harmonium* (New York, 1920), which is now expensive in the first-issue binding. His important longer poem, *Notes Towards a Supreme Fiction* (Cummington, 1942), is also expensive in the edition of 80 signed copies. Presentation copies of Stevens' work are notoriously rare, whereas Robert Frost inscribed many books, often with fragments of poetry alongside.

Other major American poets of interest to the collector include two who also wrote fiction: e.e. cummings, the popular anarchic poet renowned for his typographical experiments and song-like rhythms, and William Carlos Williams, who was influenced by the Imagists and Cubists. Robert Lowell was influenced by both Williams and Whitman, before concentrating in the 1960s on the conflicts of liberal society.

1 Edwin Arlington Robinson. *The Children of the Night.* Boston, 1897. One of approximately 500 copies of the author's second book on Batchworth paper. **£200–300/$320–480**

2 Robert Frost. *A Boy's Will.* 1913. Author's first published book. First issue in first binding of bronze cloth. **£3,000–4,000/ $4,800–6,400**

3 Wallace Stevens. *Ideas of Order.* New York, 1936. First trade edition. In the dust-jacket. **£400-600/$640–960**

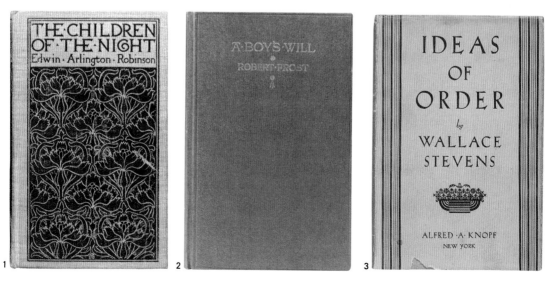

Post-war Poetry

World War II poets comprised a smaller group than those of the Great War, and were not as widely known nor as cohesive. David Gascoyne flirted with Surrealist poetry during the 1930s, and indeed translated much of the European Surrealists' work, before producing more realistic poems during the War. Keith Douglas, tutored by Edmund Blunden, is probably the best known of the war poets, but only one volume of poetry was published in his lifetime, *Selected Poems* (1943), before he was killed in 1944.

The great Welsh poet Dylan Thomas published his first book of verse, *18 Poems*, in 1934, which is found in two issues, the first with a flat spine and no advertisement leaf between half-title and title pages. His life was flamboyant, and his poetry won a huge following, especially with the publication of *Deaths and Entrances* (1946), reissued by the Gregynog Press in 1984 with illustrations by John Piper. He was also a prose writer and dramatist, and perhaps his best-known works are the play *Under Milkwood* (1954) and *A Child's Christmas in Wales* (New York, 1954). His most sought-after work is *Twenty-Six Poems* (1950), printed in an edition of 150 copies, ten signed on Japanese vellum. Apart from this and his first book, the rest of his work is readily available.

Alun Lewis was another Welsh poet who, like Keith Douglas, was killed in 1944. His first volume of verse was *Raider's Dawn* (1942) and his second, *Ha! Ha! Among the Trumpets* (1945), was published posthumously. His verse, although written during the War, referred to the landscape of Britain and India, where he was stationed.

Two poets who loom large throughout this period are John Betjeman and Philip Larkin. Poet Laureate in 1972, John Betjeman was phenomenally successful and popular, although not perhaps accorded serious critical acclaim. His *Collected Poems* (1958) sold 90,000 copies in two years: extraordinary for a volume of verse. Architectural historian, prolific prose writer and broadcaster, his first published book, *Mount Zion or In Touch with the Infinite* (1931), was of verse, the first issue of which is found in blue and gold patterned boards. Apart from this, all his other volumes of verse, most of which deal with very English themes of tradition, religion, and melancholy, can be found for very modest sums.

Philip Larkin was influenced by Thomas Hardy and W.B. Yeats and admired Betjeman's poetry while often ignoring that of his other contemporaries. In the mid-1940s he wrote two novels, *Jill* (1946) and *A Girl in Winter* (1947), and his first volume of verse, *The North Ship* (1945), the first issue of which is bound in black cloth. There was a second, unauthorized issue in maroon cloth. It was his fourth volume, *The Less Deceived* (1955), that made his name as a poet, and his two later volumes, *The Whitsun Weddings* (1964) and *High Windows* (1974), that cemented this. The key poet of this post-war period, he charted social and cultural changes with a distinctive and sardonic voice, often deliberately provocative.

1 Dylan Thomas. *Collected Poems 1934–1952*. 1952. In the dust-jacket. First trade edition. **£150–200/$240–320**

2 Philip Larkin. *High Windows*. 1974. In the dust-jacket. **£60–80/$96–128**

3 Geoffrey Hill. *The Fantasy Poets Number Eleven*. Eynsham, 1952. One of approximately 300 copies, original paper wrappers. **£200–300/$320–480**

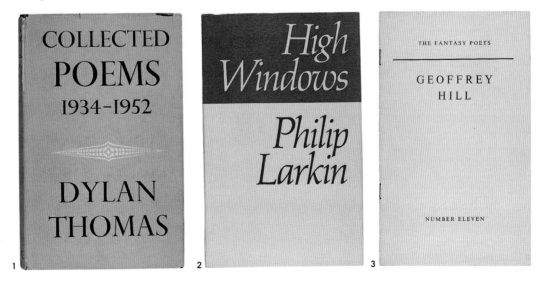

COLLECTED POEMS 1934–1952 DYLAN THOMAS

High Windows Philip Larkin

THE FANTASY POETS GEOFFREY HILL NUMBER ELEVEN

1   2   3

Contemporary Poetry

Ted Hughes, Poet Laureate until his death in 2000, is best known for his poetry of the animal world, in which he depicts its cruelty, beauty, and often surprising tenderness. His first volume was *The Hawk in the Rain* (1957), which contains the important and striking poems "The Thought-Fox" and "Hawk Roosting". The central figure of the crow, which recurs in numerous later works, was first introduced in *Crow* (1970). This predatory and mocking dark bird enables Ted Hughes to retell legends of creation, birth, and death. It was his meeting with the American artist Leonard Baskin, who has illustrated several of his volumes, that was the direct inspiration for this use of the symbol of the crow. In 1997 he published *Tales from Ovid: Twenty-Four Passages from the Metamorphoses* in which Hughes returns to his earlier themes of violence and the fusion of the wild and the human. The following year he published the remarkable series of autobiographical, frank, and moving poems about his relationship with his wife, the American poet Sylvia Plath who committed suicide, *Birthday Letters* (1998). A prolific poet, he has also published several volumes of verse and prose for children, including *Meet My Folks!* (1961) and *The Earth-Owl and Other Moon-People*

(1963). His work is often issued in limited signed editions with illustrations by Leonard Baskin and Ralph Steadman and as individual broadsheet poems. The ordinary editions of his books can easily be found under £50/$75, with these special printings usually available for around £150–200/$225–300.

Other contemporary poets worth looking at include the current Poet Laureate Andrew Motion, Thom Gunn, Geoffrey Hill, Douglas Dunn, Tony Harrison, and the Caribbean poet Derek Walcott who won the Nobel Prize for Literature in 1992. His first collection was *Selected Poems* (New York, 1964). Walcott founded the Trinidad Theatre Workshop in 1959 where many of his own plays were performed. His work concentrates on the national identity of the West Indies and its conflict with its European heritage. Using Creole vocabulary and the rhythm of calypso, it is also full of classical references.

Poetry has not been as widely read and collected in the latter part of the century as the novel, but this could be about to change. In the late 1990s there developed a vogue among creative people for acquiring volumes of poetry, and with the London Underground series "Poets of the Underground" perhaps more people will turn to poetry.

1 Ted Hughes. *Scapegoats and Rabies*. 1967. Original wrappers, one of approximately 400 copies. **£200–250/$320–400**

2 Ted Hughes. *Remains of Elmet*. 1979. Photographs by Fay Godwin. In the dust-jacket. First trade edition. **£40–60/$64–96**

3 Ted Hughes. *Cave Birds*. 1978. Illustrated by Leonard Baskin. First trade edition. **£40–60/$64–96**

4 Ted Hughes. *Crow*. 1970. In the dust-jacket. **£200–250/$320–400**

Women Poets

There are several women poets to collect in the 20th century, both American and British, although they are not as numerous as the novelists, and perhaps the best are American. Two of the earliest poets of the century, Alice Meynell and Charlotte Mew, are not widely read today. Alice Meynell's later volumes won her considerable acclaim in her lifetime, including *Later Poems* (1902) and *Last Poems* (1923). Charlotte Mew was much admired by Thomas Hardy, and with publication of *The Farmer's Bride* in 1915 she became well known. Interest in her work was revived in the 1980s with the publication of her biography.

The American poet Amy Lowell met Ezra Pound in London and became an enthusiastic convert to Imagism. Her collections include *Sword Blades and Poppy Seed* (1914). Marianne Moore, born in St Louis in 1887, contributed to the Imagist magazine *Egoist* and her first volume, *Poems*, was published in 1921. From 1925 until 1929 she edited the magazine *Dial*, which attracted important writers such as T.S. Eliot who introduced her *Selected Poems* (1935). Her *Collected Poems* won the Pulitzer Prize in 1951. The starting-point for much of her poetry is often rare or fabulous animals.

A British contemporary was Edith Sitwell, who began to write poetry as a child. Actively encouraging Modernist writers and opposing the romantic ruralism of the Georgian poets, her first volume of verse was *The Mother and Other Poems* (1915), and she quickly achieved a reputation as an eccentric and controversial writer of poetry, prose, and drama. Her best-known poems are perhaps those inspired by the Blitz and the atom bomb, *Street Songs* (1942) and *The Shadow of Cain* (1947).

The poet and novelist Stevie Smith published her first work of verse, *A Good Time Was Had by All*, in 1937, but it was not until the 1960s that she won a wide and younger audience with the publication of *Not Waving But Drowning* in 1957. Perhaps because she has only fairly recently been rediscovered, her works have climbed in value over the past few years.

However, possibly the best-known woman poet of this century is the American Sylvia Plath. Born in Boston in 1932, she met and married the poet Ted Hughes and made England her home until her suicide in 1963. Her brilliant poetry is full of undercurrents of terror and loss, and is intensely personal. Her first collection of verse was a small pamphlet of 25 copies, *Sculptor* (1959), which is expensive, as is *A Winter Ship* (Edinburgh, 1960). Her first published collection, which established her reputation, was *The Colossus and Other Poems* (1960). All her other work was published posthumously and includes *Ariel* (1965) and *Winter Trees* (1971). Several volumes of her work were published in limited editions by the Rainbow Press, including *Crystal Gazer* (1971), *Lyonesse* (1971), and *Pursuit* (1973). She also wrote a fine novel, *The Bell Jar* (1963), under the pseudonym "Victoria Lucas". Her work is generally highly sought-after and hence more expensive than most poets of the later 20th century. With the release of a new film on her life with Ted Hughes prices may well increase.

1 Laura Riding. *Collected Poems*. 1938. In the dust-jacket. **£300–350/$480–560**

2 Marianne Moore. *Collected Poems*. 1951. First English edition. In the dust-jacket. **£50–70/$80–112**

3 Sylvia Plath. *Winter Trees*. 1971. In the dust-jacket. **£70–100/$112–160**

Irish Literature

There is a distinct Irish literature of the 20th century that encompasses some of the greatest writers of the Modern movement: James Joyce (whose work is discussed on p. 35) William Butler Yeats, Samuel Beckett, and Seamus Heaney are four. W.B. Yeats trained as a painter, and helped found the Irish Literary Society in London in 1891 and another in Dublin in 1892. He was determined to establish a national theatre in Dublin, and this goal was finally achieved in 1904 when the Abbey Theatre was acquired, with the help of Lady Gregory, for the newly established Irish National Theatre Company. The plays performed on the opening night were by W.B. Yeats and Lady Gregory. The Abbey Theatre became the centre of the new Irish drama, and it was there that J.M. Synge's *The Playboy of the Western World* (1907), which provoked riots, and Sean O'Casey's *Shadow of a Gunman* (1923) and *Juno and the Paycock* (1924) were first performed.

W.B. Yeats' early work, *Fairy and Folk Tales of the Irish Peasantry* (1888) and *The Secret Rose* (1897), was concerned with the folklore and legends of Ireland. Irish traditionalism, nationalism, and unrequited love were the themes that ran through many of his works during the 1890s such as *The Wanderings of Oisin and Other Poems* (1889). His later work was influenced by his wife's experiments with automatic writing, which provided him with the Symbolist themes found in *A Vision* (1925), *The Tower* (1928), and *The Winding Stair* (1929). He received the Nobel Prize for Literature in 1923 and in 1934 edited the *Oxford Book of Modern Verse*. He was a hugely prolific writer of poetry, drama, and prose and many of his works can be found in beautiful decorative cloth bindings or in editions published by the Cuala Press, a private press, initially called the Dun Emer Press, founded in 1902 by his sisters, Elizabeth and Lily, to stimulate local crafts and employment. The Cuala Press could form the basis for a fine collection of Irish literature, for it published works by Yeats, Synge, Lady Gregory, O'Casey, and many others until the 1940s, several of which contain illustrations by Jack Yeats, brother of William.

Samuel Beckett was born near Dublin but settled permanently in France, publishing much of his work there first. A playwright, novelist, and poet, he was one of the most individual and experimental writers of the century, with a prodigious output. He was a great friend of James Joyce and his first published work appeared in *Our Exagmination Round His Factification for Incamination* of "*Work in Progress*" (Paris, 1929), a collection of articles on Joyce, published in an edition of 396 copies, of which 96 were on large paper. His first published book was the poem *Whoroscope* (Paris, 1930), published in an edition of 300 copies by the Hours Press. His first collection of short stories was *More Pricks than Kicks* (1934), which was first published in London and remains one of his most sought-after works. He wrote several full-length novels, including *Murphy* (1938), and the later trilogy *Molloy, Malone Meurt* (Paris, 1951), and *L'Innommable* (Paris, 1953). In 1953 in Paris he received huge public acclaim for the first performance of *En Attendant Godot*, published in 1952 in Paris, and translated into English in 1954 (*Waiting for Godot*). This play revolutionized drama in England and greatly influenced the new generation of playwrights such as Harold Pinter and Tom Stoppard. His distinct use of dialogue and his subtle comedy was cemented in his later plays for the stage and television such as *Endgame* (1958), *Happy Days* (New York, 1961), and *Eh Joe* (1967). He wrote in English and French, the French often taking precedence and translated all his own work. He was awarded the Nobel Prize in 1969 and died in 1989. His work can be found in various formats, such as limited signed editions and French, English, and American imprints, affording the collector many levels at which to acquire his work.

The poet Seamus Heaney was also awarded the Nobel Prize in 1995. Initially one of a group of poets based in Belfast, he moved to the Republic of Ireland in 1972, settling in Dublin. His early poetry was based around the farmland of his youth, emanating a powerful sense of the physical environment. His first collection was *Eleven Poems* (Belfast, 1965), the first issue of which was printed on laid paper and has the sun printed in red-violet. His later work became more political and cultural, as seen in collections such as *Wintering Out* (1972) and *North* (1975). Most of his works were also issued in limited signed editions, but the ordinary editions remain easily affordable for the average collector.

Other Irish writers whose work would be worth looking for could include George Moore, who was hugely influential in helping to establish the new literary stature of Irish writing during the 1920s, but today is often overlooked. The playwright Brendan Behan (*The Quare Fellow*, 1956) was arrested in 1939 for his involvement with the IRA, and his time in borstal is recorded in his well-known autobiographical *Borstal Boy* (1958). The novelists Brian Moore (*Wreath for a Redhead*, 1951), Edna O'Brien (*Girls in their Married Bliss*, 1963), Liam O'Flaherty (*Thy Neighbour's Wife*, 1923), and Flann O'Brien (*At Swim Two Birds*, 1939) are just a few of the fine Irish writers worth searching for.

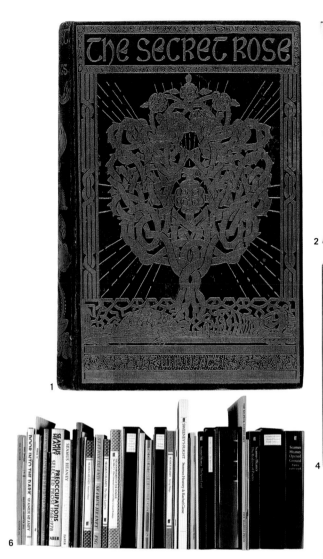

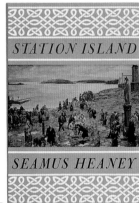

1 W.B. Yeats. *The Secret Rose.* 1897 Regular issue in smooth cloth. **£200–300/$320–480**

2 John W. Synge. *Deirdre of the Sorrows.* Dundrum: the Cuala Press, 1910.

3 Samuel Beckett. *Eh Joe and Other writings.* 1967. In the dust-jacket. **£30–50/$48–80**

4 Brendan Behan. *Borstal Boy.* 1958. In the dust-jacket. **£100–150/$160–240**

5 Seamus Heaney. *Station Island.* 1984. In the dust-jacket. **£150–200/$240–320**

6 Seamus Heaney. Collection of first editions, in dust-jackets, including early works and signed limited editions. **£3,000–5,000/$4,800–8,000**

7 Brian Moore. *The Colour of Blood.* 1987. First English edition, in the dust-jacket. **£20–30/$32–48**

Science Fiction and Horror

In 1885 Robert Louis Stevenson published *The Strange Case of Dr Jekyll and Mr Hyde*. The first edition was published in New York and the first English edition can be found in two issues, the first of which is bound in wrappers with the date on the upper cover changed by hand to 1886. This important work on dual personality was the forerunner of many later horror novels. This was soon followed by Bram Stoker's *Dracula* (1897), the first issue of which has an integral rear final blank leaf and no advertisement. The subject of and inspiration for many films, it has become an extremely sought-after book which is hard to find in good condition.

The American H.P. Lovecraft wrote numerous horror stories, mostly based in and around his native New England. These often refer to ancient mystical tomes containing secrets not known to man, especially the Necronomicon, most of which were his own invention. He still has a huge cult following and most of his works have been reissued by Arkham House in recent years. His early works remain rare and expensive, especially his first, which exists only as a mimeographed pamphlet, *The Crime of Crimes* (1915). His second work, *The Shunned House*, was first published by the Recluse Press in 1928 in an edition of 600 copies. The earliest issue comprises 300 sets of unbound sheets, of which only about 75 are thought to have survived. The second issue comprises 300 bound copies, of which probably about eight remain. His post-war books become easier to find with correspondingly lower prices.

M.R. James was a distinguished scholar who was fascinated by the macabre and supernatural, and is collected for his ghost stories. His first of five volumes was *Ghost Stories of an Antiquary* (1904). Anne Rice is a modern-day writer of the macabre. Her first book, *Interview with the Vampire* (New York, 1976), quickly became a cult bestseller and was turned into a film. This was the first in the series of "Vampire Chronicles", but she has also written "The Witch Chronicles" and several ghost stories. Her "Vampire Chronicles" were issued simultaneously in limited signed editions. Stephen King is one of the most successful living writers and his first published book was *Carrie* (New York, 1974), the first issue of which has a date code of "P6" on the inner margin of page 199. Most of his work was also issued in limited signed editions, some of which precede the regular edition, and these remain fairly expensive today.

Mary Shelley's *Frankenstein* (1818), now a rare and very expensive work, especially if found in the original boards, was the early precursor to books written about imaginary advances in science, known today as "science fiction". H.G. Wells was a hugely prolific writer, but it is his science-fiction stories for which he is best remembered and collected today. *The Time Machine* (New York, 1895) was his first published book. The American imprint precedes the English, but it is the first English issue bound in grey cloth that most collectors desire. This was followed by *The Invisible Man* (1897) and *The War of the Worlds* (1898), the first issue of which has 16 pages of advertisements. The dramatization of the latter on American radio, famously performed by Orson Welles, caused huge consternation, listeners not realizing it was fictional.

Science fiction and fantasy provides the collector with a wide variety of material to collect. There are numerous magazines and pulp publications such as *Weird Tales* and *The Fantasy Fan*, many with lurid covers and often containing stories of variable quality. Writers to look for include John Wyndham, J.G. Ballard, Brian Aldiss, Michael Moorcock, Arthur C. Clarke, Ray Bradbury, and Terry Pratchett. John Wyndham's first work was *The Secret People* (1935), but it was *The Day of the Triffids* (New York, 1951) that first brought him public acclaim. J.G. Ballard became known during the 1960s as the most prominent of the "New Wave" science-fiction writers. His first short story was published in 1956 in the influential periodical *New Worlds*. His first novel was *The Wind from Nowhere* (New York, 1962), but his first important novel was *The Drowned World* (New York, 1962). Michael Moorcock was the influential editor of *New Worlds* from 1964 to 1971, encouraging many of the best writers of this period. His own first published book was *The Stealer of Souls* (1963), the first issue of which is bound in orange boards.

Brian Aldiss wrote many different works, but is best known for his science fiction, the first of which is *Non-Stop* (1958), the earliest issue having red boards. Arthur C. Clarke's many novels have perhaps made the genre more widely known than any other writer, especially *2001: A Space Odyssey* (New York, 1968); his first work was *Prelude to Space* (New York, 1951). In 1953 Ray Bradbury published the futuristic fable *Fahrenheit 451* (New York, 1953), his first novel. The ordinary edition was issued in wrappers, with a few author's copies bound in cloth and 200 numbered signed copies. It was published in the UK in 1954 and by the Limited Editions Club with illustrations in 1982. Terry Pratchett's hugely popular "Discworld" books have earned him a fortune, and the first, *The Colour of Magic* (1983), is now rare and expensive. The second and third titles, *The Light Fantastic* (1986) and *Equal Rites* (1987), are also hard to find, but once Gollancz became his publisher larger editions were printed and titles from 1987 on are easier to come across.

1 Bram Stoker. *Dracula*. 1897. **£4,000–6,000/$6,400–9,600**

2 Isaac Asimov. *I, Robot*. 1952. First English edition, in the dust-jacket. **£100–150/$160–240**

3 Arthur C. Clarke. *2001: A Space Odyssey*. 1968. First English edition, in the dust-jacket. **£150–200/$240–320**

4 H.G. Wells. *The First Men in the Moon*. 1901. First binding in dark blue with gilt lettering. **£300–400/$480–640**

5 John Wyndham. *The Day of the Triffids*. 1951. In the dust-jacket. **£500–600/$800–960**

6 Frank Herbert. *Dune*. Philadelphia, 1965. In the dust-jacket. **£800-1,200/$1,280–1,920**

7 Stephen King. *Pet Sematary*. 1983. In the dust-jacket. **£30–50/$48–80**

Spy Stories

The 1960s was the era of the Cold War and the spy novel. An important and popular genre that was very much a product of its time, the books are a fascinating insight into a period that has only recently ended. John Le Carré, pseudonym of David John Moore Cornwell, was educated at Oxford, taught at Eton and joined the Foreign Office. His first novel, *Call for the Dead* (1961), introduced the secret agent George Smiley, who reappeared in several later books. This and his second book, *A Murder of Quality* (1962), remain his most sought-after and expensive works. These were issued, along with *The Spy Who Came in from the Cold* (1963), in distinctive bright typographical dust-jackets by Victor Gollancz. It was this third novel that brought him immediate fame and acclaim from Graham Greene, who stated it was the best spy story he had read. His later works became more complex and perceptive. From the publication of *The Honourable Schoolboy* in 1977, many of his books have been issued in collector's editions as well.

Len Deighton worked as an illustrator until the publication of his first novel, *The Ipcress File*, in 1962. His books tend to be less complex, and the earlier novels are easier to find than those of Le Carré. His second book, *Horse under Water* (1963), is found in two issues; the first contains a loose crossword competition. The American editions of *Billion Dollar Brain* (1966) and *An Expensive Place to Die* (1967) precede the English editions. The first issue of the latter contains a wallet with "in-transit" documents.

Frederick Forsyth also wrote hugely popular and easily read stories mostly relating to government agents. His first book, *The Day of the Jackal* (1971), was an immediate and huge success and was quickly turned into a film. *The Odessa File* followed in 1972, with *The Dogs of War* in 1974, and he continues to write today. Published in large editions, his works are easy to find and remain at low prices.

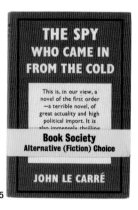

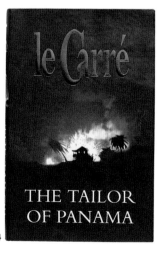

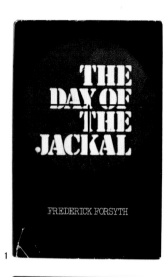

1 Frederick Forsyth. *The Day of the Jackal*. 1971. In the dust-jacket. **£150–200/$240–320**

2 Len Deighton. *An Expensive Place to Die*. 1967. First UK edition, in the dust-jacket. **£60–80/$96–128**

3 *An Expensive Place to Die* – the original brochure containing 10 full-page and folded reproductions of fictitious documents. Book and brochure: **£50–100/$80–160**.

4 John le Carré. *The Tailor of Panama*. 1996. In the dust-jacket. **£30–50/$48–80**

5 John Le Carré. *The Spy Who Came in from the Cold*. 1963. In the dust-jacket. With the original wrap-around band. **£800–1,200/ $1,280–1,920**

IAN FLEMING

In January 1962 Ian Fleming, a journalist, sat down in his house, Goldeneye, in Jamaica, and began to write a story. Seven weeks later, and fearing it was rather a joke, he sent the manuscript of *Casino Royale* to an agent. By July Jonathan Cape had agreed to publish it and soon found themselves with an instant success. Fourteen more titles followed, and numerous films, starting with *Dr No* in 1962, starring Sean Connery. It was the films that created the cult phenomenon of James Bond, the tough, witty, sexually charged and yet romantic hero, with sales of the book shooting up after each film's release. The first two films were not a success, especially in America, and it took the release of *Goldfinger* in 1964 for box-office records to break and the mania to set in. During the 1960s many boys were not allowed to read the books because of their high sexual content and occasional lurid detail, and this too helped fuel the cult following.

The books have always been collected in first edition, but recently the prices have rocketed and there appears to be no sign of this interest waning. The books were issued in wonderful vivid pictorial dust jackets designed by Richard Chopping (although the first two were simply bright and typographical), and the condition of these determines the values. It is the rare first two titles, *Casino Royale* (1953) and *Live and Let Die* (1954), for which collectors are prepared to pay large sums, and the third, *Moonraker* (1955), also reaches four figures. *On Her Majesty's Secret Service* (1963) was issued in an edition of 250 signed copies in a glassine dust jacket, which collectors seek avidly. The earliest issue of his last full-length novel, *The Man with the Golden Gun* (1965), has a revolver blocked in gilt on the upper cover of the black boards and is worth ten times the later issue.

Ian Fleming also wrote the fantastical children's story *Chitty-Chitty-Bang-Bang*, issued in three books between 1964 and 1966, with illustrations by John Burningham. This was made into a successful film in 1968 and later into a stage musical in 2001, which led to an increased interest from collectors in the children's books as well as the spy stories.

1 Ian Fleming. *Casino Royale*. 1953. The first James Bond novel. In the dust-jacket. **£7,000–10,000/$12,800–16,000**

2 Ian Fleming. *Live and Let Die*. 1954. In the second issue dust-jacket with note on jacket design by Kenneth Lewis. **£900–1,200/$1,440–1,920**

3 and **4** Ian Fleming. *For Your Eyes Only*. 1960. In cloth with "eye" design and dust-jacket. **£140–180/$224–288**

Detective Fiction

The middle years of the 19th century had seen an increase in the sensational and popular literature of crime and mystery. There were cheap thrillers and more complex darker mystery stories such as some of Charles Dickens' works and Wilkie Collins' novels *The Woman in White* (1863) and *The Moonstone* (1868). Detective fiction is avidly collected, and has been the subject of numerous specialist books. Books written before World War II remain generally fairly expensive, and there are strong prices for contemporary work. Fine new authors are appearing all the time, and these are worth watching out for.

It was the introduction of the great sleuth Sherlock Holmes in Arthur Conan Doyle's *A Study in Scarlet* in 1887 that paved the way for the explosion of crime and mystery writing in the 20th century. This story first appeared in the opening 95 pages of the 28th *Beeton's Christmas Annual* (1886). This is exceptionally rare in the original wrappers, and rebound still commands five figures. The first separate book edition of 1888, bound in wrappers in the first issue with "younger" spelt correctly in the preface, is now one of the most expensive titles listed in this book – even the second issue fetches a five-figure sum. *The Sign of Four* was the second Sherlock Holmes story and first appeared on pages 147–223 of *Lippincott's Magazine* in February 1890. The first book edition was published in the same year and the first issue has several points to check, including the misprinting of page 138 on the contents page. These first two

stories received only moderate acclaim, but it was with the publication of *The Adventures of Sherlock Holmes* (1892) and *The Memoirs of Sherlock Holmes* (1894) that success came. The values for these and for *The Hound of the Baskervilles* (1902) in fine condition have markedly increased over the past five years. Copies of *The Adventures of Sherlock Holmes* are known in the dust-jacket, but are very rare, and only two copies of *The Hound of the Baskervilles* are thought to exist in the jacket, putting these beyond the reach of the collector.

The detective short story was the earliest form of this genre, and indeed many of the Sherlock Holmes stories were in this format. G. K. Chesterton's "Father Brown" stories were very popular and today remain some of his most sought-after works. The first was *The Innocence of Father Brown* (1911). The prototype of the full-length modern detective novel was E.C. Bentley's *Trent's Last Case* (1913), which appeared in the US under the title *The Woman in Black*. E.C. Bentley set the pattern of the fuller characterization of a gentlemanly amateur detective that was to remain to the fore for the next quarter-century, the period generally known as the "Golden Age" of detective fiction. Puzzles and role-play between author and reader

1 Sir Arthur Conan Doyle. *The Memoirs of Sherlock Holmes*. 1893. Original pictorial cloth. **£1,000–1,500/$1,600–2,400**

2 Sir Arthur Conan Doyle. *The Hound of the Baskervilles*. 1902. In the original cloth. **£1,500–2,500/$2,400–4,000**

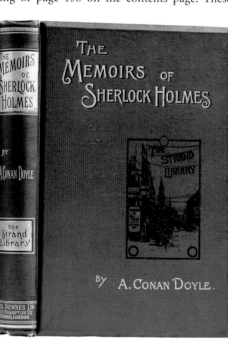
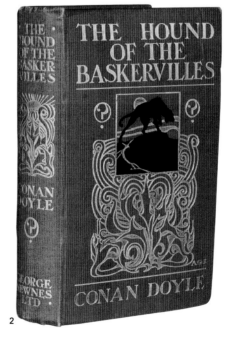

were set, law and order was always vindicated and crime punished.

Three authors from this period worth looking for are R. Austin Freeman and Freeman Wills Croft, masters of scientific and technical expertise, and John Dickson Carr, who specialized in locked-room puzzles. R. Austin Freeman's best-known character was Dr Thorndyke, and the first of the Thorndyke novels was *The Red Thumb Mark* (New York, 1907). His first detective fiction book is very rare and was written with Dr John James Pitcairn under the pseudonym "Clifford Ashdown" and titled *The Adventures of Romney Pringle* (1902). The earliest Thorndyke books are not generally known in dust-jackets, but from about 1922 they can usually be found, although they remain expensive. Freeman Wills Croft was one of the first to use police procedure methodically and his main character was Inspector French who initially appeared in *Inspector French's Greatest Case* (1924). The author's first book was *The Cask* (1920), which remains his most expensive. John Dickson Carr created two sleuths, Dr Gideon Fell, who first appeared in *Hag's Nook* (New York, 1933), and Henri Bencolin, who made his debut in *It Walks by Night* (New York, 1930). He also wrote a series of books about Sir Henry Merrivale under the pseudonym "Carter Dixon", of which *The Plague Court Murders* (New York, 1934) was the first.

Other collectable writers from the 1930s include Michael Innes, the pseudonym of J.I.M. Stewart, and Nicholas Blake, the pseudonym of Cecil Day Lewis. There are also John Buchan's mystery novels featuring Richard Hannay, the best-known of which is the first, *The Thirty-Nine Steps* (1915), which is rare in the dust-jacket.

In the US, Dashiell Hammett and Raymond Chandler are the two most important writers of the 1930s, whose style of tough fiction, with street-wise protagonists, began to erode and alter the softer British fiction. Dashiell Hammett's first book, *Red Harvest* (New York, 1929), is now generally considered his best. The hero was simply the anonymous "Continental Operative", but Hammett's greatest character was Sam Spade, who first appeared in *The Maltese Falcon* (New York, 1930), perhaps his best-known and most sought-after work, coming after *The Dain Curse* (New York, 1929). All of these are now extremely rare in the striking pictorial dust-jackets and command five-figure sums if the jacket is present and in fine condition.

Raymond Chandler, influenced by Hammett, created one of the most famous detectives of all time: Philip Marlowe. His first appearance was in *The Big Sleep* (New York, 1939). Like Dashiell Hammett, many of his earliest stories were initially printed in the important periodical *Black Mask*. Subsequent novels were *Farewell My Lovely* (New York, 1940) and *The High Window* (New York, 1942). Set in Los Angeles, the novels are

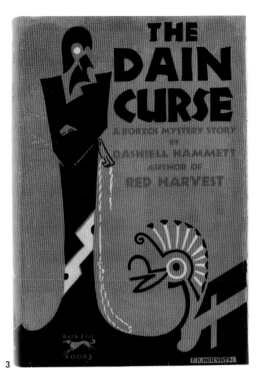

3

4

3 Dashiell Hammett. *The Dain Curse*. New York, 1929. Author's second book, in the dust-jacket, with some restoration. **£5,000–8,000/$8,000–12,800**

4 Raymond Chandler. *The Big Sleep*. New York, 1939. Author's first book, in the dust-jacket. **£7,000–10,000/$11,200–16,000**

highly moral, as Philip Marlowe searches for a hidden truth without reference to either individual gain or abstract justice.

Post-war detective fiction is more complex: truth and order do not always reign, and the conflict is not always seen from the side of justice. Writers who stuck with the earlier formula tended to abandon the amateur sleuth and to concentrate on realistic characterization or technical and scientific detail. There are many detective fiction writers from this period that one could collect, and the majority remain easily available and affordable. Writers worth looking for could include Eric Ambler, the master of fast-moving plots, whose first book was *The Dark Frontier* (1936), Ross Macdonald, the pseudonym for the American Kenneth Millar, whose *The Barbarous Coast* (New York, 1956) is still his most sought-after work, and John Creasey who remains possibly the most prolific of all crime writers. Creasey published under several pseudonyms and his most famous characters were Inspector Gideon and Inspector West. His first books were published in 1932, and his first Inspector West novel, *Inspector West Tales*, appeared in 1942. Writers of detective fiction are often extraordinarily prolific and Denis Wheatley was no exception. His dark, satanic thrillers remain hugely popular today, although they do not command high prices. His first published book was *The Forbidden Territory* (1933).

Contemporary detective fiction is perhaps stronger than ever, partly fuelled by the successful television adaptations of authors such as Colin Dexter ("Inspector Morse") and R.D. Wingfield ("Jack Frost"), and several of these novels are at the moment some of the most expensive of all contemporary fiction. Colin Dexter first introduced Inspector Morse in *Last Bus to Woodstock* (1975), and Jack Frost appeared in *Frost at Christmas*, first published in a Canadian edition by Paperjacks in 1984 and in England in 1990. *A Touch of Frost* initially appeared in the US in 1987 and was first published in England in 1990, and this is to date one of the most collected and expensive contemporary novels.

5 R.D. Wingfield. *A Touch of Frost.* 1990. In the dust-jacket. Second of the "DI Frost" novels. **£600–800/$960–1,280**

6 Colin Dexter. *Last Bus to Woodstock.* 1975. The first "Inspector Morse" novel. In the dust-jacket. **£600–800/$960–1,280**

7 "John Ross Macdonald" [Kenneth Millar]. *The Ivory Grin.* New York, 1952. In the dust-jacket. **£300–400/$480–640**

Crime Writers Association

The Crime Writers Association was formed by the author John Creasey in 1953, initially as an informal group where crime writers, both of fiction and non-fiction, could meet and discuss their work. In 1956 sponsorship was acquired, enabling the Association to provide financial awards. Titles are shortlisted every year for its prestigious Golden and Silver Dagger awards and memorial awards. The standards are high and these titles could well make an interesting collection. Robert Wilson was awarded the Gold Dagger in 1999 for *A Small Death in Lisbon*, and his works have subsequently started to climb steeply in value. His new work *The Blind Man of Seville* (2003) would be worth watching. Previous winners comprise a roll-call of the best writers of crime fiction and have included authors such as Patricia Cornwell, Ruth Rendell, Michael Dibdin, Peter Hoeg, Ian Rankin, Leslie Charteris, Colin Dexter, and John Le Carré.

5   6   7

Women Crime Writers

Women have excelled at crime fiction and the most famous is Agatha Christie, creator of the heroes Hercule Poirot and Miss Marple. Her works continue to increase sharply in value. The prices quoted for the early works from the 1920s and 1930s in the 2002/2003 edition of *Guide to First Edition Prices* have subsequently doubled or tripled since the book went to press. Born in 1890, she worked as a hospital dispenser during World War I where she gained her knowledge of poisons that proved so useful in her later writing. Her first novel was *The Mysterious Affair at Styles*, which was initially published in the US by John Lane in 1920, appearing the following year in England. Her second book was *The Secret Adversary* (1922), and the second Poirot mystery was *Murder on the Links* (1923). All these early titles are exceptionally rare in the dust-jackets and will regularly command five-figure sums if the jacket is present in fine condition. Even in the original cloth they are becoming increasingly hard to find in fine condition – *The Mysterious Affair at Styles* now reaches between £5,000/$7,500 and £7,000/$10,500 in cloth alone. This is the kind of figure the collector will have to pay for any of the other titles in dust-jackets from the 1920s and 1930s.

Death on the Nile (1937) is widely regarded as one of her best books, and the dust-jacket is particularly distinctive and rare, resulting in a five-figure sum. The jacket was designed by Robin Macartney, the architect and painter who accompanied Agatha Christie and her husband Max Mallowan on archaeological expeditions to Syria and Iraq. The first appearance of Hercule Poirot was the beginning of a prolific writing career in which she published 66 detective novels, other novels under the pseudonym of "Mary Westmacott", self-portraits, plays, including the long-running *The Mousetrap* (1954), and volumes of verse. Her earliest books were published by John Lane, but in 1926 Collins took over with the publication of *The Murder of Roger Ackroyd*. Later works from the 1940s on can be acquired easily for modest sums and could form a good introduction to her work.

1

2

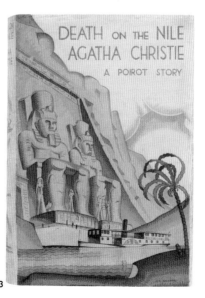

3

1 Agatha Christie. *The Mysterious Affair at Styles*. 1921. First English edition of the author's first book, the first "Hercule Poirot" novel. **£2,500–3,500/$4,000–5,600**

2 Agatha Christie. *Hercule Poirot's Christmas*. 1938. In the dust-jacket. **£1,800–2,200/$£2,880–3,520**

3 Agatha Christie. *Death on the Nile*. 1937. In the dust-jacket, this copy with some slight restoration. **£4,500–5,500/$7,200–8,800**

Her contemporary, Dorothy L. Sayers, is also regarded as one of the masters of the genre, her most famous invention being Lord Peter Wimsey. An accomplished scholar, her detective fiction is characterized by well-researched backgrounds, distinguished style, observant characterization and ingenious plots. The first "Lord Peter Wimsey" novel was *Whose Body?* (New York, 1923), the first issue of which does not have "Inc." present in the publisher's imprint on the title page. It appeared a few months later in England under the imprint of T. Fisher Unwin with a few authorial corrections. Her most widely regarded books are *Murder Must Advertise* (1933) and *The Nine Tailors* (1934). Far more affordable than Agatha Christie, her books from the 1920s command the highest prices. Publishing only a few novels, all her work is sought-after, but titles from the 1930s can be found in dust-jackets for well under £1,000/$1,500. Her last novel was *Busman's Honeymoon* (1937).

Others writing during this period whose work is more readily available include Margery Allingham, whose hero was the aristocratic Albert Campion, and Ngaio Marsh. Margery Allingham's first crime book was *The White Cottage Mystery* (1928), and the first to feature Albert Campion was *The Crime at Black Dudley* (1929). Ngaio Marsh was born in New Zealand, and is regarded as one of the most gifted of the genre. Her hero was Chief Detective Inspector Roderick Alleyn, who first appears in *A Man Lay Dead* (1934), the author's first book. Her early work from the 1930s is becoming more expensive and copies in fine dust-jackets will regularly exceed £1,000/$1,500.

Patricia Highsmith's novels contain a distinctive black humour. Her first thriller was *Strangers on a Train* (New York, 1950), which was filmed by Alfred Hitchcock in 1951, but her best known is *The Talented Mr. Ripley* (New York, 1955), only recently made into a film, which has caused its value to increase sharply. Edith Pargeter wrote many books under her own name, the first of which was *Hortensius, Friend of Nero* (1936), and under the pseudonym of "Jolyon Carr", the first being *Murder in the Dispensary* (1938). But she is best known as "Ellis Peters", creator of the Benedictine monk, Brother Cadfael, who has now been televised. The first book to feature the monk was *A Morbid Taste for Bones: A Mediaeval Whodunnit* (1977). This remains her most sought-after book.

Other contemporary writers to collect include P.D. James, whose first "Adam Dalgliesh" novel was *Cover her Face* (1962), and Ruth Rendell, whose first Inspector Wexford novel under her own name was *From Doon with Death* (1964). She also publishes darker, more psychological thrillers under the pseudonym "Barbara Vine", the first of which was *A Dark Adapted Eye* (1986). Patricia Cornwell's first novel featuring the forensic pathologist

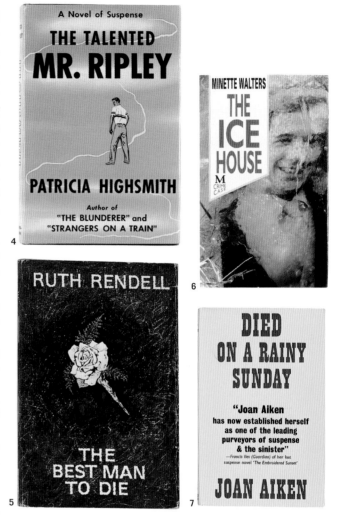

4 Patricia Highsmith. *The Talented Mr. Ripley*. New York, 1955. First of the celebrated "Mr. Ripley" crime novels. In the dust-jacket. **£800–1,000/$1,280–1,600**

5 Ruth Rendell. *The Best Man to Die*. 1969. In the dust-jacket. **£300–400/$480–640**

6 Minette Walters. *The Ice House*. 1992. In the dust-jacket. Author's first detective novel. **£300–400/$480–640**

7 Joan Aiken. *Died on a Rainy Sunday*. 1972. In the dust-jacket. **£50–100/$80–160**

Kay Scarpetta, *Postmortem* (New York, 1990), won her four major awards. Her most recent, *The Last Precinct* (New York, 2000), has recently been filmed, which will no doubt cause her books to rise in price. Minette Walters' first book, *The Ice House* (1992), was televised, as were most of her subsequent works, and this has led to increasing interest from collectors. There is a variant dust-jacket for *The Ice House* which depicts two heads under the ice, and this commands a sum in excess of £1,000/$1,500 today, twice the value of the normal edition.

Other Areas

While we have looked at the major fields of literature, there are numerous other areas on which a collector could choose to concentrate.

One of the biggest growth areas over the past few years has been in the works of Winston Churchill. A prolific writer and the most important British statesman of the 20th century, his books on history, military history, travel and politics have a strong following, especially in the US. Titles include his first book, *The Story of the Malakand Field Force* (1898), which has issue points to check, *The River War* (1899), *London to Ladysmith via Pretoria* (1900), *My African Journey* (1908), the six-volume *The Second World War* (1948–54), and the four-volume *A History of the English-Speaking Peoples* (1956–8). Several of his works are found in signed limited editions with additional presentation inscriptions, and these can command five-figure sums. Two rare works are *Mr Broderick's Army* (1903), not seen at auction for over 30 years, and the pamphlet *For Free Trade* (1906).

A good area for the collector interested in foreign travel is, of course, travel writing. There are many fine 20th-century writers whose books would make a satisfying collection, with titles ranged at various price levels. Probably the most expensive will be *The Seven Pillars of Wisdom* (1922) by T.E. Lawrence, of which there are only eight copies known: the author's own copy was sold at auction in New York in 2001 for $850,000 (£566,600). However, the book can be found in several other editions: proof copies of 1924 and 1925, subscribers' copies of 1926, which regularly fetch £20,000–30,000/ $30,000–45,000 at auction, the American copyright edition of 1926, the English printing of 1935, comprising a limited edition and the ordinary edition, and the 1935 American edition, also present in three states – something for all pockets.

Wilfred Thesiger's classic books *The Marsh Arabs* (1964) and *The Arabian Sands* (1959) document the life of the Marsh Arabs and Bedouins almost hounded to extinction by Saddam Hussein. Other travel writers worth looking for include Karen Blixen, who wrote *Out of Africa* (1937) under the name of Isak Dinesen, which was made into a film starring Robert Redford, Robert Bruce whose books from the 1930s were picked up by the generation of the 1960s and given cult status, Paul Theroux, Eric Newby, Gavin Young, and Bruce Chatwin, whose first book, *In Patagonia* (1977), won the Hawthornden Prize. The UK edition of *In Patagonia* contains photographs of Chatwin's trip to South America that are not included in the US edition of 1978. There are many fine books written about Africa and the Middle East in the early part of the 20th century which document worlds that have all but vanished.

1 Freya Stark. *Riding to the Tigris*. 1959. In the dust-jacket. **£20–30/$32–48**

2 Paul Theroux. *The Old Patagonian Express*. 1979. First American edition, in the dust-jacket. The author's second travel book. **£40–50/$64–80**

3 Bruce Chatwin. *In Patagonia*. 1977. In the dust-jacket. The author's first book. **£350–450/$560–720**

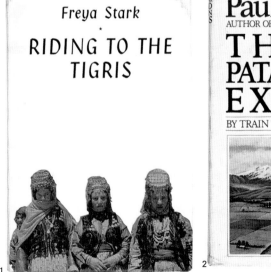

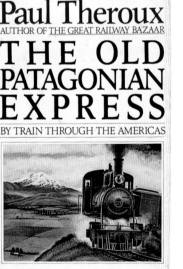

Children's Books

Many of the children's books that are most collected today have their roots in previous centuries, and indeed in non-English-speaking countries. The early 18th century had seen the appearance in print, in English, of the great fairy tales collected by Madame d'Aulnoy and Charles Perrault, such as "Little Red Riding-Hood", "Sleeping Beauty", and "Cinderella". In 1812 the Brothers Grimm began to publish their tales (first English edition, 1823), and in 1846 Hans Andersen's stories were first published in English. Edward Lear's *A Book of Nonsense* appeared the same year. It is these, and Lewis Carroll's *Alice's Adventures in Wonderland* (1865), that stand out as possibly the most important children's books of the 19th century, and their impact continues to be felt today. As with many of the most rare children's books, only a few copies of each title survive in first edition, making them extremely expensive for collectors. However, there is a wealth of later editions worth collecting.

On 4 July 1862 Charles Lutwidge Dodgson rowed up the river from Oxford to Godstow with a friend and three young girls, Lorina, Alice, and Edith Liddell, daughters of the Dean of Christ Church. It was on this expedition that he told them a story about a little girl called Alice and her adventures underground. At the end of the day Alice begged Dodgson to write down the tale for her, and after some persuasion he published it, under the pseudonym "Lewis Carroll". However, he was unhappy with the printing of John Tenniel's illustrations and asked for the book to be recalled and reprinted. The majority of the books were returned, the sheets were sent to America where they were reissued with a new title page (first edition, second issue), and the whole book was reprinted for the English market (second [first published] edition). All are highly prized by collectors today, although only about 25 copies of the true first edition remain in existence.

In 1907 the copyright of the illustrations expired and in the closing months numerous editions of the tale and its sequel, *Through the Looking-Glass* (1872), were published with illustrations by various artists. The story has proved to be arguably the greatest fantasy story ever written in the English language and is frequently cited as one of the most influential and oft-quoted books after the Bible and the works of Shakespeare. It is no wonder that it remains as popular

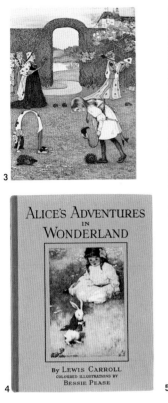

3

5

6

4

and sought-after as ever, with collectors eagerly seeking modern editions illustrated by artists as diverse as Arthur Rackham, Peter Newell, Mabel Lucie Attwell, Walt Disney, Barry Moser, Salvador Dalí, and Ralph Steadman. One of the most interesting editions was that translated into Russian by Vladimir Nabokov, accompanied by Constructivist illustrations, in 1932, 32 years prior to his own masterpiece about a young girl, *Lolita*.

The 19th century witnessed the flowering of children's literature, with publishers such as John Newbery and John Harris, and the Darton and Wallis families producing books of fables, nursery rhymes, fairy tales, and light-hearted educational books. As literacy spread and printing processes improved and cheapened, the demand for children's books increased. At the end of the century, advances in colour printing enabled printers such as Marcus Ward and Edmund Evans and publishers such as George Routledge, Frederick Warne, and Ernest Nister to produce the superb illustrated books for children by Kate Greenaway, Walter Crane, and Randolph Caldecott. The style of illustration at this time was most often firmly rooted in the whimsical, cosy world of the

1 Walt Disney's *Alice in Wonderland*. New York, 1951. Illustrations by the Walt Disney Studio. Signature of the real "Alice" on the endpaper. **£1,500–2,000/$2,400–3,200**

2 Lewis Carroll. *Alice's Adventures in Wonderland*. 1907. Illustrated by Arthur Rackham. Original cloth. **£300–400/$480–640**. Also a limited edition of 550 copies.

3 Lewis Carroll. *Alice's Adventures in Wonderland*. 1907. Illustrated by Margaret Sowerby, **£100–150/$160–240**. The first English edition to be issued without Tenniel's illustrations.

4 Lewis Carroll. *Alice's Adventures in Wonderland*. Enlarged edition, [1931]. Illustrated by Bessie Pease, first published in 1907. **£100–150/$160–240**

5 Lewis Carroll. *Alice in Wonderland*. [1932]. 12 coloured plates and other Illustrations by Gwynedd Hudson. **£40–60/$64–96**

6 Hans Andersen. *Stories*. 1911. Illustrated by Edmund Dulac. Original cloth. **£150–200/$240–320**. Limited signed edition of 750 copies. £600–800/$960–1,280.

Victorian child, but the work of these artists was becoming more modern in tone and technique.

The latter part of the 19th century also saw the rise of the adventure story, fuelled by the greater knowledge and awareness brought by the expansion of the British Empire, foreign travel, and exploration. Several of those authors most collected today successfully bridged the gap between the Victorian and modern worlds, producing adventure stories or thrillers but with modern political, social or psychological tendencies. Jack London and Robert Louis Stevenson are prime examples, and *Treasure Island* (1883), with its psychologically complex characters, is widely regarded as the first modern adventure story. Jack London's books, *The Son of the Wolf* (New York, 1900) and *The Call of the Wild* (New York, 1903), tell of lone animals working within the confines of the collective, social pack – themes taken up later in George Orwell's *Animal Farm*.

Prior to the 1970s very few people collected children's books except for a small band of dealers and private collectors, most of whom knew each other, and today they are legendary names in the book world. Then, in the mid-1970s, came the sale by auction of the collection of Edgar Oppenheimer, comprising children's books throughout the centuries and across many continents. The past three decades have seen vast changes in this area of collecting with many dealers now specializing solely in children's books and entire auctions dedicated to this field, which has thus slowly become a legitimate and respected area of collecting. Many collectors are first prompted by a sentimental affection for the tales they read as a child, others re-discover the books of childhood as their own children grow. This often coincides with increasing levels of disposable income and it is perhaps the past few years' healthy financial climate that has helped fuel the rapid increase in the value of children's books. As the older, classic books become harder to find, with correspondingly higher prices, so collectors seek out alternative authors and illustrators. This area – perhaps more than any other – is constantly changing and producing fine material, with children's writers and illustrators receiving greater recognition every year. Quentin Blake was made the first Children's Laureate in 1999 and in 2001 Philip Pullman's *The Amber Spyglass*, the third volume in his trilogy "His Dark Materials", was the first children's book ever to win the Whitbread Book of the Year award.

7 Barefoot Books. Aleksei Tolstoy. *The Gigantic Turnip*. 1998. Illustrated by Niamh Sharkey. **£10–15/$16–24**. Winner of Books for Children Mother Goose Award.

8 Jack London. *The Call of the Wild*. New York, 1903. **£3,000–4,000/$4,800–6,400**. Rare in dust-jacket. First issue has vertical ribbing to cloth.

9 Robert Louis Stevenson. *Treasure Island*. 1883. Original cloth, early issue with advertisements dated 5R-1083. **£3,000–4,000/$4,800–6,400**

Fairies and Fairy Tales

It is perhaps the fairy tale that many think of first when they turn to children's books. The French first called them *contés des fées*, but these stories were actually traditional narratives deriving mostly from oral culture and set in print from the 17th century. These are the tales of *The Arabian Nights*, of Madame d'Aulnoy and Charles Perrault, of the Brothers Grimm, and Hans Andersen, in which fairies rarely play a major role, but which involve magic or fantasy. It was in 1889 that Andrew Lang issued the first of his 12 volumes of "Fairy Books", *The Blue Fairy Book*, with illustrations by Henry Ford and other artists. These are collected as much for their beautiful bindings, each colour reflecting the title of the book, as for the content.

The 20th century saw a blossoming of editions of fairy tales, with the greatest illustrators of each generation embellishing them. The books were not initially intended for children, often being expensively bound, but were soon taken up and adopted by them as their own. Arthur Rackham's edition of Grimm, Edmund Dulac's editions of *The Arabian Nights* and tales of Hans Andersen, Kay Nielsen's version of Hansel and Gretel and tales from further afield, *East of the Sun and West of the Moon* (1914) are some of the greatest illustrated books of the century (see the next chapter). All were issued as trade editions bound in pictorial cloth, and in de-luxe editions in pictorial vellum stamped in gilt with silk ties. It was probably Walt Disney, however, who brought these tales to subsequent generations of children, starting with his 1937 film and book of *Snow White and the Seven Dwarfs*. The ensuing films and books of *Cinderella*, *Sleeping Beauty*, *Beauty and the Beast*, and other tales have ensured these ancient stories remain in vogue. Iona and Peter Opie's *The Classic Fairy Tales* (1974) is the indispensable book for enthusiasts, presenting the exact text of the first publication in English of 24 of the best-known tales.

Actual fairies and other-worldly creatures were taken seriously in the 19th century, and several attempts were made to hoax the public. They were often portrayed as grotesque (as in Christina Rossetti's *Goblin Market*, illustrated by Dante Gabriel Rossetti in 1862, and Laurence Housman in 1893). By the 20th century these airy beings had generally been relegated to the nursery, to be depicted by Cicely Mary Barker in her 1920s "Flower Fairy" series or by the great Australian artist Ida Rentoul Outhwaite in works such as *Elves and Fairies* (Melbourne, 1916, the first great illustrated book published in Australia and prohibitively expensive at the time) and *Fairyland* (Melbourne, 1926). More recently Brian Froud and Alan Lee have produced a fine series of books as much for adults as for children, *Faeries* (1978) and *Good Faeries, Bad Faeries* (1998). The close of the 20th century saw a revival of interest in fairies and a major exhibition of "Victorian Fairy Paintings" in London and abroad. Important works by Rackham and Dulac were included.

1 Andrew Lang. *The Fairy Books*. 1889–1907. 12 volumes with illustrations by Henry Ford and others, original pictorial cloth. **£1,500–3,000/$2,400–4,800**

2 Ida Rentoul Outhwaite. *Elves and Fairies*. Melbourne, 1916. Illustrated by the author. **£500–700/$800–1,120**

3 Brian Froud. *Good Faeries, Bad Faeries*. 1998. Illustrated by the author. **£10–15/$16–24**

Animals

The association of animals with children's literature goes back a long way to the time of the early fables of Aesop and other ancient writers. Initially used mainly as moral emblems, animals come alive to children and can easily and memorably be given different attributes. Animals, whether realistic or anthropomorphized, in a natural or make-believe setting, bring home the sense of wonder and variety in the world, two of the most important factors in determining the children's literature that rises above the norm and proves to be timeless.

The great 19th-century animal stories were the precursors of many of the finest and most sought-after modern tales and paved the way for the explosion of books about animals published for children in the 20th century. William Roscoe's fantastical *The Butterfly's Ball* of 1805 leads through Leslie L. Brooke's humorous verse and nonsensical animals in the early 1900s directly to Alan Aldridge's 1973 *The Butterfly Ball and the Grasshopper's Feast*. Anna Sewell's moral and realistic *Black Beauty* (1877), one of the most widely read novels of all time, explores the theme of cruelty to animals, which was taken up in Felix Salten's *Bambi*, published in Berlin in 1923 and made popular by Walt Disney's film of 1942, and later in Dodie Smith's *The Hundred and One Dalmatians* (1956, animated in 1961).

Rudyard Kipling's *The Jungle Book* (1894) is generally regarded as the first attempt to enter the animal world and paves the way for great classic animal books as diverse as *Watership Down*, *The Wind in the Willows*, and *The Story of Babar*. Working from earlier myths, Kipling created a totally new world where it was entirely credible that the animals could walk and talk and befriend Mowgli. Until recently relatively common in the original cloth, copies in fine condition now command quite high prices, and the exceptionally rare printed dust-jacket which appears to have only been issued for *The Second Jungle Book* (1895) can easily increase the value by a factor of five.

Beatrix Potter generally depicted her animals, mostly domestic or woodland, in a human setting, wearing clothes and behaving much as children or adults would. This theme continues through the century with Alison Uttley's "Little Grey Rabbit" series, the first book, *The Squirrel, the Hare and the Little Grey-Rabbit*, appearing in 1929 and the last in 1975. As with the Beatrix Potter books, the format remained the same, the animals wore clothes and the environment was domestic. A similar theme can be found today in Dick Bruna's "Miffy" books, the first of which was published in 1964. Much loved by children, collectors have

1 William Plomer. *The Butterfly Ball and the Grasshopper's Feast*. 1973. Illustrated by Alan Aldridge. **£10–15/$16–24**

2 Dodie Smith. *The Hundred and One Dalmatians*. 1956. Illustrated by Janet and Anne Grahame-Johnstone. **£120–180/$192–288**

3 Rudyard Kipling. *The Jungle Book*. 1894. *The Second Jungle Book*. 1895. Illustrated by J. Lockwood Kipling. The pair in original cloth. **£1,000–1,500/$1,600–2,400**

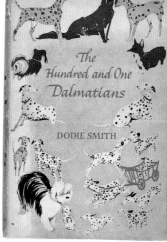

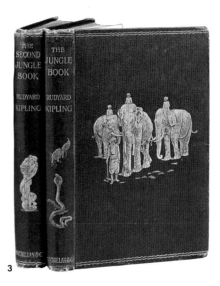

BEATRIX POTTER

As the 20th century dawned, arguably the most famous animal in children's literature found his way into print: Peter Rabbit. It was in 1893 that Beatrix Potter had written to the sick child of her governess, Noel Moore, one of her typical picture letters in which she tells the tale of "four little rabbits whose names were Flopsy, Mopsy, Cottontail and Peter".

Several years later she asked whether she might borrow back the letter to expand it into a book for publication. She sent the manuscript with black-and-white illustrations to several publishers, all of whom turned it down. Eventually, in December 1901, she decided to publish it herself, in an edition of 250 copies bound in green paper covered boards with a flat spine (first edition, first issue). This was given away or sold quickly, and in the following February she issued a further 200 copies with a round spine (first edition, second issue). In October the publishers Frederick Warne decided to reconsider their initial rejection, asking her to colour the illustrations and to reduce the length of the story and the number of illustrations from the initial 42 to 31. The story was issued in paper-covered boards with a pictorial label pasted to the upper cover and endpapers with a lavender-grey leaf pattern (first published edition). A few months later a further four illustrations were dropped, and pictorial endpapers were introduced. This format has never altered. Special de-luxe editions of several of the tales were issued in cloth bindings with gilt decoration and gilt-edged pages, and all of the titles originally came in protective glassine dust wrappers. The presence of these or an inscription from the author increases the value quite considerably.

The keenest demand is for the earliest tales – *Peter Rabbit*, *The Tailor of Gloucester*, *Squirrel Nutkin*, and *Benjamin Bunny* – being issued in shorter print-runs, and beloved of so many. The books were reprinted almost immediately and have never been out of print. A first edition has the date on the front of the title page at the bottom where the publisher's imprint is (to confuse matters a few titles do not have this date in the first edition). Collectors should check the endpapers, since the characters were changed as additional titles came out, and ideally consult a good bibliography or trusted dealer.

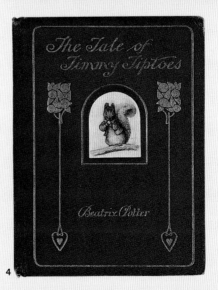

1 Beatrix Potter. *The Tale of Peter Rabbit*. [December 1901]. Illustrated by the author. Privately printed, 250 copies with flat spine. **£30,000–40,000/$48,000–64,000**

2 Beatrix Potter. *The Tale of Peter Rabbit*. 1902. Illustrated by the author. First published edition, first issue, 31 coloured plates and leaf endpapers. **£5,000–7,000/$8,000–11,200**

3 Beatrix Potter. *The Tale of Tom Kitten*. 1907. Illustrated by the author. The books were originally issued in printed glassine wrappers, now rare. **£3,000–5,000/$4,800–8,000**

4 Beatrix Potter. *The Tale of Timmy Tiptoes*. 1911. Illustrated by the author. Several of the tales were issued in a de-luxe gilt and cloth binding. **£3,000–4,000/$4,800–6,400**

recently begun to acquire his books, partly as a result of an increase in the merchandizing.

As the "Little Grey Rabbit" series developed, the tales became more imaginative, with the animals becoming part of a more comprehensive community. At about the same time that Little Grey Rabbit first appeared, the greatest animal society story, Kenneth Grahame's *The Wind in the Willows*, became a massive popular success with the addition of E.H. Shepard's illustrations, although it had first been published some years before. It is a fine example of a book that is present in several desirable editions for the collector to acquire: the 1908 first edition (issued in a dust-jacket but known by only a handful of copies); the 1931 Shepard first edition found as a trade edition and a limited signed edition of 200 copies; the first English edition illustrated by Arthur Rackham and the limited Rackham edition, both published after the artist's death, in 1950 and 1951; and the 1971 edition with the illustrations by E.H. Shepard in colour. As with Beatrix Potter's *Peter Rabbit*, these tales began life as a series of letters, to Grahame's son, Alastair. The riverbank world is peaceful, fun, and full of adventure, and although the animals wage a battle the story is ultimately full of charm and humour and not too threatening. The darker side of animal society is portrayed in tales such as Richard Adams' *Watership Down* (1972) and Colin Dann's series *The Animals of Farthing Wood* (1979–82). Richard Adams' tale, as with Beatrix Potter's (and in more recent times, J.K. Rowling's) was initially turned down by the major publishers. One of the most influential of modern animal stories, it has won both the Carnegie Medal and the Guardian Award as well as being made into a film. While the book undoubtedly looks at human behaviour and society, it remains essentially a children's tale about a community of rabbits.

Doctor Dolittle lived in the entirely imaginative world of Puddleby-on-the-Marsh where he learned to talk to his animals, Polynesia the parrot, Dab-Dab the duck and others. Hugh Lofting wrote 12 books in all, the first being *The Story of Dr. Dolittle* (New York, 1920) and the last three published posthumously. Although born in England, Lofting was educated in the US and moved there in 1912, hence the majority of his books were first published there, with first English editions appearing the following year. The first book commands considerably more than subsequent titles and the true first editions more than the first English editions. His work has risen steadily in value over the past few years.

Further developing these fantastical animal worlds were authors who created an animal protagonist and wrote a series of stories around their adventures, such as Mary Tourtel, succeeded by Alfred Bestall, who brought Rupert the Bear to life, and Jean de Brunhoff who created Babar. Each wrote and also illustrated their stories depicting the ever-increasing adventures of their characters. Rupert first appeared in print in the *Daily Express* on 8 November 1920. The strips were collected into book form and issued in distinctive yellow boards. The annuals, as they are known today, were first issued in 1936 when Alfred Bestall took over (until 1976). The 1936 annual was issued in a dust-jacket and copies in this state along with the annuals prior to 1943 remain the most sought-after. Cecile de Brunhoff first told her children a story about a little elephant in 1931. The tale was related to their father, the painter Jean de Brunhoff, who created the familiar picture-books. The stories were written in French but all were quickly translated and published in English, initially in New York, and it was this market that ensured his success. The first was *L'Histoire de Babar* (Paris, 1931; *The Story of Babar*, New York, 1933). Jean de Brunhoff wrote only seven titles before he died and the series was continued by his son. It is these early titles most collectors seek to acquire.

Whereas Babar soon came to rule over his kingdom and Rupert's adventures became ever more exotic, Michael Bond's Paddington Bear fell into small-scale scrapes within a domestic, suburban setting, which were both appealing to children and all-too-familiar to adults. There is a strong emphasis on the illustration in these books, and indeed it is the symbiosis between text and picture that has made them so enduring, whereas it is the stories themselves that have made authors Dick King-Smith and E.B. White so sought-after. White's *Charlotte's Web* (New York, 1952) and *Stuart Little* (New York, 1945) are much in demand, especially since the latter was made into the film. The story of Stuart the mouse came to E.B. White in a dream which he shared with his nephews and nieces before writing it down. *Charlotte's Web* won numerous awards and was listed as a Newbery Honor Book in 1953, and White was given a Pulitzer Prize special citation for his work in 1978. The magical worlds of such books, so loved by children and sought by adults, is what has attracted collectors to Dick King-Smith's work (helped by the filming of *The Sheep-Pig*, 1983, as *Babe*). Sales of his work, over 50 titles, are thought to have been exceeded only by Enid Blyton and Roald Dahl. His books combine humour, adventure, and a wit much appreciated by older children, and once again create the feelings of magic and wonder sought by collectors.

One of the most important and enduring themes in children's books is the magical or fantastical relationship between a child and its toys, usually animals. The toys come to life and embark upon adventures within the nursery or beyond, turning into the child's closest friends. It is perhaps these stories that often evoke the strongest feelings of nostalgia from adult collectors today: Christopher Robin and Winnie the Pooh; the Boy and his Velveteen Rabbit; Max and his Wolf Suit and the fruit of his imagination, the Wild Things. It was in 1922 that Margery

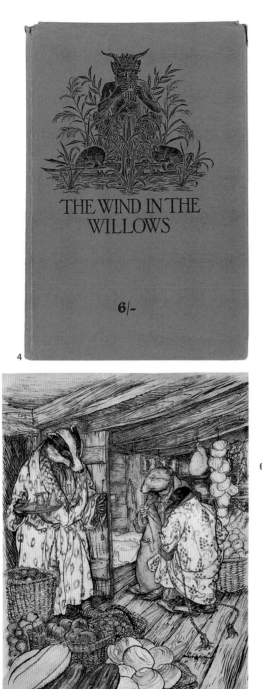

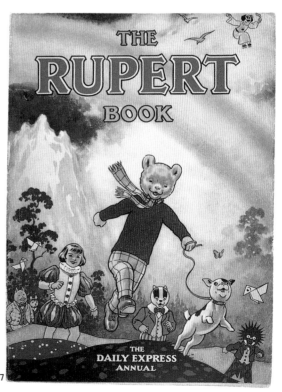

4 and **5** Kenneth Grahame. *The Wind in the Willows.* 1908.
Frontispiece by Graham Robertson. With the rare first-issue dust-
jacket, £60,000–80,000/$96,000–128,000. Without dust-jacket,
£1,500–3,000/$2,400–4,800. Illustrated by Arthur Rackham, one of
2,020 copies, New York, 1940, **£600–800/$960–1,280**; one of 500
copies, 1951, £700–900/$1,120–1,440.

6 Hugh Lofting. *Doctor Dolittle's Caravan.* 1927. **£100–150/
$160–240**. Illustrated by the author. First UK edition, originally
published in New York in 1926.

7 A.E. Bestall. *The Rupert Book.* 1948. **£60–80/$96–128**. Illustrated
by the author. The first Rupert annual was published in 1936.

Williams Bianco wrote her story *The Velveteen Rabbit, or How Toys Became Real*, based on her own toy rabbit, Fluffy, and inspired by the experiences of her own young children. The extremely rare first edition was illustrated with coloured lithographs by William Nicholson, although it has been reissued many times since (see page 104). In the book children explore complex themes about love and loss through the familiar world of toys. When Maurice Sendak wrote and illustrated *Where the Wild Things Are* (New York, 1963), a child's behaviour and feelings became the starting-point for a great fantasy tale. Max, who has behaved like a monster and been sent to bed with no supper, dons his suit, turns to his imagination and creates an adventure where he sails away to find monsters, the Wild Things. Calming down, banishing the monsters, he returns home to supper. Controversial when it was first published, the book soon received great acclaim, winning the Caldecott Award, selling millions of copies and inspiring an opera. This was really the first of the darker and more psychological fantasy books prevalent and so appealing to both child and collector during the closing years of the 20th century (see page 112).

9

10

11

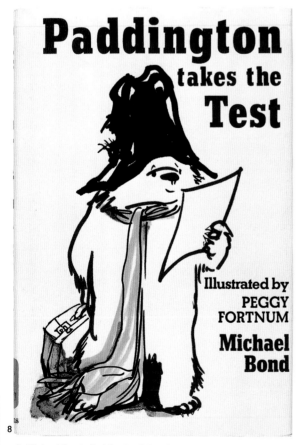

8 Michael Bond. *Paddington Takes the Test*. 1979. Illustrated by Peggy Fortnum, **£15–20/$24–32**.

9 Richard Adams. *Watership Down*. 1972. **£500–700/$800–1,120**. Illustrated by John Lawrence, 1976, in an ordinary edition, and 250 copies with a drawing by the artist.

10 Jean de Brunhoff. *Histoire de Babar le petit elephant*. Paris, 1950. Moving illustrations by the author. **£1,500–2,000/$2,400–3,200**. Rare in the dust-jacket.

11 E.B. White. *Charlotte's Web*. New York, 1952. Illustrated by Garth Williams. First-issue dust-jacket priced $2.50. **£400–600/$640–960**

BEARS

Possibly the best known and most collected books of the child-toy genre are the tales of Christopher Robin and Winnie the Pooh. A freelance writer, A.A. Milne became assistant editor of *Punch* in 1906, and a successful playwright in London and on Broadway throughout the 1920s. He also wrote numerous novels and books of verse, which today are overlooked by collectors. All of these can be found for very modest sums, but the verses and tales he wrote with his son Christopher in his mind command high prices. Milne was asked to contribute some light-hearted verse to *Merry-Go-Round*, a new magazine for children, in 1922. These proved popular and were collected into book form in 1924, dedicated to his son as *When We Were Very Young*. Pooh himself first appeared on Christmas Eve 1925 in the *Evening News*, and the book was published in 1926. It was a success from the start, thanks in part to Ernest Shepard's illustrations. His animals are very definitely modelled on soft toys, and indeed Winnie the Pooh was based on Shepard's own son's bear "Growler". Their world is one of constant summer, safe and idealized, and yet fantastical, encapsulating adult nostalgia for childhood. The books were quickly issued in various special de-luxe editions to enhance the market: bound in soft roan leather; in a signed and limited edition on hand-made paper with a dust-jacket: and the ultimate edition of 20 copies of all but the first title printed on Japanese vellum, bound in limp vellum. There are issue points to the dust-jackets for the first and second books to check relating to the wording on the inside lower flap (referring to other publications). Books of music soon followed, various spin-offs and of course the merchandizing and films, all of which have conspired to make Winnie the Pooh probably the best-known toy animal in the world.

It is the Americans, though, who can lay claim to the "teddy bear", with the Roosevelt Bears, which although largely unknown outside the US are part of American childhood. Holidaying in 1902, President Theodore, or "Teddy", Roosevelt attended a bear hunt. The only bear he was given a chance to kill was a cub tethered to a tree. He declined, and the incident was illustrated in the *Washington Post* by the cartoonist Clifford Berryman. The bear came to symbolize the President, and within a year it had been transformed into a toy for children called "Teddy's Bear". In 1906 Seymour Eaton wrote a book about two toy bears, Teddy G and Teddy T, followed by three further books, and numerous novelties were issued as a result of its popularity. It would be fair to say that *The Roosevelt Bears, their Travels and Adventures* (Philadelphia, 1906) was the precursor of all other bear stories and is thus highly sought-after by collectors.

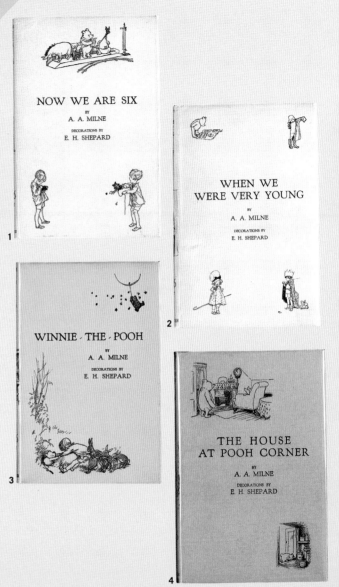

1 A.A. Milne. *Now We Are Six.* 1927. Illustrations by E.H. Shepard. **£400–600/$640–960**. Without dust-jacket, £150–200/$240–320.

2 A.A. Milne. *When We Were Very Young.* 1924. Illustrations by E.H. Shepard. **£2,000–3,000/$3,200–4,800**. Without dust-jacket, £700–900/$1,120–1,440.

3 A.A. Milne. *Winnie the Pooh.* 1926. Illustrations by E.H. Shepard. **£1,000–1,500/$1,600–2,400**. Without dust-jacket, £500–700/$800–1,120.

4 A.A. Milne. *The House at Pooh Corner.* 1928. Illustrations by E.H. Shepard. **£400–600/$640–960**. Without dust-jacket, £150–200/$240–320. Complete set of the four books with dust jackets, £8,000–12,000/$12,800–19,200.

Fantasy Worlds: Oz to Hogwarts

Although fairy tales date from the 17th century, and literature created especially for children dates back to the 18th century, fantasy as an extended form of story does not. Apart from the fairy tales and myths and legends of ancient lore adapted for children, the first major, and still perhaps the greatest, fantasy tale written for children was Lewis Carroll's *Alice's Adventures in Wonderland* (1865). This and Charles Kingsley's *The Water Babies* (1863), more often now collected in its later illustrated editions, really stood on their own until the publication of George MacDonald's powerful stories *At the Back of the North Wind* (1871) and *The Princess and the Goblin* (1872). Both are rare and sought-after by collectors in the original cloth.

Modern children's literature draws on earlier fairy tales, myths, and legends to enhance and create its own fantasy worlds, whether it be the world of Peter Rabbit, Peter Pan, Dorothy, Alice, or Harry Potter, and it would probably be correct to say that an element of fantasy runs through the best and certainly the most collected of children's literature, lending it a timeless quality and for adults an escape from the stresses of the real world.

Peter Pan and Alice have been until recently the two children who best embody childhood fantasy literature, but some say it is Peter Pan who perhaps remains more influential or relevant today. Initially appearing in J.M. Barrie's 1902 novel *The White Bird*, Peter's character was fleshed out in the 1904 stage play *Peter Pan*, which was a resounding success but remained unpublished until 1928. Barrie turned the play into a novel, *Peter and Wendy*, which was published in 1911 with illustrations by F.D. Bedford. However, in 1906 he had published a story titled *Peter Pan in Kensington Gardens* with illustrations by Arthur Rackham. Although both stories deal with a child called Peter Pan who does not grow up, and his adventures in a fantasy world, they are actually different stories. The 1906 story has Peter as a one-week old baby who, as with all babies, was a bird before birth. By the force of

1

2

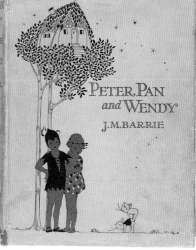

3

1 J.M. Barrie. *Peter and Wendy.* 1911. Illustrated by F.D. Bedford. **£150–200/$240–320**

2 J.M. Barrie. *Peter Pan in Kensington Gardens.* 1906. Illustrated by Arthur Rackham. Limited edition of 500 copies, **£2,000–3,000/ $3,200–4,800**. Ordinary edition without dust-jacket, £300–500/ $480–800; with dust-jacket, £800–1,200/$1,280–1,920.

3 J.M. Barrie. *Peter Pan and Wendy.* [1921]. Illustrated by Mabel Lucie Attwell. **£500–700/$800–1,120**. Without dust-jacket, £100–150/$160–240.

BAUM and OZ

The 20th century saw the development and coming-of-age of the phenomenon of the "alternative" or "fantasy" world first seen underground in *Alice*. L. Frank Baum's *The Wonderful Wizard of Oz* (Chicago, 1900) has been called "the first distinctive attempt to construct a fairyland out of American materials". Dorothy and her fantastical friends, the Tin Woodman, the Scarecrow, and the Cowardly Lion, explore the new and magical world of Oz, but they are also particularly American. Baum's first published book for children was *Mother Goose in Prose* (Chicago, 1897), illustrated by Maxfield Parrish. This wonderfully imaginative book "explains" and elaborates on 22 classic nursery rhymes. It is quite a rarity, with a complicated binding history leading to two issues of the first edition.

The author's second book for children was also the first important American coloured picture book for children, *Father Goose. His Book* (Chicago, 1899), with coloured illustrations by W.W. Denslow. It was such a popular book that only a handful of copies of the first print run are known to have survived today. It was Baum's second collaboration, however, with W.W. Denslow, the first of the Oz books, that was to make his name. The story was so successful that Baum produced one new book a year until his death in 1919. Baum fell out with Denslow and the subsequent Oz books were illustrated by John R. Neill. After Baum's death many other titles were added by Ruth Plumly Thompson in collaboration with Neill. The Oz books are rare in fine condition. *The Wonderful Wizard of Oz* has a complex series of issue points concerning priority of the binding, the endpapers, text, the inserted plates, and the verso of the title page, making a bibliography or expert help essential in determining a rare and expensive true first issue. The majority of copies that come on to the market are of mixed issue, displaying a variety of points from one of three states of binding, text, and plates. The second title, *The Marvelous Land of Oz* (Chicago, 1910), is probably the next hardest to find as a first issue, and all titles where the decorative binding has been enhanced with a metallic pictorial label, such as *Emerald City of Oz* (Chicago, 1910), are rare in fine condition.

1 L. Frank Baum. *The Wonderful Wizard of Oz*. Chicago, 1900. Illustrated by W.W. Denslow. First-issue text, binding variant B with imprint in red. **£8,000–12,000/$12,800–19,200**

2 L. Frank Baum. *The Wonderful Wizard of Oz*. 1982. Illustrated by Michael Hague. **£15–20/$24–32**. Also 500 copies signed by the artist.

his imagination he regains his ability to fly through his nursery windows to Kensington Gardens. Ultimately it is too late for him to return and he has to remain in the Gardens. This story is mostly sought-after by collectors of Arthur Rackham for his superb illustrations. The book was issued in a trade edition and a de-luxe signed and limited edition. It was reissued in 1912 with additional coloured plates and also as a portfolio of larger-format plates in the same year, and has been reprinted many times. The 1911 story of Peter and Wendy derives from the play: Peter is a young boy verging on manhood but not wishing to cross that boundary. His world is that of Never Never Land, to which he entices the Darling family. It is this story that is generally known by children and adults today and which has been illustrated by numerous artists including Arthur Rackham and Mabel Lucie Attwell. Well-loved and read by children, copies in fine condition, especially in dust-jackets, are hard to find but worth looking out for.

First and foremost, John Masefield wrote poetry for adults, becoming Poet Laureate in 1930; however, he is best remembered today for two fantasy stories for children, *The Midnight Folk* (1927) and its sequel, *The Box of Delights* (1935), in which a young orphan, Kay, gets caught up in a world full of magic and movement in time, witches, and mermaids. Hugely popular during his lifetime, but out of fashion for much of the latter part of the 20th century, Masefield's verse and prose has been discovered by a new generation of collectors and the values of these books is starting to climb again. The theme of lonely children discovering a world full of magic that enables them to escape their real life has long had attractions for collectors, and P.L. Travers' tale of the adventures of Mary Poppins and the Banks children epitomizes this. The success of the first book, *Mary Poppins* (1934), led to a further six stories and the release of the film ensured its

place in the sights of collectors. There is a huge difference in price between the first title and later titles of the 1970s and 1980s.

Other authors who have created classic fantasy worlds range from Mary Norton and her tales of the little people, starting with *The Borrowers* in 1952, to Alan Garner, whose first great book, *The Weirdstone of Brisingamen* (1960), is becoming more and more sought-after. His equally fine *The Stone Quartet* (1976–8) can be acquired fairly easily. The American Ursula Le Guin is another name worth looking out for. A writer of science fiction and fiction for adults, she is nevertheless perhaps best known for her "Earthsea Quartet". Written for older children, *A Wizard of Earthsea* (1968) and its sequels *The Tombs of Atuan* and *The Farthest Shore* recount the life of Archmage Ged in a faraway archipelago. The island nations are ruled and maintained by magic. In 1993 she finished the series with *Tehanu*. Still relatively inexpensive, these would make a good introduction to the fantasy genre of children's literature.

The Whitbread Book of the Year Award ensured a huge increase in value for Philip Pullman's *His Dark Materials* trilogy, with its cast of lonely children discovering a world full of magic enabling them to escape their own time and find fantastical and mythical figures.

4 P.L. Travers. *Mary Poppins Opens the Door.* New York, 1943. Illustrated by Mary Shepard and Agnes Sims. **£60–80/$96–128**. Precedes English edition of 1944.

5 Alan Garner. *Elidor.* 1965. Illustrated by Charles Keeping. **£70–100/$112–160**

6 Mary Norton. *The Borrowers Afloat.* 1959. Illustrated by D. Stanley. **£20–30/$32–48**

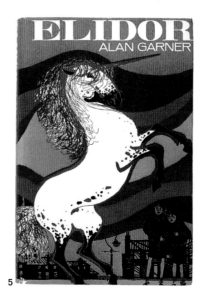

J.R.R TOLKIEN and C.S. LEWIS

For most of the 20th century, two great authors remained unrivalled in their creation of complex fantasy worlds for children. Like Lewis Carroll, they were academics and initially wrote for adults. Oxford-based, as were Carroll, John Masefield and now Philip Pullman, the two were close friends and members of the writing group "The Inklings". They were J.R.R. Tolkien and C.S. Lewis. Their stories have grown in stature throughout the years, quickly gaining cult followings, and during the past five years have shot up in price as demand has grown. South-African born, and appointed Professor of Anglo-Saxon at Oxford at the age of 33, J.R.R. Tolkien wrote *The Hobbit* (1937) for children and *The Lord of the Rings* (1954–6) for adults, although the latter acquired a cult following in the 1960s and has long been read by older children. It is *The Hobbit*, however, that has become the most sought-after today. It is relatively easy to find a copy of the first edition in the cloth, but to find a fine copy in the pictorial dust-jacket designed by Tolkien is exceptionally hard and can cost 25 times more than a copy without. (The first-issue jacket has an ink correction to the printed name "Dodgeson" on the inside lower flap.) As with Philip Pullman's stories, *The Hobbit* combines elements of ancient myths alongside the author's own creations, in this instance the hobbit people. Written for children, it is a more approachable and light-hearted work than his later

trilogy. Despite being peopled by goblins, hobbits and trolls, its Middle-Earth world is essentially safe, unlike the dark world of *The Lord of the Rings*. While the latter is certainly collected and has also increased in value over the past few years, particularly with the release of the three films, *The Hobbit* was important because it was the first of Tolkien's great fantasies. His other work for children, such as *Farmer Giles of Ham* (1949), can be found quite readily and commands very reasonable prices.

Tolkien and C.S. Lewis worked together and influenced each other. The artist Pauline Baynes worked on both their books, having been chosen by Tolkien to illustrate *Farmer Giles of Ham* and was subsequently introduced by Tolkien to Lewis. Lewis was the author of many academic and theological works, but it was through "The Chronicles of Narnia" that he found fame. The land of Narnia was discovered by a young girl called Lucy through the back of a wardrobe and the children move freely between it and their own real world. Although Narnia is a dark place, emphasized by the black-and-white illustrations of Pauline Baynes, the chronicles are about quests, the nature of desire, and finding oneself, reminiscent of *The Hobbit*. Such themes appeal to adults today and often mean more with the hindsight of time and distance. It is the first of C.S. Lewis' Narnia tales, *The Lion, the Witch and the Wardrobe* (1950), that commands the highest price.

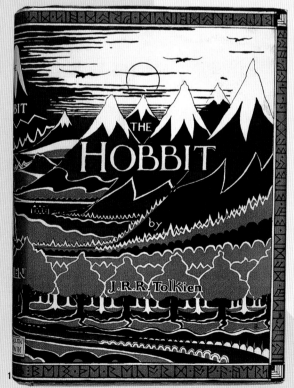

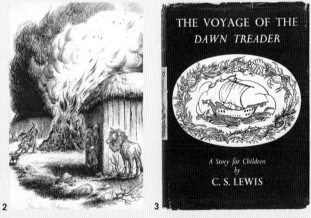

1 J.R.R. Tolkien. *The Hobbit*. 1937. Illustrated by the author. First issue with "Dodgeson" corrected on flap, **£20,000–30,000/ $32,000–48,000**. Without dust-jacket, **£4,000–6,000/ $6,400–9,600**.

2 C.S. Lewis. *The Last Battle*. 1956. Illustrated by Pauline Baynes. **£500–700/$800–1,120**

3 C.S. Lewis. *The Voyage of the Dawn Treader*. 1952. Illustrated by Pauline Baynes. **£300–400/$480–640**. Without dust-jacket, £80–120/$128–192.

J.K. ROWLING

J.K. Rowling is the creator of the most important fantasy figure in children's literature for many years: Harry Potter. Harry has to take his place alongside Alice and Peter Pan and possibly for many even above Christopher Robin and Dorothy as the most important child protagonist in children's fantasy literature. As with many great writers, J.K. Rowling initially found it hard to get her first book published, but in 1997 Bloomsbury issued a tiny print-run of 500 copies of *Harry Potter and the Philosopher's Stone*, of which 200 were paper-covered advance proof copies and the remainder bound in pictorial glazed boards. The majority of these copies were sent to specialist bookshops, schools, and libraries for children's opinions, and the remainder shipped to Australia. As early as November 1999, a copy of this first edition in hardback, signed by the author, was sold over the Internet on www.sothebys.com for $14,000 (£9,300). This was an unheard-of sum of money for such a recent book and the Harry Potter phenomenon had begun. The first title was issued in 1998 in the US under the alternative title of *Harry Potter and the Sorcerer's Stone* by Scholastic Press and is worth considerably less than then 1997 UK edition.

There are issue points to all four of the titles published to date which indicate a true first edition, from the correct numbering inside the book opposite the title page ranging from 10 to 1, to misprints to the author's name on the copyright page and indeed misprints of text in the third book. Although the value of each successive title has dropped as the print-run has increased dramatically, all remain avidly sought-after at the moment. While the value of the first book, *Harry Potter and the Philosopher's Stone* (1997), will probably remain high because of its tiny print-run and the fact that it is the first of the series, collectors should be careful about paying too much for subsequent titles, for the de-luxe editions issued for the more adult market or for those copies with inserted original watercolours by Cliff Wright, the illustrator of the covers of the second and third books. There may well be some shaking down of the market in years to come, and at the moment the books are being traded rather as a commodity. However, it is entirely fitting that the 20th century should close and the 21st open with the birth of a truly great childhood fantasy figure.

Signed copies will always be sold at a premium, but the collector should be aware of the difference between copies signed prior to the publicity tour for the fourth book in 2001 and those signed at a later date. Inscriptions contemporary with the date of publication will always be preferable.

1 J.K. Rowling. *Harry Potter and the Philosopher's Stone*. 1997. **£4,000–6,000/$6,400–9,600**

2 J.K. Rowling. *Harry Potter and the Prisoner of Azkaban*. 1999. With watercolour drawing by Cliff Wright, **£2,000–4,000/ $3,200–6,400**. Ordinary copy, dust-jacket, first issue with "Joanne" Rowling on copyright page, £150–200/$240–320.

3 J.K. Rowling. *Harry Potter and the Philosopher's Stone*. 1997. De-luxe edition signed by the author, original cloth with pictorial label. **£800–1,200/$1,280–1,920**

1

2

3

Writers: Stevenson to Garfield

tories of adventure, exploration or history, or simply stories by one particular author, could form the basis of a collection. Robert Louis Stevenson's innovative *Treasure Island* (1883) led the way for classic adventure stories such as Rider Haggard's *King Solomon's Mines* (1885) and John Meade Falkner's *Moonfleet* (1898). While the earliest issue of *Treasure Island* is now expensive in fine condition in the original cloth (the collector should check the issue by the date of the advertisements at the end), Stevenson's other adventure books for children can be acquired for very little.

Richard Jefferies wrote mostly adult works, but he published two important books for children, *Wood Magic* (1881) and *Bevis: The Story of a Boy* (1882), which had a great influence on Arthur Ransome, a master of adventure stories. *Swallows and Amazons*, the first of 12 titles devoted to the adventures of the Walker and Blackett families, was published in 1930 and at first sold slowly. It was later reissued ten times in the first six years and has subsequently never been out of print. The book sold well in the US and he was encouraged to publish a sequel, *Swallowdale* (1931). The sixth story, *Pigeon Post* (1936), was the first winner of the Carnegie Medal. Ransome's stories of adventures on land and sea are full of make-believe alongside realistic detail. They draw on mythology, folk tales, *The Arabian Nights*, traditional sea-shanties and the adventure stories of the 19th century, and had a huge influence not only on children but also on a later group of authors. The value of the first book far exceeds that of the later titles, although all are uncommon in the original dust-jackets.

Frances Hodgson Burnett spent much of her life in the US and wrote many adult novels, but is best known and certainly collected for two of her children's books, *Little Lord Fauntleroy* (New York, 1886), first issue with the De Vinne imprint, and *The Secret Garden* (New York, 1911). Both were first published by Scribner in New York and immediately afterwards by Warne in England, and these editions are becoming harder to find and hence more expensive. The English edition of *The Secret Garden* was illustrated by Charles Robinson, and is the costlier of the two, although it is one of her later works. Her stories begin with children as outsiders or neglected in some way, and are among the first to look at the whole development of a child. The Canadian writer Lucy Maud Montgomery wrote *Anne of Green Gables* in 1908 and issued seven sequels. Grounded very much in earlier works such as Louisa May Alcott's *Little Women* (Boston, 1868), the stories tell of the orphan Anne as she grows up at the turn of the century. Unlike 19th-century heroines, she is well educated and spends hours in an imaginary world. The earliest "Anne" titles are now fairly expensive, but the later ones and her many

1 Arthur Ransome. *The Picts and the Martyrs.* 1943. Illustrated by the author. **£150–200/$240–320**

2 E.Nesbit. *The Phoenix and the Carpet.* [1904]. Illustrated by H.R. Millar. **£100–150/$160–240**

3 L.M. Montgomery. *Anne of the Island.* 1925. Frontispiece. First UK edition, **£40–60/$64–96**. First edition, New York, 1915.

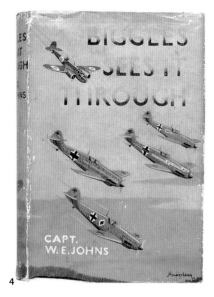

4

5

6

other works for children can be found without much difficulty.

E[dith] Nesbit also has her children developing or learning through play, but whereas Frances Hodgson Burnett's and Anne Montgomery's children were loners, E. Nesbit's children form tight-knit family groups. A prolific writer, she first published poetry before turning to children's stories with *The Story of the Treasure Seekers* (1899). Its success encouraged her to continue in this vein and her other most sought-after works are *Five Children and It* (1902), *The Phoenix and the Carpet* (1904), and the much-loved and collected *The Railway Children* (1906), one of her later books, which is her most expensive work. Her other titles can be found for quite small sums, unless a rare dust-jacket is present.

Three young girls who were adopted, chose their own surname ("Fossil") and undergo a voyage of self-discovery are the protagonists in Noel Streatfield's hugely popular and sought-after *Ballet Shoes* (1936), although it was her second work, *Tennis Shoes* (1937), that remained the author's favourite. A prolific author, she wrote over 90 books for adults and children and her other works can be acquired for very little.

These four authors wrote mainly for girls, whereas another top best-selling author of children's books, Captain W.E. Johns, wrote mostly for boys (although also publishing science-fiction novels for young readers). His greatest creation was Biggles (Major James Bigglesworth), the hero of 102 stories. The first book, *The Camels are Coming* (1932), was written under the pseudonym of "William Earle" and was published by John Hamilton. This and the early titles issued by John Hamilton or Oxford University Press between 1932 and 1943 are now exceptionally hard to find in fine condition in the original dust-jackets and therefore command large sums. In 1943 Hodder and Stoughton took over publication with much larger print-runs and these later titles are much easier to find for modest sums. His other books, including the "Worrals" and "Gimlet" series, are also much less expensive. A sensitive, lonely individual, Biggles was the leader of a group of friends. Their flying adventures proved irresistible to generations of children who are today's collectors.

Another famous wooden toy is, of course, Pinocchio. He was brought to life by Carlo Collodi, pseudonym of

4 Capt. W.E. Johns. *Biggles Sees It Through*. 1941. Illustrated by H. Leigh and A. Sindall. **£400–600/$640–960**. First edition dust-jacket priced 4/-.

5 William Mayne. *Summer Visitors*. 1961. Illustrated by William Stobbs. **£10–15/$16–24**

6 Leon Garfield. *The Confidence Man*. 1978. **£8–10/$12–16**.

ENID BLYTON

Enid Blyton, the best-selling children's author of all time, wrote adventure stories, schoolgirl stories, strip books and the phenomenally popular "Noddy" books. Born in 1897, she began writing at an early age but had her work rejected until *Child Whispers*, a volume of poems, was issued in pictorial card covers by J. Saville in 1922 and in 1923 with a dust-jacket. A second volume, *Real Fairies*, was also issued in 1923, appearing simultaneously in card covers and with a dust-jacket. These are some of her most sought-after works, but the "Famous Five" and "Adventure" series, both now scarce in fine condition in the dust-jacket, remain most desirable. The 24 volumes of the "Noddy Library" are everywhere in reprint, but first editions in dust-jackets are hard to find. Later editions were issued in glazed pictorial boards with no dust-jacket. Harmsen van der Beek illustrated the first seven titles, providing a guide for the many later illustrators. The Enid Blyton Company sold all the original artwork in 1997–8, when the Beek originals fetched high prices.

Enid Blyton wrote over 700 books and 4,500 short stories in 46 years, and is the third most translated author in the world. Her books remain widely read and avidly collected today, although ten years ago they were overlooked and could be found for next to nothing. *The Island of Adventure*, the first in the series (1944), would fetch about £10–15, but now it would cost 50 times that. Her first full-length work of fiction was *The Adventures of the Wishing Chair* (1937), and in 1939 the first of the "Magic Faraway Tree" stories, *The Enchanted Wood*, was published. These are also avidly collected and therefore hard to find. Children wrote to her daily, and she answered every one, so such letters have little scarcity value. Although read throughout the world, her books have never properly taken off in the US and until a recent TV series most Americans had never even heard of Noddy.

1 Enid Blyton. *Five Get Into Trouble*. 1949. Illustrated by E. Soper. **£80–120/$128–192**

2 Enid Blyton. *Noddy Goes to Sea*. 1959. Illustrations. Without dust jacket, **£10–15/$16–24**. With jacket, £30–40/$48–64. Number 18 in series "Noddy in Toytown".

3 Enid Blyton. *Shock for the Secret Seven*. 1961. **£30–40/$48–64**. Illustrated by B. Shorrocks.

4 Enid Blyton. *The Island of Adventure*. 1944. Illustrated by Stuart Tresilian. **£500–700/$800–1,120**. The first of the "Adventure" series.

Italian journalist Carlo Lorenzini. The story was initially serialized in the magazine *Giornale per i bambini* in 1881 and appeared in book form in Italy in 1883. It was first published in English in 1892 under the title of *The Story of a Puppet, or the Adventures of Pinocchio*. Regarded as one of the finest works of children's literature, the first edition is extraordinarily rare and expensive, with even the first English edition commanding several thousand pounds. The first-issue binding is of blue and cream cloth with a variant binding of green cloth stamped in gilt. There are many good modern editions available to collectors with illustrations by, among others, Emily Hall Chamberlin (New York, 1909), Charles Folkard (1911), and Walt Disney, of which there is a signed and limited edition of 100 copies.

Also at the turn of the century Florence and Bertha Upton created a series of books around a group of wooden dolls and other toys who later became controversial: the Golliwoggs. Florence Kate Upton was born in the US but moved to England where she illustrated a series of books written by her mother, Bertha. The first, *The Adventures of Two Dutch Dolls and a Golliwogg*, was published in 1895. Thirteen titles were published in all, spawning a huge and long-lasting "golliwogg" craze. Notoriously fragile in the first edition, the books have long outlived the period when they were deemed politically incorrect and a bad influence. Collectors eagerly seek the series, so prices have risen in the past few years.

A few years later Honor C. Appleton produced beautiful and delicate illustrations for Mrs H.C. Cradock's "Josephine" books. *Josephine and her Dolls* (1916) was the first in a series of 20 books relating the adventures of Josephine and her dolls. Still relatively inexpensive, they are worth looking out for. In the US Johnny Gruelle created the hugely popular "Raggedy Anne" series about a rag doll, and the author designed and patented a doll to be marketed at the same time as the books were published. The first title was *Raggedy Anne Stories* (New York, 1918) and is highly sought-after by American collectors, although not so well known in England. Although Gruelle died in 1938, books continued to be issued up to 1977 under his name but compiled by other authors. The discerning collector should really concentrate on the titles published before his death in 1938. There were four titles published posthumously in 1939–40 that may possibly have been written by him prior to his death.

In 1943 an important fantasy work was translated from the French and issued in a limited edition of 525 copies in America. This first edition of *The Little Prince* (New York, 1943) preceded both the French and English editions. Antoine de Saint-Exupery, a French aviator who died in 1944 in the War, wrote and illustrated this story, which tells the tale of an aviator who has crashed his plane in the Sahara desert and meets the Little Prince.

He is the ruler and only occupant of a tiny asteroid the size of a house on which his beloved flower is in danger of becoming overwhelmed by baobab trees. The Prince journeys across countries, but the end remains a mystery. Does the Prince die, or return to his asteroid? Its central theme, however, is unambiguous. "It is only with the heart that can one see rightly. What is essential is invisible to the eye." Although the American limited edition is expensive, the first English edition can be found relatively easily.

A genre of children's adventure stories that developed from the late 19th-century novel during the 1930s but became particularly popular during the 1950s and 1960s is historical fiction. Often overlooked by collectors, these works can be found for very little and are worth looking out for. Geoffrey Trease wrote over 120 books over seven decades and brought a new realism to historical fiction. His first novel was *Bows against the Barons* (1934), but he is perhaps best known for *Cue for Treason* (1940). Henry Treece is another interesting historical writer. His first book is *Legions of the Eagle* (1954), but it is his "Viking" trilogy that remains best known: *Viking's Dawn* (1955), *The Road to Miklagard* (1957), and *Viking's Sunset* (1960). Rosemary Sutcliff wrote many historical novels, as well as stories retelling ancient myths and legends such as those of King Arthur. *The Lantern Bearers* (1959), which won the Carnegie Medal, and *The Eagle of the Ninth* (1954) are probably her best-known books. Leon Garfield set many of his adventure books in the past. His first work, *Jack Holborn* (1964), was initially intended for adults, but was rewritten for a younger audience. This and *Black Jack* (1968) are the most well known. Joan Aiken wrote many books for adults, including horror and fantasy, as well as several books for children, notably the "James III" series, of which *The Wolves of Willoughby Chase* (1962) is the first and most famous. This highly acclaimed series of nine books set in the 18th century chronicles a fantastical history that never actually happened.

School stories

The theme of school adventure stories for girls and boys has flourished throughout the century and today many of these books command quite high prices. Angela Brazil was one of the earliest to write about the adventures of girls at school, setting the tone that was later taken up by Elsie Oxenham with the "Abbey Girls" books, Elinor Brent-Dyer in the "Chalet School" series, and Enid Blyton with "Malory Towers". For boys there was Charles Hamilton's "Greyfriars" series and the adventures of Billy Bunter which first appeared in the comic *The Magnet* in 1908 under the pseudonym of Frank Richards. Anthony Buckeridge's "Jennings" stories are also school-based, as are Richmal Crompton's "William" books to a certain extent.

7 Carlo Collodi [Carlo Lorenzini]. *The Story of a Puppet, or the Adventures of Pinocchio*. 1892. Illustrated by C. Mazzanti. First English edition. **£1,500–2,000/$2,400–3,200**

8 Florence and Bertha Upton. *The Golliwogg's Christmas*. 1907. Illustrated by Florence Upton. **£300–400/$480–640**. The most scarce of the "Golliwogg" titles.

9 Richmal Crompton. *William and the Space Animal*. 1956. Illustrated by Thomas Henry. **£60–100/$96–160**

10 Carlo Collodi. *Pinocchio. The Story of a Puppet*. 1911. Illustrated by Charles Folkard. **£70–100/$112–160**. Reprinted many times.

11 Mrs H.C. Craddock. *Josephine Goes Shopping*. 1926. Illustrated by Honor Appleton. **£20–30/$32–48**

12 Antoine de Saint-Exupery. *The Little Prince*. New York, 1943. Illustrated by the author. First issue. **£1,000–1,500/$1,600–2,400**

13 Elinor Brent-Dyer. *The Highland Twins at the Chalet School*. 1942. Illustrated. **£150–200/$240–320**

ROALD DAHL

In 1943 in New York another book was published by a pilot which also related a fantastical adventure of the skies: *The Gremlins*, by Flight Lieutenant Roald Dahl. Dahl had been seconded to Washington with the Royal Air Force and he became known for his stories about his adventures. One such story he wrote down as "The Gremlin Lore". Under military rules the story was passed to the authorities, one of whom showed it to Walt Disney who was looking for war material for his company. A film was planned, but gradually problems overtook the project and it was abandoned. The book, however, was published by Random House with illustrations by the Walt Disney studios. As his first book, it is rare and prized by collectors, although the first English edition of 1944 is relatively common.

Although Dahl wrote numerous books for adults, his most famous and sought-after those are for children. *James and the Giant Peach* (1961), *Charlie and the Chocolate Factory* (1964), and *Charlie and the Great Glass Elevator* (1972) were all published first in the US, where the "Charlie" books were illustrated by Joseph Schindelman. It is the first English editions illustrated by Faith Jaques, however, that most people know today. These were issued in pictorial glazed boards without dust-jackets. It is the American editions in dust-jackets that command the highest prices, however. His later works, such as *Fantastic Mr Fox* (1970) and *Danny, the Champion of the World* (1975), are relatively easy to find for quite modest sums and make a good start for collectors. Roald Dahl formed a working partnership with the artist Quentin Blake and their books are some of the most harmonious collaborations ever produced between author and artist. *The Enormous Crocodile* (1978) was the first, and they worked together constantly until the author's death in 1990.

1 Roald Dahl. *The Gremlins*. New York, 1943. **£1,000–1,500/ $1,600–2,400**. Precedes English edition of 1944.

2 Roald Dahl. *Charlie and the Chocolate Factory*. New York, 1964. Illustrated by Joseph Schindelman. **£1,000–1,500/$1,600–2,400**. Precedes English edition of 1967.

3 Roald Dahl. *Charlie and the Great Glass Elevator*. 1973. First UK edition with illustrations by Faith Jaques. **£150–200/$240–320**. First US edition, 1972.

Picture-books

One of the most exciting areas for collectors of 20th-century children's books is the picture-book. Picture-books may be defined as books that rely on the complete interplay of words and pictures to achieve their effect, unlike illustrated books where the pictures tend to complement an existing text. The picture-book is a peculiarly 20th-century phenomenon, although its roots lie in the earlier 17th- and 18th-century chapbooks. These chapbooks comprised simple text or verse illustrated with crude woodcuts and were sold cheaply by travelling salesmen or pedlars.

Printmakers such as William Hogarth, Thomas Rowlandson, and George Cruikshank influenced the development of the picture-book during the 19th century, but it was the improvements to printing processes pioneered by Edmund Evans that led to the fine picture-books of Kate Greenaway, Walter Crane, and Randolph Caldecott at the century's close. All three produced fine picture-books, or "toy books", as Walter Crane's publishers referred to many of his. They illustrated titles by other authors as well as creating their own books, and their work was faithfully reproduced by Edmund Evans from 1865 on. Their work comes and goes in fashion among collectors but they remain fundamentally important in this field, and Caldecott's witty and humorous work influenced many later artists. L. Leslie Brooke produced some fine and amusing pic-ture-books, such as *Johnny Crow's Garden* (1903) and *Johnny Crow's Party* (1907), but the colour printing processes were still in their infancy and the colour plates had to be produced on different glossy paper. Beatrix Potter had the same problem and was never entirely happy with the finish of the paper that had to be used to print her illustrations.

During the early years of the century, the publishers Blackie and Son in Glasgow issued many fine picture-books by artists such as Frank Adams, Gordon Browne, and John Hassall. These are relatively easy to find today for modest sums and could form the basis of a collection.

The Glasgow-based and trained Jessie M. King illustrated many books, some of her greatest being for the adult market, such as *The High History of the Holy Grail* (1903) or Oscar Wilde's *The House of Pomegranates* (1915). She produced several fine children's books, often small in format and delicate in binding, and in 1929 issued a fine picture-book, *Mummy's Bedtime Story Book*. During the 1940s and 1950s there was a steady stream

1 *Goody Two-Shoes Picture Book*. 1875. Illustrated by Walter Crane. **£150–200/$240–320**

2 Marion [Mrs Alexander Gemmell]. *Mummy's Bedtime Story Book*. 1929. Illustrated by Jessie M. King, in the rare glassine wrapper. **£1,500–2,000/$2,400–3,200**

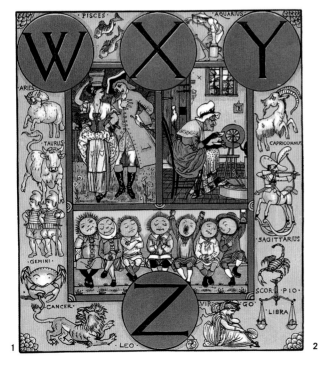

LITHOGRAPHY

It was the development of colour photo-offset lithography during the 1920s that heralded the burst of superb picture-books in the 1930s, and this has continued unabated until the present day. The artist William Nicholson had a great impact on the picture-book through a small body of work. He and his brother-in-law James Pryde were inspired by the Art Nouveau posters of France to produce their own under the name the Beggarstaff Brothers. Nicholson brought these techniques to children's books, in which he cut large bold images on wood to be printed lithographically for the mass market. *An Alphabet* (1898) and *A Square Book of Animals* (1900) were issued for children, but it was three books published during the 1920s, hard to find today, that instigated the change to come in the picture-book: *The Velveteen Rabbit* (1922), *Clever Bill* (1926), and *The Pirate Twins* (1929). Nicholson's designs and, for the later two, hand-written text, were produced by this offset lithographic process. The artist Edward Bawden used lithography for several of his books including the small book *Take the Broom*, written for his children in 1944 and issued in 1952 with text and illustrations drawn lithographically on to the plates by the artist.

Colour offset lithography also helped Edward Ardizzone create his timeless series of books about a boy called Tim. The first, *Little Tim and the Brave Sea Captain*, was published in 1936. This and the two subsequent titles, *Lucy Brown and Mr. Grimes* (1937) and *Tim and Lucy go to Sea* (1938), also used the juxtaposition of image and hand-written text. The series was revised after the War in 1949 and continued until his death in 1979.

As well as the "Tim" books, both written and illustrated by Ardizzone, he illustrated many others, forming particularly successful partnerships with authors James Reeves, Eleanor Farjeon and his cousin Christianna Brand. While the very first "Tim" book in its dust-jacket is now becoming a little more expensive, the remainder of his work can be acquired for very modest sums. Kathleen Hale used the similar format of hand-written text and illustrations in her successful series of "Orlando" books, the first of which, *Orlando the Marmalade Cat: A Camping Holiday*, was published in 1938. All are now avidly collected.

1

Christmas morning

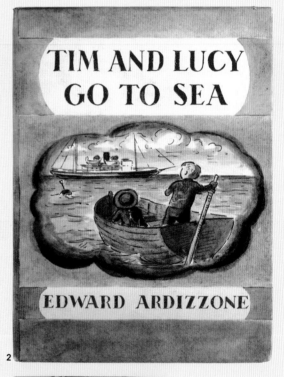

2

3

scales & he said, turning to Ant Ann
& giving her a bow "I am amazed!"
The property consisted of a fungus
garden & a herd of Aldernay milch
aphis. The Head Gardener gave her
some delicious truffles & the Milk-
man offered her a glass of honey-milk.

1 Margery Williams Bianco. *The Velveteen Rabbit*. 1922. Illustrated by William Nicholson. **£5,000–7,000/$8,000–11,200**

2 Edward Ardizzone. *Tim and Lucy Go To Sea*. [1938]. Illustrated by the author. **£300–400/$480–640**

3 Edward Bawden. *Take the Broom*. Christmas, 1952. Illustrated by the author, limited to 350 copies. **£30–50/$48–80**

of good books being published in which new text and illustration provided by author and artist worked particularly well together. Some of the most interesting names that are still avidly read by children today and are being acquired by collectors are Ludwig Bemelmans, the Reverend Awdry, and Kay Thompson. Bemelmans was Austrian by birth but settled in the US in 1914. The first of his "Madeline" books, *Madeline* (New York, 1939), was conceived while the author was on holiday in France. Written in rhyming couplets with deceptively simple illustrations, some in half-tone, others in full colour, they relate the adventures of Madeline and her school friends. Only six books were written, the last of which was completed by his wife and daughter after his death. The second title, *Madeline's Rescue* (New York, 1953), won the Caldecott Medal.

Kay Thompson wrote only four books about the adventures of a young girl living in the Plaza Hotel in New York; the first, *Eloise: A Book for Precocious Grown-ups* (New York, 1957), was hugely successful and sold 150,000 copies in two years. All four titles were illustrated by Hilary Knight, and it is the interplay of text and illustrations that make them so successful.

These books were generally read by girls but a series of picture-books more usually read by boys of a younger age was begun in 1945 that remain in print today: the "Thomas the Tank Engine" books. The Reverend W. Awdry began his series in 1945 with *The Three Railway Engines*, and in the following year the most famous title was published, *Thomas the Tank Engine*. The first story was illustrated by William Middleton and the second by Reginald Payne, but it is the illustrations provided by C. Reginald Dalby, which appeared in the third book right up to the 11th title in 1956, that made the series so successful. Subsequent artists who worked in Dalby's style included John Kenney and Gunvor and Peter Edwards. The later books of the 1980s and 1990s were written by his son, Christopher Awdry. The books have only recently begun to be collected seriously and can consequently be acquired very reasonably, although condition can be difficult as they were generally well read and loved.

In 1930 a book was published in Belgium that was quite alternative in style to anything that had gone before: *Les Aventures du Tintin Reporter du 'Petit Vingtième' au Pays de Soviets* ("Tintin in the Land of the Soviets"). The creator of this comic-style strip book was George Remi, working under the pseudonym "Hergé". First appearing in the children's magazine *Le Petit Vingtième* in 1929, "Tintin" proved to be universally popular. Twenty-two books were issued but they did not appear in English until 1958 when *The Crab with the Golden Claws* was published. The year after this René Goscinny and Albert Uderzo published the first of their "Asterix" books in

3

4

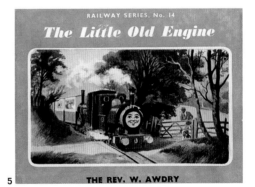

5

3 Ludwig Bemelmans. *Madeline*. [1952]. First UK edition. Illustrated by the author. **£80–120/$128–192**. First edition, New York, 1939.

4 Kay Thompson. *Eloise in Paris*. 1959. Illustrated by Hilary Knight. **£100–150/$160–240**.

5 Reverend W. Awdry. *The Little Old Engine*. 1959. Illustrated by C. Reginald Dalby. **£30–40/$48–64**. The 14th "Thomas the Tank Engine" book.

SAVING SINBAD!

Michael Foreman

For the crew of the St. Ives Lifeboat – past, present and future.

Andersen Press
London

6

7

Oi! Get Off Our Train

JOHN BURNINGHAM

9

Quentin Blake's

ABC

8

The
CLOTHES
HORSE
AND OTHER STORIES

Janet & Allan Ahlberg

10

11

THE
MOUSEHOLE
CAT

Antonia Barber · Nicola Bayley

12

Paris, not translated into English until 1969 as *Asterix the Gaul* (1969). Both series still have huge followings, from new readers to collectors, and have also had a great deal of influence on the evolution of these strip-style picture books and comics.

Two contemporary picture-book creators, Shirley Hughes and Raymond Briggs, have taken this style of illustration and made it their own. Raymond Briggs has created some of the most memorable and innovative picture-books detailing the adventures of his three great protagonists: Father Christmas, Fungus the Bogeyman, and the Snowman. His first illustrated book was *Midnight Adventure* (1961), and in 1966 he won the Kate Greenaway medal for the most distinguished British book of illustrations for *The Mother Goose Treasury*, but it was with the appearance of *Father Christmas* in 1973 that he formulated his particular style. This book took many months to come to fruition and won him the Kate Greenaway medal again. He has not shied away from difficult or unpleasant themes: *Fungus the Bogeyman* (1977) was adored by children but perplexed many adults, and *When the Wind Blows* (1982) deals with the after-effects of a nuclear war. His most expensive work is *The Mother Goose Treasury*, although still very reasonable, and the remainder can be found easily for modest sums and would make a good collection.

Shirley Hughes has illustrated well over 200 works, initially those by other authors, but latterly concentrating on her own picture-books. Her work ranges from the popular series "My Naughty Little Sister" by Dorothy Edwards to works by Noel Streatfield and Nina Bawden. She has won numerous awards, including the Kate Greenaway award for *Dogger* (1977), and the Eleanor Farjeon award for services to children's literature in 1984.

6 Michael Foreman. *Saving Sinbad!* 2001. Illustrated by the author. Signed by the author, issued without dust-jacket. **£15–20/$24–32**

7 Raymond Briggs. *The Snowman.* 1978. Illustrated by the author. Issued without dust-jacket. **£15–20/$24–32**

8 Quentin Blake. *Quentin Blake's ABC.* 1989. Illustrated by the author. **£15–20/$24–32**

9 John Burningham. *Oi! Get Off Our Train.* 1989. Illustrated by the author. Issued without dust-jacket. **£10–15/$24–32**

10 Janet and Allan Ahlberg. *The Clothes Horse and Other Stories.* 1987. Illustrated by Janet Ahlberg. **£10–15/$24–32**

11 *The White Cat.* 1973. Illustrated and retold by Errol Le Cain. **£15–20/$24–32**

12 Antonia Barber. *The Mousehole Cat.* 1990. Illustrated by Nicola Bayley. **£15–20/$24–32**

Her style is quite distinctive, almost sketchbook in tone, with definition of characters by fine brush-strokes. Her best-known series are the "Lucy and Tom" and "Alfie" books, with *Lucy and Tom's Day* first appearing in 1960 and *Alfie Gets in First* in 1981.

Allan and Janet Ahlberg were an extremely successful and popular husband and wife team who have published many fine picture-books. Their first collaboration was *Here Are the Brick Street Boys* (1975), but possibly their best known is *Each Peach Pear Plum* (1978). They won the Kurt Maschler award for excellence in text and illustration in 1986 for *The Jolly Postman*.

There are some very fine contemporary illustrators who began working in the 1960s, most of whom are still creating important and beautiful picture books today and their names are well worth looking out for. They include Brian Wildsmith, Charles Keeping, Michael Hague, Michael Foreman, Alan Aldridge, Quentin Blake, Nicola Bayley, Babette Cole, and John Burningham. Their work can be found quite cheaply, and may prove an affordable way to start a collection that can be added to as new works are published. The quality of their work was enhanced by developments in colour printing in the 1960s, which enabled almost any kind of art to be reproduced cheaply and accurately for the children's market. New artists are producing fine work all the time and are worth watching for; one of the newest is Helen Cooper, whose picture-books *The Baby Who Wouldn't Go to Bed* and *Pumpkin Soup* won the Kate Greenaway award in 1996 and 1998.

The strength of the contemporary picture-book market and the technological advances that allowed it to happen take one back in time to the early part of the 20th century when huge changes in colour printing and book production took place. There was a vogue for illustrated gift books, usually for the adult market but filtering through to the children's market, and these are often seen today as children's books. Not strictly picture-books, they are nonetheless collected for their pictures. Arthur Rackham, Edmund Dulac, Kay Nielsen, and the three Robinson brothers are the best known and most collected today. Their work is looked at in more detail in the next chapter. Other illustrators who are collected for illustrating classic children's tales are Margaret Tarrant, Helen Jacobs, Mabel Lucie Attwell, Charles Folkard, and Anne Anderson. Their work is often found for very reasonable prices and in many different formats. Helen Jacobs and Margaret Tarrant produced many fairy images, and Mabel Lucie Attwell is best known for plump little children. Charles Folkard produced highly detailed images for many of the great classic tales such as Carlo Collodi's *Pinocchio* and George MacDonald's *The Princess and the Goblin*.

America: Baum to Sendak

The most collectable children's books tend to have universal appeal, but many important books that originated in the United States have either specific relevance for the American market, or are well known and collected there but have a limited appeal elsewhere. In 1956 the bibliographer Jacob Blanck published a book titled *Peter Parley to Penrod: A Bibliographical Description of the Best-Loved American Juvenile Books*. This makes fascinating reading today, since many of the books are still known and collected, while others have sunk into obscurity. Most books were published in New York, Boston or Chicago.

In 1900 two quintessential books for children were published, *The Wonderful Wizard of Oz* (see page 93) and Gellett Burgess' *Goops and How to Be Them*, the first in a series of hugely popular books, and now highly sought-after by American collectors. The Goops were a series of balloon-headed children who satirized different intellectual postures and first appeared in the periodical *The Lark*. Burgess soon turned them into characters for children's books where each personified a kind of misbehaviour. In 1903 Kate Douglas Wiggin published *Rebecca of Sunnybrook Farm*, her only work that has endured. She was an educational theorist who was heavily involved with the teaching of Friedrich Froebel, founder of the kindergarten.

Two important illustrators published their most collectable work within three years of each other. E. Boyd Smith's *The Story of Noah's Ark* was published in 1905 and can be regarded as perhaps the pioneer of American picture-books; as such, it is sought-after today. In 1908 Peter Newell published *The Hole Book*. The format of his books is unusual: this one has a hole running through the entire book, whereas *Topsy & Turvys* (New York, 1893) is a series of pictures that can be turned upside-down for humorous effect. Newell's challenge to the traditional format can be seen as a forerunner of several more modern classic American books such as Eric Carle's *The Very Hungry Caterpillar* (New York, 1968). Newell also illustrated Lewis Carroll's two "Alice" stories in 1901 and 1902, to great acclaim.

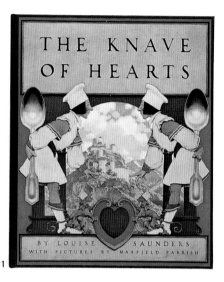

1

2

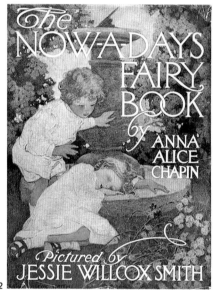

3

1 Louise Saunders. *The Knave of Hearts*. New York, 1925. Illustrated by Maxfield Parrish. **£1,200–1,600/$1,920–2,560**. The artist's last and greatest book.

2 Anna Alice Chapin. *The Now-a-days Fairy Book*. New York, 1911. Illustrated by Jessie Wilcox Smith. **£100–150/$160–240**

3 Diane Lampert. *Twyllyp. A Down-to-Earth Story*. New York, 1963. Illustrated by Peter Farrow. **£15–20/$24–32**

DR SEUSS

Arguably the most famous American picture-book author has to be Dr Seuss. His extraordinary books, which celebrate the subversive and the power of a child's imagination, constitute some of the greatest nonsense literature of the 20th century. Born Theodor Seuss Geisel in 1904, he studied at Dartmouth College where he edited and drew cartoons for the campus magazine *Jack-o-Lantern*, under his middle name. He spent a year in England at Oxford University but returned to the States, where he drew humorous advertising material for Shell Oil. His first and most sought-after book was *And To Think I Saw It on Mulberry Street* (New York, 1937). Many publishers rejected it until an editor who was an old college friend accepted it. Seuss named the boy in the story "Marco" after his friend's son. This is now an expensive book, and rare in fine condition in the original dust-jacket. He wrote and illustrated a series of prose fairy tales, including *The 500 Hats of Bartholomew Cubbins* (New York, 1938).

It was *The Cat in the Hat* (1957) that made him a household name. Devised as a controlled vocabulary after complaints about dull school reading schemes, it became hugely successful throughout the world. A further 17 other vocabularies followed, with mixed success. *Green Eggs and Ham* (New York, 1960) and *Hop on Pop* (New York, 1963) were probably the most popular. The titles he chose not to illustrate were issued under the name "Theo. LeSieg" (his surname spelt in reverse). *The Cat in the Hat* is expensive today and there are issue points collectors need to be aware of. The earliest issues were bound in matt boards, whereas the later issues had laminated boards. The first-issue dust-jacket is priced at $2.00 with the second issue at $1.95. His third most sought-after book today is probably *How the Grinch Stole Christmas!* (New York, 1958). This was televised in 1971 with narration by Boris Karloff and is regularly reshown. The first-issue dust-jacket lists 14 titles by Seuss on the front flap. He was given the Laura Ingalls Wilder Award in 1980 for his contribution to children's literature. As with the most enduring English authors, Beatrix Potter and A.A. Milne, the authorization by the estate of merchandise featuring many of his characters after his death in 1991, has helped ensure his name and creations live on.

1 Dr Seuss [Theodore Geisel]. *How the Grinch Stole Christmas!* New York, 1957. Illustrated by the author. First-issue dust-jacket with 14 titles listed. **£600–800/$960–1,280**

2 Dr Seuss. *The 500 Hats of Bartholomew Cubbins.* New York, 1938. Illustrated by the author. Inscribed copy, first issue, priced $1.50 on inner flap. $1.00 price for author's first book. **£1,500–2,000/$2,400–3,200**

3 Dr Seuss. *And To Think That I Saw It On Mulberry Street.* New York, 1937. Illustrated by the author. Dedication copy inscribed by the author. **£10,000–15,000**. The author's first book.

Howard Pyle, whose first great work, *The Merry Adventures of Robin Hood*, was published in 1883, founded the "Brandywine School" of American illustration. Among his students were Maxfield Parrish, Jessie Wilcox Smith, and N.C. Wyeth. Parrish's first published book was L. Frank Baum's *Mother Goose in Prose* (Chicago, 1897), which remains scarce; the black-and-white illustrations are especially fine. However, he is best known for his bold and extraordinary colour illustrations, which can be seen to good effect in Eugene Field's *Poems of Childhood* (New York, 1904), the 1909 edition of *The Arabian Nights Entertainment* by Kate Douglas Wiggins and A. Smith, and his greatest work, Louise Saunders' *The Knave of Hearts* (1925). Jessie Wilcox Smith found that Pyle's teaching encouraged students to connect emotionally with their subjects and brought out the best of her whimsical yet realistic children. Perhaps her best-known work was the 1905 edition of Robert Louis Stevenson's *A Child's Garden of Verse*. In 1914 she published the highly sought-after Jessie Wilcox Smith *Mother Goose Treasury*. It was in 1911 that N.C. Wyeth's edition of *Treasure Island* was published, to great acclaim. This was the first in a long series of "Illustrated Classics" published by Scribner.

There were few great picture-books published in the US during the next decade but the early 1920s saw a revival, brought about by improvements in colour printing and an influx of European artists. C.B. Falls' *ABC Book* (New York, 1923) was followed by *Maud and Miska Petersham's Poppy Seed Cakes* (New York, 1924). One of the most sought-after picture-books from this period, and perhaps the most innovative, is Wanda Gag's *Millions of Cats* (New York, 1928). The layout of double-page black-and-white illustrations and hand-lettering flows across the pages. It was awarded the Newbery Honor in 1929, and several of her other books were awarded

Caldecott or Newbery Honor status. She issued a series of highly praised illustrated tales from the Brothers Grimm, including *Snow White and the Seven Dwarfs* (New York, 1938), intended to counter the Disney version. Both the *ABC Book* and *Millions of Cats* were issued in the standard edition as well as a de-luxe edition, and the latter commands a considerably higher price. *Millions of Cats* is uncommon in a dust-jacket, and also has issue points: the correct first issue has red and yellow endpapers and "Jersey City Printing" on the copyright page. One of the first great collaborative picture-books was *The Story about Ping* (New York, 1933), written by Marjorie Flack and illustrated by Kurt Wiese. The close of the 1930s saw several fine picture-books, including Tasha Tudor's first picture-book, *Pumpkin Moonshine* (New York, 1938), and Virginia Lee Burton's *Mike Milligan and his Steam Shovel* (New York, 1939). In 1941 came the publication of the first of seven volumes about a monkey, *Curious George*. The story was smuggled out of Nazi Germany by bicycle and taken to New York by its authors, H.A. and Margaret Elizabeth Rey, where they settled. Margaret Wise Brown wrote several books for children, but it is the picture-book *Goodnight Moon* (New York, 1947), illustrated by Clement Hurd, that has remained her best known and most collected work.

4 Eleanor H. Porter. *Pollyanna*. 1924. **£80–120/$128–192**. First edition, New York, 1913.

5 Robert E. Howard. *The Pride of Bear Creek*. New York, 1966. **£20–30/$32–48**

6 Lewis Carroll. *Alice's Adventures in Wonderland*. New York, 1901. Illustrated by Peter Newell. **£150–200/$240–320**. The first important American edition of "Alice", which precedes the artist's famous *The Hole Book*.

4

5

6

WALT DISNEY

1

Walt Disney had begun his career as an animator in Kansas City and moved to Hollywood in 1923. It was in 1928 that he produced *Steamboat Willie*, in which he introduced his most famous and enduring character: Mickey Mouse. By 1929 there were Mickey Mouse clubs worldwide, and the first comic strip appeared on 13 January 1930. That same year the first annual was published by Dean and Son in England, and the first book dedicated to Mickey, *Mickey Mouse*, was published in New York. This was quickly followed by *Adventures of Mickey Mouse Book I* (Philadelphia, 1931), found in two issues, one in cloth over boards, the other in cloth-backed boards; it was published in England in the same year by George Harrap, now rare in fine condition in the dust-jacket. A steady stream of Mickey and Minnie Mouse, and from 1935, Donald Duck, books followed. Pop-up editions were issued, of which one of the most complex was *Mickey Mouse in King Arthur's Court* (New York, 1933).

It was in 1937 that Walt Disney produced the first full-length animated feature film, *Snow White and the Seven Dwarfs*, which resulted in many book spin-offs. Each of the feature films adapted from fairy tales and children's classic stories was accompanied by one or more books, and these are some of the most collectable Disney books. The "*Sketchbook*" (of *Snow White and the Seven Dwarfs*) was first published in London in 1938. Work on the film had begun in 1934 and this book comprises the early sketches and concept drawings leading to the more finished work. Walt Disney's version of *Pinocchio* (New York, 1939) was first published in a spiral-bound limited edition of 100 copies signed by Walt Disney and the animators of the film. The trade edition was issued in cloth-backed pictorial boards later the same year. There are numerous later editions of the Disney books that can be collected for very little, but copies of the informative *Art of Animation: The Story of the Disney Studio* (New York, 1958), signed by Walt Disney and many of his animators, now command high prices.

2

3

1 Walt Disney. *Snow White and the Seven Dwarfs.* 1938. **£100–150/$160–240**. The only edition published to coincide with the release of the film.

2 Walt Disney. *Fantasia. The Nutcracker Suite.* [1943]. First UK edition. Illustrated by the Walt Disney Studios. **£50–60/$80–96**

3 Walt Disney. *The Adventures of Mickey Mouse. Book 1.* Philadelphia, [1931]. Illustrated by the Walt Disney Studios. **£300–400/$480–640**

MAURICE SENDAK

The 1960s and 1970s saw an explosion of fine picture-books, and names worth looking out for are Nancy Ekholm Burkert, Alice and Martin Provensen, and Chris Van Allsburg. However, the greatest contemporary American picture-book maker, illustrator, and writer and one of the most important on the international scene is Maurice Sendak. Sendak won the important Hans Christian Andersen Medal in 1970, the first American to do so. Working in Manhattan in window display, he studied art in evening school. He met the children's book editor Ursula Nordstrom, who commissioned him to illustrate children's books. His pictures for Ruth Kraus' *A Hole is to Dig* (New York, 1952), established his credentials.

Sendak has written extensively about the role of the illustrator and his art and he has a deep fascination with the state of childhood, both his own and that of others. He cites the profound influence that Disney's *Fantasia* had on him aged 12. His picture-books record how children live in a dual world of fantasy and reality, constantly moving between the two. The earliest examples are *Kenny's Window* (New York, 1956) and *The Sign on Rosie's Door* (New York, 1960). In 1962 he issued his popular "Nutshell Library" comprising four miniature books, and illustrated Charlotte Zolotow's *Mr Rabbit and the Lovely Present*.

It is his own picture-book about a boy named Max, *Where the Wild Things Are* (New York, 1963), that is the greatest exponent of his art and beliefs and his best-known book. As discussed earlier (page 90), this work broke new ground in the theme and appearance of children's books. A first edition in the first-issue dust-jacket is now an expensive book, but one can find the 1967 first English edition and the 1988 25th anniversary editions for more reasonable figures. The first-issue dust-jacket must not list the book as being the recipient of the 1964 Caldecott Medal on the flap. The correct price of $3.50 should also be printed. The work was so popular that in 1971 a portfolio of four prints taken directly from the original drawings was issued in a limited edition. Relatively easy to find as issued, sets of the prints signed by the artist are becoming increasingly valuable. Two further stories, *In the Night Kitchen* (New York, 1970) and *Outside Over There* (New York, 1981), complete this trilogy of stories about a journey, dangers to be surmounted and a resolution which provides a healing or wholeness. He has produced numerous other important works including a fine two-volume set of the tales of the Grimm brothers, *The Juniper Tree* (New York, 1973) and the "Little Bear" series of reading books.

1

2

1 Maurice Sendak. *Where the Wild Things Are*. New York, 1963. Illustrated by the author. First edition, first issue priced at $3.50 and does not mention the Caldecott Award. **£3,000–4,000/ $4,800–6,400**

2 Maurice Sendak. *Outside Over There*. 1981. First UK edition. Illustrated by the author. **£30–40/$48–64**

Moving Picture-books

Many collectors of 20th-century children's books choose to concentrate on the more ephemeral or novelty publications such as moving picture-books. The moving picture-book was perfected in the 19th century, although its roots lay in the much earlier "volvelles" or turning discs used in astronomical or geographical books of the 16th century and the harlequinades of the late 1600s and early 1700s. The English publishers Dean and Son issued a fine series titled "Dean's New Scenic Books" which were mostly fairy tales, the first and most scarce being *Little Red Riding Hood* (1866).

It was the German artist Lothar Meggendorfer who produced the most innovative series of picture-books with moving parts and sliding flaps towards the end of the 19th century. His moving picture-books were the first in which each scene was able to have multiple moving parts. Initially published in Germany from the 1880s, they were soon translated into English. The publisher Ernest Nister began to issue his own moving picture-books at about the same time, the fine chromolithographed illustrations being printed in Nuremberg. Nister's publications most often comprised books with sliding slats or revolving images such as *The Land of Long Ago: A Visit to Fairyland with Humpty Dumpty* (1890). In

the 1880s in New York the firm McLoughlin Brothers issued the first American moving picture-books, usually comprising large three-dimensional tableaux scenes such as zoos and aquariums, including *The Snake Charmer* (New York, 1884).

During World War I, German production of the best moving picture-books had to cease and there was little of note until the 1930s. It was then that the actual "pop-up" was invented and patented by Theodore Brown, an engineer, in conjunction with S. Louis Giraud. These images that unfolded and stood up when the page was turned were issued under the Bookano imprint in England and were soon copied in the US by the New York firm of Blue Ribbon Books, who published the Disney pop-ups. The next leap in style and content was not until the 1960s when the Czech architect Voitech Kubasta began to issue a series of extraordinary pop-up books, often on educational or engineering themes, such as *How Columbus Discovered America* (Prague, 1960). His original style, bold illustration, and technical skills were the forerunner to complicated contemporary works by artists such as Jan Pieńkowksi. It is imperative when collecting these moving picture books to check the moving parts and tabs carefully, for once replaced the value begins to fall.

1 and **2** Jan Pieńkowski. *Haunted House.* 1979. Illustrated by the author, with moving parts by Tor Loknig. Issued without dust-jacket. **£40–60/$64–96**

No, I don't have many visitors.

1

2

Illustrated Books

British book illustration of the 20th century is outstanding in its diversity. It encompasses Arthur Rackham's fantasy illustrations, Chris Foss' science-fiction art, Aubrey Beardsley's black-and-white line drawings, David Low's humorous pen-and-ink caricatures, Eric Gill's wood-engravings, Eric Ravilious' colour-stencilled images, David Hockney's photographic illustration, and architectural lithographs by John Piper. Examples can be found within a wide price range, from expensively produced gift books bound in vellum to ordinary books in pictorial dust-jackets.

At the turn of the century, three movements dominated the field: William Morris and the Pre-Raphaelites; Aubrey Beardsley and Art Nouveau; and Edmund Evans and his illustrators. Although medievalist and aimed at a limited market, William Morris' work at the Kelmscott Press had an enormous impact throughout the 20th century. Morris' primary importance is as a printer and designer, and he is discussed in the next chapter. He did, however, revive the use of engraving on wood to reproduce an artist's drawing. Initially, all book illustration had been printed from wood, but towards the end of the 19th

century, photomechanical methods of transfer were widely used. Delicacy of line was often lost, but the method enabled a wide range of artists to work in book illustration. Burne-Jones and the Pre-Raphaelites in particular were thus able to illustrate many books and their style was copied by artists such as Henry Ford and J.D. Batten. Initially influenced by the Pre-Raphaelites, Beardsley later embraced Art Nouveau and Japanese-inspired wood-block work. He was one of the first to design specifically for the line block. His best-known work is probably for Thomas Malory's *Morte D'Arthur* (1893–4), Oscar Wilde's *Salome* (1894), and Alexander Pope's *The Rape of the Lock* (1896). He edited and illustrated the influential periodical *The Yellow Book*, which epitomizes the extraordinary literary and artistic activity of the time.

The printer Edmund Evans perfected the use of colour printing. His best-known artists, Walter Crane, Randolph Caldecott, and Kate Greenaway, would provide the key design on wood, which Evans would engrave. The artists would then colour a proof in simple tones and the illustration would be printed using the same oil colours. The finished result was much more delicate than the heavier

3

4

chromolithograph used elsewhere. It particularly suited the nostalgic work of Greenaway, whose first book, *Under the Window* (1878), sold the entire first edition of 20,000 copies almost immediately, and Caldecott, whose nursery-rhyme series "Shilling Picture Books" (1878–85) embodied a rustic and idealized countryside. Walter Crane produced a wide range of work, from his toy books and floral fantasies such as *Flora's Feast* (1889) to wood-blocks printed by William Morris at his Kelmscott Press.

Much of the best illustration in the first two decades of the 20th century came from the private press movement. The expense of such books meant that they were not widely available, and it was some time before commercial book production responded. The new photomechanical techniques had brought about a wealth of illustrated magazines and periodicals in the closing years of the 19th century, such as *The Idler*, *The Sketch*, *The Savoy*, and *The Pageant*, and it was often these that saw the first appearance in print of many of the most important illustrators of the 20th century.

It was in 1910 that Noel Rooke revived the teaching of wood-engraving as an original art form at the

1 Laurence Housman. Christina Rossetti. *Goblin Market*. 1893. 12 plates and decorations by Laurence Housman. **£300–400/$480–640**. Also in a large-paper edition.

2 Edward Burne-Jones. *The Flower Book*. 1905. 38 facsimile watercolours by Edward Burne-Jones. Limited to 300 copies. **£4,000–6,000/$6,400–9,600**

3 Jessie M. King. Oscar Wilde. *A House of Pomegranates*. 1915. Sixteen coloured plates by Jessie M. King. In original pictorial box. **£1,000–1,500/$1,600–2,400**

4 Aubrey Beardsley. Thomas Malory. *Le Morte D'Arthur*. 1893–4. Two volumes, many illustrations by Aubrey Beardsley. Limited to 1500 copies, **£500–700/$800–1,120**. 300 copies on hand-made paper bound in 3 volumes. £2,000–3,000/$3,200–4,800

Central School of Arts and Crafts, and in the same year Roger Fry curated the influential exhibition "Manet and the Post-Impressionists" at the Grafton Galleries in London. This exhibition provoked a reaction against Edwardian art and gave direction to a sense of protest. Modern art and illustration had begun to emerge.

Gift Books

It was the advance in colour-printing techniques that produced some of the finest, and most collected, illustrated work at the start of the 20th century, when the three- and four-colour printing process emerged as the best method of printing in colour. The three-colour printing system, in use as early as the 18th century, was now employed together with the half-tone screen, a method patented in 1882; many artists used a final fourth block to provide black, darker tones. The process could reproduce an extraordinary range and brilliance of colour, but it had to be done on special coated paper. This requirement meant that publishers had to look at ways of incorporating the paper into the actual book. Once the costs and technical processes were under control, this method of printing revolutionized illustrated books and enabled artists to see their original work as a painting rather than a linear interpretation. The resulting diversity has meant that this period is often referred to as the "golden age of illustration". Whereas Beatrix Potter's books simply had the illustrations printed on one side of this coated paper, publishers such as Hodder and Stoughton, William Heinemann, and J.M. Dent came up with a special format to accommodate this paper: the gift book with tipped-in plates and tissue guards. The necessity of interleaving thick art paper with ordinary text paper was made a virtue, and the public was persuaded to purchase these special editions.

The ordinary copies were bound in cloth, usually with detailed pictorial designs provided by the artist and stamped in gilt over the covers and spine. Pictorial endpapers were often included, the edges, either the top only or all three, were gilded, and the illustrations were printed on thick paper, tipped-in often on a different coloured paper and protected with a tissue guard, usually overprinted with a caption from the text. Relatively swiftly the publishers decided there was a market for more luxurious, limited editions of these books, numbered and signed by the author, occasionally with the text printed on Japanese vellum ("Japon"). The binding would be of full vellum, parchment-backed cream cloth, or cream cloth. Finished with silk ties, the book would be housed in a special numbered box.

It was commissions by publishers such as J.M. Dent, Hodder and Stoughton, and William Heinemann that enabled artists such as Arthur Rackham and Edmund Dulac to earn a living. Joseph Malaby Dent was born in 1849 and at the age of 13 was apprenticed to a printer, turning shortly thereafter to bookbinding. He moved to London in 1867, setting up his own bookbinding shop where he acquired a reputation for fine craftsmanship. In 1888 he founded the publishing firm J.M. Dent and Company. His first production in that year was Charles Lamb's *Essays of Elia*, illustrated by Herbert Railton. In 1893 the bookseller Frederick Evans suggested he publish

1 Arthur Rackham. Edgar Allan Poe. *Tales of Mystery and Imagination*. 1935. 12 coloured plates and other illustrations by Arthur Rackham. In dust-jacket. **£300–400/$480–640**. Also limited signed edition of 460 copies.

2 Arthur Rackham. Richard Wagner. *The Rhinegold and the Valkyrie*. 1910. 34 coloured plates by Arthur Rackham. **£100–150/$160–240**. Also limited signed edition of 1,150 copies.

3 Millicent Sowerby. Robert Louis Stevenson. *A Child's Garden of Verses*. 1908. 12 coloured plates by Millicent Sowerby. De-luxe edition. **£500–700/$800–1,120**

ARTHUR RACKHAM

The best-known and also most collected illustrator of these gift books is Arthur Rackham. Born in London in 1867, he trained at the Lambeth School of Art and became a staff artist on the magazine *The Westminster Budget* in 1892. His first book illustrations, in black and white, were for Thomas Rhodes' *To the Other Side* (1893), a travelogue about America. He frequently contributed to periodicals and searching for these can be a fascinating way to come by his early work. His style at this time was linear, influenced by a variety of artists that included George Cruikshank, Richard Doyle, Aubrey Beardsley, and Albrecht Dürer. With the publication of his first major illustrated book, *Rip van Winkle* (1905), his reputation was assured. With 50 colour illustrations commissioned by William Heinemann, it was the first of the illustrated de-luxe editions to be published: the gift book was created. Today it is one of the most sought-after of his books, superseded only by his second title, *Peter Pan in Kensington Gardens* (1906).

Arthur Rackham has illustrated Shakespeare and Milton, Wagner and Swinburne, but it is his editions of classic tales such as *Alice's Adventures in Wonderland* (1907), Edgar Allan Poe's *Tales of Mystery and Imagination* (1935), *Hans Andersen's Fairy Tales* (1932), and his final, posthumously published work, *The Wind in the Willows* (1950), for which he is most collected. These editions were never intended for children, but they quickly took them to heart. Each of these titles was issued in an unlimited edition bound in cloth, alongside a special limited edition signed by the artist. The unlimited editions were reprinted many times and were also sold in cheaper editions through outlets such as Boots the Chemist. In his final years his publishers, George Harrap, decided to issue some of his books in a special collector's edition, bound in green morocco, with an original watercolour by the artist on one of the preliminary blank leaves. It is uncertain exactly how many titles were issued in this format, or precisely how many copies of each, but it is thought that about ten titles were issued thus, of which about ten copies of the entire print-run were in this format. These remain the most expensive and eagerly sought-after examples of Rackham's work.

Rackham exhibited and usually sold the work for each book, at the time of publication, at the Leicester Galleries in London, and these watercolours were as much in demand then, both in Europe and the US, as they are today.

1 S.J. Adair-Fitzgerald. *The Zankiwank and the Bletherwitch.* 1896. 17 full-page and other illustrations by Arthur Rackham. **£600–800/$960–1,280**

2 Washington Irving. *Rip van Winkle.* 1905. 51 coloured plates by Arthur Rackham. **£300–500**. Also a limited signed edition of 250 copies.

3 William Shakespeare. *A Midsummer Night's Dream.* 1908. 40 coloured plates by Arthur Rackham. **£150–200**. Also a limited signed edition of 1,000 copies.

EDMUND DULAC

French by birth, the Anglophile and book illustrator Edmund Dulac emigrated to England in 1904 at the age of 22. He was commissioned by the publisher J.M. Dent to provide a series of illustrations to the novels of the Brontë sisters. He also contributed to periodicals such as *The Pall Mall Magazine* and joined the London Sketch Club. It was the Leicester Galleries who commissioned Dulac to paint a series of watercolour illustrations to the tales of *The Arabian Nights*, and through their recommendation he was retained by the publishers Hodder and Stoughton. *Stories from the Arabian Nights* was published in 1907, the watercolours were exhibited at a sell-out show at the Leicester Galleries and he illustrated several similar works, including *The Rubaiyat of Omar Khayyam* (1909) and *Stories from Hans Andersen* (1911). *The Sleeping Beauty and Other Fairy Tales* (1910) was an instant success and the 30 watercolours for this book show his work at its most complex. Often known as his "Blue Period" as they display a predominant use of shades of blue, these are generally the works most eagerly sought-after by collectors. From 1914 on, the influence of Persian manuscripts and Eastern art was more noticeable and his style altered. He also began to draw cartoons, caricatures and portraiture. He produced several gift books for charities such as the French Red Cross, which are usually the least expensive of his works. During the 1930s much of his output was for American periodicals such as *American Weekly* and *Good Housekeeping*, or commercial designs for playing cards, stamps and medals. During World War II he designed bank notes and stamps for the Free French. One of his last designs prior to his death in 1953 was a coronation stamp for Queen Elizabeth II in 1952.

HAND'S DEATH

3

1 Hans Andersen. *Stories*. 1911. 28 coloured plates by Edmund Dulac. **£200–300/$320–480**. Also signed limited edition of 750 copies.

2 *Fairy Book*. 1916. 15 coloured plates by Edmund Dulac. **£100–150/$160–240**. Also signed limited edition of 350 copies.

3 Robert Louis Stevenson. *Treasure Island*. 1927. 12 coloured plates and other illustrations by Edmund Dulac. **£80–120/$128–192**

a pocket edition of the works of William Shakespeare, and the Temple Shakespeare series was born. J.M. Dent produced many other series, such as the Everyman Library and the Medieval Towns series. The hallmarks of the Dent publications were classic texts, fine illustrations (newly commissioned), and elaborate bindings tooled in gilt. Many of the most important illustrators of this early period, such as Aubrey Beardsley, Arthur Rackham, Maxwell Armfield, Robert Anning Bell, Charles and Henry Brock, and the three Robinson brothers, William Heath, Thomas Heath and Charles, established their name through his commissions. In 1987 the archive of original artwork was sold at auction and the company itself was sold to Weidenfeld and Nicholson in 1988.

Other major contributors to these gift books were Kay Nielsen, Harry Clarke, Warwick Goble, Willy Pogany, and Edward Detmold. Of these, the books by Kay Nielsen are probably the most sought-after today. Kay Nielsen was born in Denmark in 1886 and brought up in the Scandinavian theatre world. At the age of 17 he left to study art in Paris and in his free time began to illustrate writers such as Verlaine and Hans Christian Andersen. He was encouraged by English friends to settle in London in 1911, and in 1912 he exhibited a series of haunting ink drawings for a proposed work titled *Book of Death.* These were never published, but the exhibition prompted the publishers Hodder and Stoughton to commission illustrations for Sir Arthur Quiller Couch's compilation of folk tales, *In Powder and Crinoline* (1913). Kay Nielsen produced a tiny number of books compared to Arthur Rackham and Edmund Dulac, yet his work is among the greatest of the century and as such generally commands higher prices than the other illustrators. His work was usually for fairy tales or ancient myths such as *East of the Sun and West of the Moon: Old Tales from the North* (1914), which is perhaps his most famous book. Kay Nielsen worked on stage productions for the Royal Theatre in Copenhagen during the 1920s and in 1939 he moved to California where he worked on the Walt Disney film *Fantasia.* His work is usually elaborate, with beautiful patterned and jewelled detail, often exhibiting oriental influences.

Harry Clarke was born in Dublin in 1889 and educated by the Jesuits. Initially apprenticed as an

4

5

6

4 Kay Nielsen. J.L.C. and W.C. Grimm. *Hansel and Gretel.* 1925. 12 coloured plates and other illustrations by Kay Nielsen. Limited to 600 copies. **£1,500–2,000/$2,400–3,200**

5 Harry Clarke. J.W. von Goethe. *Faust.* 1925. 21 coloured plates and other illustrations by Harry Clarke. Limited to 1,000 copies. **£300–400/$480–640**

6 Edward Detmold. 16 illustrations of subjects from Kipling's *Jungle Book.* 1903. 16 coloured plates by Edward and Maurice Detmold. **£1,500–2,000/$2,400–3,200**

architect, he soon joined his father's firm of stained-glass designers. Studying glass design in Paris and winning coveted medals, he produced designs of a delicate intensity that can be seen echoed in his illustrative work. Often in black ink only, his evocative, ethereal, and often chilling drawings were sought-after by publishers for intense tales such as Edgar Allan Poe's *Tales of Mystery and Imagination* (1919) and Samuel Taylor Coleridge's *The Rime of the Ancient Mariner* (1916). His watercolours are very reminiscent of stained-glass designs, with deep, intense colour and elaborate use of black line.

The three Robinson brothers were hugely talented and amassed a prodigious and varied output of artistic work. Thomas Heath was the eldest, born in 1869, followed by Charles in 1870 and William Heath in 1872. Much of Thomas Heath's work was in ink and for periodicals. His books were often historical, religious or mythical in subject-matter, such as Thomas à Kempis' *Of the Imitation of Christ* (1935). Charles Robinson also did much work in ink, but his illustrative style is very different, often comprising cherubic children and swirling decorative borders in an Art Nouveau style. His most famous work is Robert Louis Stevenson's *A Child's Garden of Verses* (1895), and other works included Oscar Wilde's *The Happy Prince* (1913), Hans Andersen's *Fairy Tales*, and a three-volume series titled "Annals of Fairyland", published in 1902.

It is probably William Heath Robinson who is the best known of the brothers; his illustrations vary from those for *Don Quixote* (1929) and Rudyard Kipling's *A Song of the English* (1909) to his own works *Uncle Lubin* (1902) and *Bill the Minder* (1912). He contributed a series of wonderful, imaginative pictures and cartoons, detailing absurd inventions, sports, life in London and the country, to periodicals such as *The Bystander*, and to a series of comic manuals including *How to Live in a Flat* and *Railway Ribaldry* (both 1936). Initially a landscape painter, he soon turned to illustration, often working with line drawing only. His first gift book was *Twelfth Night* (1908), but perhaps his most sought-after books are his edition of *Hans Andersen's Fairy Tales* (1913) and his own two works. His style of cartoon was immensely popular and he was soon being commissioned to provide commercial work such as posters. He is one of very few 20th-century illustrators whose work was equally fine whether serious or humorous.

Warwick Goble also contributed to early periodicals and illustrated a few books during the 1890s, including the 1898 edition of H.G. Wells' *War of the Worlds*. Goble was fascinated by Japanese techniques, and his fine watercolours were suited to the gift book, producing ten between 1909 and 1913. These included his best works, *The Water Babies* (1909) and *Queen Willow and Other Japanese Fairy Tales* (1910).

Willy Pogany was born in Hungary and, after studying in Paris, settled in London and later America. He illustrated many books of fairy tales, myths, and legends. His most sought-after today is Samuel Taylor Coleridge's *The Ancient Mariner* (1910).

7 Thomas Heath Robinson. *The Arabian Nights Entertainment*. 1899. Coloured frontispiece and ten other illustrations by Thomas Heath Robinson. **£40–60/$64–96**

8 Charles Robinson. Percy Bysshe Shelly. *The Sensitive Plant*. 1911. 18 coloured plates and other illustrations by Charles Robinson. **£150–200/$240–320**

9 William Heath Robinson. Hans Andersen. *Fairy Tales*. N.d. 16 coloured plates and other illustrations by W.H. Robinson. This later edition for Boots. **£150–200/$240–320**

7

8

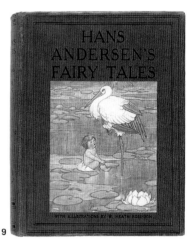

9

Wood-engravings

Images engraved and cut on wood had for centuries formed the basis for illustration in books. Early images had been cut on the soft flat edge of the wood with a knife, providing a rough, coarse line, whereas at the end of the 18th century Thomas Bewick perfected the art of engraving on the hardened grain of the wood using a graver and producing a relief block. Delicacy of line and detail was now possible. The huge increase in book production throughout the 19th century put pressure on these artists. Thousands of wood-blocks were turned out to meet the demand, but these were engraved not by the artist but by jobbing engravers. Wood-engraving, no matter how skilled, was reduced to a reproductive medium. The best-known firm of engravers was the Dalziel Brothers, who produced much of the finest work during the middle of the century for artists such as John Tenniel, Dante Gabriel Rossetti, and William Holman Hunt. Even though William Morris revived the use of the wood-engraving with his Kelmscott Press, artists such as Edward Burne-Jones and Walter Crane did not engrave their own designs.

Charles Ricketts and Charles Shannon at the Vale Press and Lucien Pissarro at his Eragny Press were the first to revive original wood-engraving at the turn of the century (see the next chapter). Lucien Pissarro, in particular, was most inventive, employing the coloured woodcut in most of his books. Ricketts and Thomas Sturge Moore both provided wood-engravings for commercial publishers and Ricketts' *The Sphinx* (1894) is a fine book to look for. Also in the 1890s Edward Gordon Craig, William Nicholson, and Claud Lovat Fraser worked with woodcuts, cutting the design themselves. Edward Gordon Craig used the woodcut as a quick and practical method of reproducing his theatrical designs, and in doing so created some of the finest books of the 20th century, including the Cranach Press *Hamlet* (1927) and his *Book of Penny Toys* (1899). William Nicholson was influenced by French poster design and both he and Claud Lovat Fraser admired the work of the earlier woodcut artist Joseph Crawhall, who produced many chapbooks. William Nicholson's large bold images for books such as Rudyard Kipling's *Almanac of Sports* and *London Types* (1898) were engraved by him on wood. The de-luxe editions were printed direct from the blocks with the images coloured by hand, and the ordinary editions were coloured and printed lithographically. Claud Lovat Fraser's work was much smaller in scale, reminiscent of the early chapbooks, and was often reproduced in chapbook or poster format by the Poetry Bookshop and the Curwen Press.

These artists were the exception, however, for in the early part of the century the majority of illustration on wood was cut by a commercial engraver. In 1910 Noel Rooke began teaching wood-engraving at the Central School of Arts and Crafts in London. A pupil of the great calligrapher Edward Johnston and a teacher of illustration at the Central School, Rooke was dissatisfied with the reproduction of his drawings and was determined

1 William Nicholson. W.E. Henley. *London Types*. 1898. 13 coloured plates by William Nicholson. **£150–200/$240–320**. Also de-luxe edition on japon and 40 portfolios of original woodcuts coloured by hand.

2 Paul Nash. *The Double Crown Club Records*. 1988. Wood-engravings by Paul Nash and others. **£10–15/$16–24**

3 Robert Gibbings. *Samson and Delilah*. Golden Cockerel Press, 1925. 6 wood-engravings by Robert Gibbings. Limited to 325 copies. **£300–400/$480–640**

1

3

2

to find a way in which his work would be reproduced faithfully. He chose to use wood for this and from his own work sprang the extraordinary revival of wood-engraving. Rooke himself was not a prolific print-maker, nor did he illustrate many books, but his importance lies in his role as teacher. His many pupils included some of the best wood-engravers of the century, such as Eric Gill, Robert Gibbings, John Farleigh, and Clare Leighton. Other artists, meanwhile, had also taken up the medium. At the Royal College of Art, Paul Nash began to teach wood-engraving in 1920, having begun his own experiments the year before; two of his pupils were Edward Bawden and Eric Ravilious. His brother, John Nash, Douglas Percy Bliss, and Eric Fitch Daglish began to work with him in exploring and improving the art of engraving on wood.

In 1920 many of the major practitioners formed the Society of Wood Engravers, under whose banner they held annual exhibitions. The rival or complementary organizations, the English Wood Engraving Society and the Grosvenor School of Modern Art, were formed in 1925. Iain Macnab established the latter; his staff included Blair Hughes-Stanton, a major contributor to the Gregynog Press (see page 137), Graham Sutherland, and Claude Flight, the pioneer in Britain of colour lino-cutting. These artists illustrated numerous books, many within the private press movement (discussed in the next chapter), but others were issued by commercial publishers such as J.M. Dent, Cassells, and Victor Gollancz. Some of Robert Gibbings' finest work was for a series of "River Books" published by J.M. Dent, including *Sweet Thames Run Softly* (1940), comprising personal anecdotes, natural history observations, and beautiful illustrations. These are today still very reasonably priced. Agnes Miller Parker produced two superb commercial

books, quite easy to find today, *Through the Woods* (1936) and *Down the River* (1937), and Clare Leighton's *The Farmer's Year* (1933) is a magnificent production. The wood-engravings of Joan Hasall, Eric Daglish, and Charles Tunniclife, often illustrating natural history works, are usually found in commercial editions published from the 1920s to the 1950s and as such are priced reasonably today. One of the greatest successes of commercial wood-engraved illustration was John Farleigh's work for George Bernard Shaw's *Adventures of the Black Girl in her Search for God* (1932), which was reprinted five times within a few months of its publication. An important and fine book, it can still be acquired for a very modest sum.

Wood-engraving was dropped from art schools during the 1960s and the art form languished, to be revived in 1987 by Simon Brett (Chairman of the Society of Wood Engravers from 1984), who curated an important exhibition "Engraving Then and Now: The Retrospective 50th Exhibition of the Society of Wood Engravers". Interest in the medium was revived, and much of this work today is published once again by the private presses, for some of the owners of these presses are practising engravers themselves.

4 Agnes Miller Parker. Aesop. *Fables*. Gregynog Press, 1932. 37 wood-engraved illustrations by Agnes Miller-Parker. Limited edition of 250 copies. **£1,500–2,000/$2,400–3,200**

5 John Buckland Wright. John Keats. *Endymion*. Golden Cockerel Press. 1947. 58 wood-engraved illustrations by John Buckland Wright. Limited to 500 copies. **£150–200/$240–320**

6 Clare Leighton. *Four Hedges, a Gardener's Chronicle*. 1935. 88 wood-engraved illustrations by Clare Leighton. **£40–60/$64–96**

4

5

6

ERIC GILL AND DAVID JONES

Eric Gill was one of the best wood-engravers of the 1920s and 1930s. He illustrated some of the most important books of the 20th century, although he considered himself more of a decorator. He was a fine stone mason and typographer, and his lettering for the Golden Cockerel Press and Monotype Corporation is among the most significant of the century (see the next chapter). Born in 1882 in Brighton, Gill was educated at Chichester before becoming articled at architects' offices in London and joining Edward Johnston's lettering class at the Central School of Arts and Crafts in 1899. Abandoning architecture for letter-cutting, he received his first commission in 1903 while still a student. He moved to Ditchling, Sussex, in 1907, where he began to explore wood-engraving as a medium for illustration, partly because of its compatibility with type, and founded an artistic community in which he was the master craftsman. Much of his work examines themes of faith and sexual desire. Gill became involved with book illustration through Douglas Pepler, whose *The Devil's Devices* (1915), published at the Hampshire House Workshops and illustrated by Gill, is a key work in the revival of wood-engraving. Pepler subsequently formed the St Dominic's Press. Gill illustrated many of its publications, and these could make an inexpensive collection.

In 1924 Gill moved to Capel-y-ffin in the Black Mountains of Wales, forming another community. Here he designed the typeface Perpetua, and engraved many of his greatest illustrations for the Golden Cockerel Press, notably *The Song of Songs* (1925) and Chaucer's *Troilus and Criseyde* (1927). He moved once more in 1928 to "Piggots" in High Wycombe, where most of his important work was produced, including his second typeface, Gill Sans, and the Golden Cockerel Press editions of *The Canterbury Tales* (1929–30) and *The Four Gospels* (1931). Much of his work was commissioned from within the private press movement but he also undertook fine designs for commercial publishers such as J.M. Dent's "New Temple Shakespeare" series, and published his own works, *Art, Nonsense and other Essays* (1929) and *Clothes* (1931). Gill's impact on 20th-century book production, especially his decorative borders, lettering, illustrations, and his influence on other artists such as David Jones, cannot be overestimated.

David Jones was born in 1895 and after studying at Camberwell School of Art joined the Ditchling community in 1921. It was under the influence of Pepler and Gill that Jones learnt to engrave on wood. He spent long periods of time with Gill in Wales and High Wycombe, and Gill's influence is evident in his early wood-engravings, especially in *The Book of Jonah* (1926) and *The Chester Play of the Deluge* (1927) for the Golden Cockerel Press. His later book work, including *The Rime of the Ancient Mariner* (1929, reissued 1972), was mainly engraved on copper, and here the style is all his own. Jones was also a fine watercolourist and calligrapher, and he issued several important texts and poems of his own, including *In Parenthesis* (1937) and *The Anathemata* (1952). The majority of his work, however, was published from within the private press movement.

1

2

1 Eric Gill. *The Four Gospels of the Lord Jesus Christ*. Golden Cockerel Press. 1931. 62 wood-engravings by Eric Gill. Limited to 500 copies. **£2,500–3,500/$4,000–5,600**

2 David Jones. *The Book of Jonah*. Golden Cockerel Press, 1926. 13 wood-engravings by David Jones. Limited to 175 copies. **£500–700/$800–1,120**

The Curwen Press Artists

The Curwen Press was established in 1863 but it was not until the founder's grandson, Harold Curwen, took over the management shortly before World War I that the visual content of its books and ephemera came to the fore. Harold Curwen had an unconventional education in which craft had played a prominent part. He was one of very few people at the time who believed that every single element of printing was important, the typeface, the decoration, spacing and, most of all, that the illustrations should be an integral part of the work. He was receptive to all things new and he fostered a co-operative spirit amongst his workforce. All of these factors were crucial at a time of enormous change and helped create a sympathetic atmosphere attractive to artists. Curwen also attended Edward Johnston's classes at the Central School of Arts and Crafts. He was a founder-member of the Design and Industries Association in 1915, through whom he met future customers and colleagues.

The first independent artist to work for the Press was Claud Lovat Fraser, whose woodcuts adorned many of their early publications and ephemeral pieces. Curwen printed a series of light-hearted booklets, posters, and broadsides extolling the virtues of the Press and decorated by their artists. Fascinating ephemeral pieces, these could make an inexpensive collection documenting changes in illustration and book design. Always open to experimentation, he used the colour line block to reproduce the work of Lovat Fraser and Albert Rutherston. Both worked initially with black outline and then supplied the colours on a printed proof. Great care was taken with the printing at all stages and the artists were encouraged to participate and supervise throughout.

The artists were delighted with the fine results, particularly when the French process of "pochoir" (colour added by hand through stencils) was adopted around 1925. Curwen developed this by using celluloid for each layer, so that the key design could be seen underneath. The resulting colour was exactly the same as the original used by the artist and was startling in its brilliance and freshness. Two of the very finest examples are Arnold Bennett's *Elsie and the Child* (1929), with illustrations by E. McKnight Kauffer, and Paul Nash's illustrated edition of Thomas Browne's *Urne Buriall* (1932).

Curwen also championed the use of lithography, and encouraged artists to create the lithographs themselves (autolithography). Some of the finest book illustrations and jacket designs of the 1930s–1950s were in this medium, and W. Barnett Freedman was one of the first to master the technique. His first important book was Siegfried Sassoon's *Memoirs of an Infantry Officer* (1931). He illustrated several of the Limited Editions Club books with fine lithographs, including Tolstoy's *War and Peace* (1938). Often overlooked, autolithography could make a fascinating focus for a collection (see page 104).

The typographer Oliver Simon, nephew of artists William Rothenstein and Albert Rutherston, had worked with Stanley Morison before joining the Curwen Press in 1922 (see pages 139–40). His aim was to attract more book commissions to complement the current commercial and retail work. Oliver Simon was firmly opposed to what he saw as the elitest and historical principles of the private presses and was determined to produce good books within the commerical field. Book production became an important part of the firm, with good design and newly commissioned illustration being the guiding principles.

Most of the artists Simon introduced to the Press were unknown and made their reputation with the Press. A roll-call comprises many of the most important artists in the book world from the 1920s to the 1950s, and underlines how influential Curwen and Simon were. Oliver Simon's brother, Herbert, was once asked who of the two had been more important, and he replied: "Certain it is that without the technical skill and real pioneering of Harold Curwen, Oliver Simon would have floundered; but the latter's achievement in book printing and editing have left an enduring memorial which Curwen's commercial work, splendid as it was, could never have conjured forth."

Ariel poems

One of the most interesting series printed by the Curwen Press was the "Ariel poems". These were conceived by the publishers Faber in 1927 as alternatives to Christmas cards and comprised an unpublished work by a distinguished poet illustrated by a sympathetic artist. The poems were issued in an unlimited edition and a limited edition on large paper signed by the author and artist, and each was preserved within a special envelope. Faber needed to keep the price reasonable and so devised a colour range for the artists to work within so that a set of eight poems could be printed at one time. The series ran from 1927 to 1931 and 38 titles were issued, the first being *Yuletide* by Thomas Hardy with illustrations by Albert Rutherston. A new series was issued later in the 1950s. These can make one of the most rewarding and least expensive ways of collecting the major illustrators of the period.

1

2

3

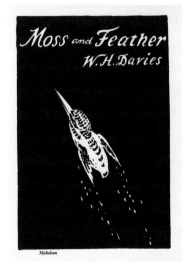

4

1 Curwen Press Newsletter. No. 1. Curwen Press. 1932. Wood-engraved illustrations by Paul Nash and Edward Bawden. **£30–50/$48–80**

2 Gino Severini. *Fleurs et Masques*. 1930. 16 plates by Gino Severini coloured by hand by pochoir, heightened with gold. Limited to 125 copies. **£10,000–15,000/$16,000/24,000**

3 Claud Lovat Fraser. *A Collection of Nursery Rhymes*. 1922. New edition, illustrations by Claud Lovat Fraser. **£15–20/$24–32**

4 William Nicholson. W.H. Davies. *Moss and Feather*. Ariel Poem. 1928. Illustration by William Nicholson. Limited to 500 signed copies. **£100–200/$160–320**

5 T.S. Eliot. *A Song for Simeon*. Ariel Poem. 1928. Illustration by E. McKnight Kauffer. Limited to 500 signed copies. **£100–200/$160–320**

5

Much of the Press's work was published under their own imprint, but the majority was executed for enterprising publishers such as Allen Lane's Puffin Books, Desmond Flower at Cassell, and Francis Meynell at the Nonesuch Press (discussed in the next chapter).

Albert Rutherston was one of the first artists to work with the Curwen Press, initially designing vignettes and pattern papers, and going on to illustrate four of the "Ariel" poems. He worked on various books, including *A Box of Paints* (1923), and the complex work *The Haggadah*, published in 1930 by the Soncino Press. Much experimental work was carried out on the printing of the illustrations, which were coloured by stencil: the result was vibrant and especially pleasing to the artist.

Paul Nash came to the Press through Claud Lovat Fraser's instigation, and as a prolific writer of articles he championed many of the artists working with the Press. He had taught at the Ruskin School alongside Albert Rutherston and later at the Royal College of Art where Eric Ravilious and Edward Bawden were his pupils. He was one of the foremost artists of his generation, and much of his work was landscape in form, often harsh and abstract. He illustrated nearly 20 books and contributed illustrations to many journals. His greatest work, *Urne Buriall* (1932), has been called one of the most beautiful books of the 20th century. Although these illustrations were coloured by stencils, the majority of his book work was cut on wood, and he was influential in the revival of the artist-engraved wood-block. *Genesis*, his first book for the Curwen Press, published by the Nonesuch Press in 1924, contains 12 striking woodcuts.

Edward Bawden studied at the Cambridge School of Art under Paul Nash and was close friends with his fellow pupil Eric Ravilious. He continued studying at the Central School and taught at the Royal College of Art. Whilst there, he was commissioned by Harold Curwen to illustrate *Pottery Making in Poole* and he began designing patterned papers and decorations for the Press. All his early books were for the Press, including *The Life and Adventures of Peter Wilkins* (1928) and *Adam and Evelyn at Kew* (1930). Harold Curwen was a friend, sponsor, and teacher, and encouraged him to draw directly on to lithographic stone, a medium particularly suited to his bold and free style. The first example of his autolithography was *The Arabs*, published by Puffin Books in 1947. He was an official war artist throughout World War II, and these years deepened his emotional range as an artist. His fine work, from the years 1928 to 1987, encompassed the woodcut, the linocut, lithography, watercolour, and gouache, and ranges from book jackets to murals, from wallpaper to ceramic tiles, poster designs, and numerous books.

His contemporary, Eric Ravilious, however, produced comparatively few books, as he was killed during World War II. His best-known work, *High Street*, is his last and one of the greatest illustrated books of the century, printed at the Curwen Press and published in 1938, with bold, coloured lithographic illustrations. The majority of his early work – patterned papers, books, and decorations for the Curwen Press – was in the form of the woodcut. He produced a fine edition of Gilbert White's *The Natural History of Selborne* for the Nonesuch Press in 1938. Later

6 Albert Rutherston. Geoffrey Scott. *A Box of Paints*. 1923. Seven coloured illustrations by Albert Rutherston. Limited to 1,000 copies. **£15–20/$24–32**

7 Edward Bawden. Jonathan Swift. *The Voyages of Lemuel Gulliver*. 1948. 12 coloured lithographs by Edward Bawden, **£15–20/$24–32**

8 Eric Ravilious. J.M. Richards. *High Street*. 1938. 25 coloured lithographs by Eric Ravilious. **£500–700/$800–1,120**

6   7   8

in his life he turned more to colour and painting, and *High Street* was an indication of how his work could have progressed had he lived.

Edward McKnight Kauffer was born in Montana. He had a troubled childhood, and it was not until he met Joseph McKnight, a professor at the University of Utah, who became his patron and gave him his middle name, that he could afford to study art. He settled in England in 1914 where he worked as an advertising artist, designing some of the greatest of the London Underground and Shell posters. He continued to work in the advertising world, and was perhaps more responsible for raising the standard of advertising and commercial art in Britain than any other artist. He also illustrated some of the finest books of the century, the majority of which were printed by the Curwen Press for Nonesuch, Cassells, and other publishers. He worked with watercolour or gouache using the stencil process, producing brilliantly coloured, bold illustrations and jacket designs. *Elsie and the Child* (1929) and *Benito Cereno* (1926) are some of his best-known works.

From this brief look at some of the artists who worked for the Curwen Press, it becomes apparent how important it was in the development of book illustration and the patronage of 20th-century artists in Britain. In the US there was a similar commercial printing operation, the Limited Editions Club (discussed in the next chapter). The Curwen Press believed in fine design and illustration, with book production comprising a large part of its output, but it was commercial, decorative work such as posters, patterned papers, and advertising leaflets that formed the bulk of its work. The influence and patronage of Harold Curwen and Oliver Simon, alongside that of Frank Pick at London Underground, Jack Beddington and Kenneth Rowntree at Shell, S. John Woods at Ealing Studios, and the advertising directors of Guinness, enabled these artists to flourish by commissioning promotional material from them. This in turn led to commissions for book work.

Other commercial publishers that commissioned and encouraged illustrators, and whose books are not expensive today, were the Folio Society and Penguin. The Folio Society was founded in 1947 "to produce editions of the world's great literature in a format worthy of the contents, at a price within the reach of everyman". Penguin's series of Puffin Picture Books (discussed in the previous chapter) and King Penguins provided work for many illustrators. The King Penguins were launched in 1939 with the aim of providing for a wide reading public a selection of informative texts illustrated by the best artists of the day at affordable prices.

Other series worth looking for are "Britain in Pictures" published by Collins, and a series established towards the end of World War II entitled "New Excursions into English Poetry", which features many of the best post-war artists working with lithographs, such as John Piper, Michael Ayrton, John Craxton, and Edward Bawden. *English, Scottish & Welsh Landscape 1700–c.1860* (1944), by John Betjeman and Geoffrey Taylor with John Piper's lithographs, printed by the Curwen Press, is probably the most important.

9 Barnett Freedman. Siegfried Sassoon. *Memoirs of an Infantry Officer.* 1931. 18 coloured lithographs by Barnett Freedman. **£100–150/$160–240**. First illustrated edition.

10 Curwen Press. Harold Curwen. *Printing.* Puffin Picture Books, 1961. Illustrations by Jack Brough. Revised edition. **£15–20/$24–32**

11 Edward McKnight Kauffer. T.S. Eliot. *A Song for Simeon.* Ariel Poem. 1928. Illustration by E. McKnight Kauffer. Limited to 500 signed copies. **£100–200/$160–320**

9

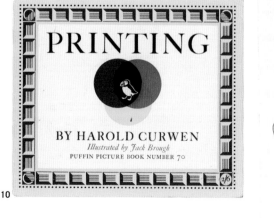
10

11

Artists

John Piper's early work also included poster designs, as did that of Frank Brangwyn. Born in 1867, Brangwyn was a prolific artist working in many media, including oil, watercolour, etching, and wood. He was a muralist, printmaker, and designer of interiors and jewellery; he produced bookplates, and illustrated numerous magazines and books. Perhaps his most famous are of bridges, including Walter Shaw-Sparrow's *A Book of Bridges* (1915) and C. Barman's *The Bridge* (1926). His illustrations are often woodcuts or reproductions of his atmospheric watercolours.

John Piper was born in 1903 and after art school in the 1920s began making topographical notebooks of English architecture. His first exhibition of wood-engravings was held in 1927 although he later turned to oils, completing his first abstract oil in 1935. In 1937 he was commissioned by John Betjeman to write the *Shell Guide to Oxfordshire.* One of his greatest works was a series of 12 aquatints, *Brighton Aquatints* (1939). The edition of 500 copies was printed at the Curwen Press, with 55 sets coloured by hand and signed by the artist. An official war artist, he was commissioned to paint shipping and agricultural subjects. He is probably best known for his watercolours and prints of British landscape and architecture. His moody and romantic illustrations, often lithographs, appeared in works such as Walter de la Mare's *The Traveller* (1946), J.M. Richards' *The Castles on the Ground* (1946), John Betjeman's *Church Poems* (1981), and Dylan Thomas' *Deaths and Entrances* (1984). He also produced murals and designs for the stage, for fabric and for stained glass.

Rex Whistler was also well known for his murals, mostly for friends' houses, and a major one in the Tate Gallery restaurant, London. He too designed posters and stage sets and painted portraits. Born in 1905, he studied at the Royal Academy and the Slade. He illustrated numerous books in a distinctive style reminiscent of 18th-century baroque, the pages surrounded with ornate, swirling borders and cherubs, and dust-jackets decorated with ornamental architectural motifs. His most important work is the two-volume Cresset Press edition of *Gulliver's Travels* (1930), which contains 12 fine full-page illustrations coloured by hand. His other works include Walter de la Mare's *The Lord Fish* (1933), several books by his brother, Laurence, including *The Emperor Heart* (1936), and Hans Andersen's *Fairy Tales* (1935). Just as he was beginning to mature as an artist, he was killed in action in World War II.

William Russell Flint, born in 1880, is perhaps best known for his paintings, but he too illustrated books, including classic texts such as *The Canterbury Tales* (1913), *The Odyssey of Homer* (1924), and *Morte D'Arthur* (1910–11), under the imprint of the Riccardi Press or Medici Society.

Books illustrated by great 20th-century photographers would make another interesting collection. Cecil Beaton, stage designer and fashion and portrait photographer, produced a series of inexpensive books, including *New York* (1938), *Near East* (1943), and *Far East* (1948). These books often contain his drawings and hand-drawn title pages as well as his photographs. Ansel Adams and Bill Brandt have published several books of photographs. Robert Mapplethorpe's work has appeared under many imprints, including that of the Limited Editions Club, who published several books illustrated by photogravures or photographs during the 1980s and 1990s, including work by Berenice Abbott, Henri Cartier-Bresson, and the Austrian mountaineer-photographer Heinrich Harrer.

American illustration in the last hundred years ranges from depictions of the Far West by Frederic Remington at the turn of the century, society drawings of Charles Dana Gibson, and realist pen-and-ink drawings by A.B. Frost and E.W. Kemble, to the romantic illustrations of Edward A. Wilson and his images of the sea, such as *Two Years before the Mast* (1924). Perhaps the best known outside the US is the prolific illustrator Rockwell Kent. His most famous work is for *Moby-Dick* (1930). Several of the best American illustrators have worked mainly on children's books, such as Howard Pyle, N.C. Wyeth, Maurice Sendak, and Edward Gorey (discussed in the previous chapter).

Book jackets

During the 1920s and 1930s many of the best artists produced pictorial dust-jackets for publishers as a means of earning a living. With publishers increasingly adopting the role of patron and artists increasingly aware of commercialism, the competitive market combined with the advances in colour printing to produce a wealth of fine pictorial or decorative jackets. W. Barnett Freedman, E. McKnight Kauffer, Rex Whistler, William Nicholson, Edward Bawden, and Eric Ravilious are some of those artists responsible. This trend has continued right through to the present day, with dust-jacket designs for authors such as Louis de Bernières becoming instantly recognizable. Pictorial dust-jackets could provide the collector with a selection of work by some of the best artists of the century, while at the same time forming a record of changing design and artistic trends. The Modernist jackets of the 1930s, often in monochrome, are particularly striking.

1 John Piper. Walter de la Mare. *The Traveller.* 1946. Four lithographs by John Piper. In rare dust-jacket. **£20–30/$32–48**

2 Rex Whistler. Jonathan Swift. *Gulliver's Travels.* Cresset Press, 1930. 12 full-page coloured engravings by Rex Whistler. Limited to 195 copies. **£2,000–3,000/$3,200–4,800**

3 Frank Brangwyn. Christian Barman. *The Bridge.* 1926. 48 plates by Frank Brangwyn, 26 coloured. Limited to 125 copies with additional plates. **£150–250/$240–400**

4 Henry Moore. *The Shelter Sketch-book.* [1945]. 80 coloured plates by Henry Moore. In dust-jacket. **£60–100/$96–160.** 1967 limited edition of 180 copies with signed lithograph.

5 Cecil Beaton. *Indian Album.* 1945–6. 100 plates by Cecil Beaton. **£15–25/$24–40**

6 Bill Brandt. *Shadow of Light.* 1966. 128 plates by Bill Brandt. **£80–120/$128–192**

Humorous and Caricature

There is a whole genre of British artists who produce comic satire or social caricature, usually through simple line drawing, often initially working for magazines such as *Lilliput*, *Punch*, the *Daily Mail*, *Radio Times*, and *Private Eye*. Their books can be found easily and could form a rewarding and light-hearted collection. Two of the earliest practitioners were H.M. Bateman and Max Beerbohm. Nicholas Bentley established his reputation as an artist with Hilaire Belloc's *New Cautionary Tales* (1930), one of his earliest commissions. He also provided drawings for the first illustrated edition of T.S. Eliot's *Old Possum's Book of Practical Cats* (1940). His witty and yet simple drawings were stylish and full of social or humorous comment and observation. He also wrote and illustrated his own books, such as *Die? I Thought I'd Laugh* (1936).

David Low was born in New Zealand in 1891. Fond of early English comics and caricatures, he came to England in 1919 at the invitation of the *London Star* for whom he had been working as a political cartoonist. He joined the *Evening Standard* and began his attacks on Hitler as early as 1933. Passionate about democracy and politics, he produced his best work during the War and helped shape public opinion. He invented the pompous "Colonel Blimp", who became a national figure. He illustrated many books, including H.G. Well's *The Autocracy of Mr. Parham* (1930) and *Low's War Cartoons* (1941).

Bentley and Low were both superb draughtsmen working mainly in pen and ink, as did Osbert Lancaster, but Lancaster, born in 1908, was influenced by Edward Bawden and Eric Ravilious and also produced much fine colour work. He worked for the Curwen Press and London Transport, designing posters and decorations, but will be best remembered for his humorous cartoons and book work. His lifelong interest in architecture, the stage and ballet is often apparent in his work. He has illustrated a diverse range of works, from C.N. Parkinson's *Parkinson's Law for the Pursuit of Progress* (1958), to his own *The Life and Times of Maudie Littlehampton* (1982).

More recently Ronald Searle, Gerald Scarfe, and Ralph Steadman have continued this tradition, although much of Steadman's work is rather bleak. Executed in pen and ink, it is often embellished with red, or in bold and striking full colour. He was voted Illustrator of the Year by the American Institute of Graphic Art in 1977 and has won many other awards. His work ranges from *Alice's Adventures Underground* (1967) to Hunter S. Thompson's *Fear and Loathing in Las Vegas* (1971). His own substantial body of work includes *I, Leonardo* (1983).

Mervyn Peake worked in pen and Indian ink to create his macabre and atmospheric illustrations. His "Gormenghast" trilogy gained him a cult following, but he has also provided fine illustrations for *The Hunting of the Snark* (1941) and *Treasure Island* (1949).

1 Osbert Lancaster. *The Littlehampton Bequest.* 1973. Numerous illustrations by Osbert Lancaster. **£8–10/$12–16**. Also limited signed edition of 75 copies.

2 Mervyn Peake. Robert Louis Stevenson. *Treasure Island.* 1949. 42 illustrations by Mervyn Peake. **£100–150/$160–240**

3 Ronald Searle. Alex Atkinson. *Escape from the Amazon.* 1964. Numerous illustrations by Ronald Searle. **£15–20/$24–32**

Contemporary Illustration

The cult following generated by Mervyn Peake's fascination with the fantastical is also a feature of science-fiction books and book illustration. Artists such as Chris Foss, Jim Burns, Mark Salwoski, and John Harris who have worked on films and designed the bright and often rather lurid covers of contemporary science-fiction literature, have generated a whole army of devotees in England and the US.

From the 1960s through to the 1990s, avant-garde and pop artists such as David Hockney, Gilbert and George, Andy Warhol, Patrick Caulfield, Jim Dine, and Tom Phillips have been involved in producing occasional illustrated books for the expensive limited-edition market. These are often portfolios of prints with text rather than books with illustrations, but they can be a good way to acquire original art from these major contemporary artists. David Hockney has produced etchings for C.P. Cavafy's *14 Poems* (1967), for the Grimm brothers' *Six Tales* (1970) and, more reasonably priced, a collaborative effort with Stephen Spender, *China Diary* (1982).

Andy Warhol's *The Index Book* (New York, 1967) is a key Pop Art book and also a pop-up book with several attachments inside, which have often perished over the years. *The Philosophy of Andy Warhol (From A to B and Back Again)* (New York) was published in 1975 and is often found embellished with an original signed drawing of the famous Campbell's soup can. Jim Dine has produced some extraordinarily complex books in which the illustrations are often multi-media, a combination of etching, sculpture, and paper making. *His Temple of Flora* (San Francisco, 1984) contains dry-point floral engravings. All his works are expensive and produced in very small limitations.

There are many talented illustrators and artists working in the book world today, but much of their work is published by the contemporary private presses (see pages 142–3) or as illustrations for children's books. It is the latter market that has enabled many artists to make a living within the book world.

1 Ralph Steadman. Roald Dahl. *The Roald Dahl Treasury.* 1997. Numerous illustrations by Ralph Steadman, Quentin Blake and others. **£10–15/$16–24**

2 John Harris. Poul Anderson. *The Corridors of Time.* 1985. Dust-jacket design by John Harris. **£15–20/$24–32**

3 David Hockney. *Cameraworks.* 1984. Numerous coloured plates by David Hockney. **£30–40/$48–64**

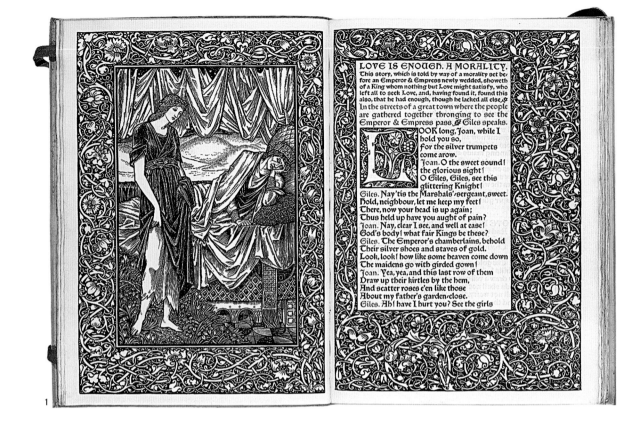

1

Fine Printing and Typography

Private Presses

On 15 November 1888, Emery Walker delivered a lecture at the Arts and Crafts Exhibition in London that raised the issue of new type design. Present was William Morris, whose eye was always set on the earliest years of printing, the second half of the 15th century, because he saw in those earliest books some of the finest ever made. In a period of industrialization and rapid spread of literacy, in which books were printed simply to be read with little thought for their appearance, he wished to recreate those past standards and set out with his press, the Kelmscott Press, to prove it could be done. Although his books have a medieval look, the principles behind the Press were always to produce books of finest quality, made with the best paper, ink, binding, type, illustration, and design avail-

able. It is these principles, rather than the style of his books, that have made Morris so important and influential throughout the 20th century; indeed he is regarded as the founder of modern book design and production. His fundamental belief that each opening spread of a book should be designed as one unit is still too often ignored. The pages of his Kelmscott Press books are bursting with decoration, but the decorative borders and initials, the text and the illustrations form one harmonious spread over each double page.

William Morris chose to have his earliest books printed by the Chiswick Press. The Press had been inherited by Charles Whittingham in the mid-19th century; both he and the publisher William Pickering had concentrated on good design and printing, and Whittingham had

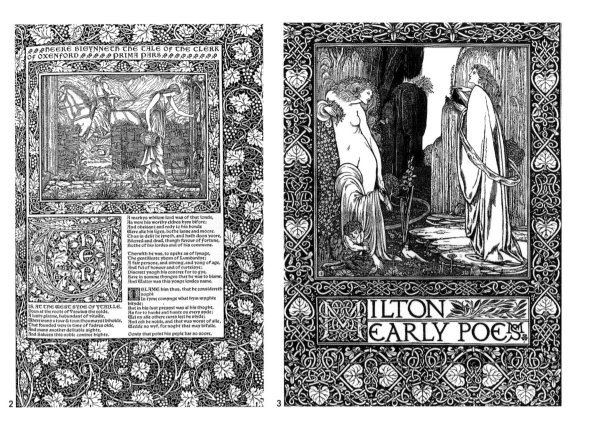

2   3

revived the use of the Caslon type-face for his books. They were, however, the sole practitioners of fine printing during the 19th century. Following Emery Walker's lecture, William Morris began designing his own type-face, the Golden type; the punches were cut and completed by the end of 1890 and the first trial page was pulled in January 1891. The first book off the press was William Morris' own *The Story of the Glittering Plain* (1891), issued in an edition of six copies printed on vellum and 200 on paper. Bound in limp vellum with uncut edges to the paper and leather ties, the book was decorated simply with an ornamental woodcut border to the title page and initials. All but two of the vellum copies sold immediately, as did 180 of the 200 paper copies. Morris had asked Walter Crane to provide illustrations but these were slow in coming, and had to wait for a later printing in 1894. In the short period between 1891 and 1898, the Kelmscott Press issued 53 books, the last few titles after Morris' death in 1896.

Unlike many of the later private presses, William Morris commissioned new texts, among them prose romances, volumes of verse, Morris' own stories, early chronicles and French tales. Each was decorated with ornamental woodcut borders and initials, printed from

1 Kelmscott Press. William Morris. *Love is Enough*. 1898. Woodcut borders and initials, wood-engraved illustrations after Edward Burne-Jones. Limited to 300 copies. **£2,500–3,000/ $4,000–4,800**. Also eight copies on vellum.

2 Kelmscott Press. Geoffrey Chaucer. *The Works*. 1896. Woodcut borders and initials, wood-engraved illustrations after Edward Burne-Jones. Limited to 425 copies. **£20,000–30,000/ $32,000–48,000**. Also 13 copies on vellum.

3 Vale Press. John Milton. *Early Poems*. 1896. Wood-engraved borders, initials and illustrations by Charles Ricketts. Limited to 310 copies. **£300–400/$480–640**

metal impressions taken of the woodblocks, and several contained wood-engraved illustrations printed from drawings by Burne-Jones, Walter Crane, Charles Gere, Arthur Gaskin, or Charles Fairfax Murray. The books were printed on thick hand-made paper or vellum in one of three type-faces designed by Morris (Golden Legend, Troy or Chaucer), and bound in limp vellum with silk ties or holland-backed boards. They were expensive to produce, and whereas the paper copies were meant for all those interested in good design and printing, Morris always intended a few copies of each title to be grand

133

examples for a more exclusive market. These vellum copies today remain at the pinnacle of the private press market. Values have risen steeply over the past few years but there is still a wide price range, from the smaller, unillustrated books to the volumes with wood-engraved illustrations after Burne-Jones. The most valuable is the Kelmscott Chaucer. The largest of the Kelmscott books (41.25cm/16.5in by 26.88cm/10.75in), it was one of Morris' last, and he spent four years planning and printing it. From the very first, the book was regarded as one of the finest ever to be produced and has long since been considered a landmark in printing and book production. The ordinary paper copy (issued in an edition of 425) cost £20 on publication, a vast sum, and today regularly commands in excess of £20,000/$30,000 at auction. Thirteen copies were on vellum, and 48 were issued in a special white pigskin binding designed by Morris, of which three were on vellum. These special bindings are eagerly sought-after. Another area for the collector to consider is the ephemera generated by the Press, which ranges from trial pages for works never published, such as Froissart's *Chronicles* (1896–7), to invitations and leaflets, book lists, and menus.

In 1896 Charles Ricketts printed John Milton's *Early Poems*, the first book from the Vale Press. Ricketts had been interested in type design and the reform of book production for ten years by this date and Morris' achievements encouraged him in his own productions. He produced a fine series of books, smaller in scale than the Kelmscott editions, and set in Ricketts' own Vale type. They were decorated with fine initial letters and occasional borders, as well as with wood-engraved illustrations by Ricketts himself and Charles Shannon.

The Vale Press books are not as grand or as perfectly finished as those from other presses, but they are important in the history of the private press movement in that Ricketts, like Morris, was much more than simply a maker of books. He was a designer and artist working in several media as well as a printer. He could draw borders and decorations with skill and as an artist he developed his own style. Unlike the Kelmscott books the illustrations on wood in the Vale Press books were actually cut by the artist and not by a commercial engraver. He too was concerned with the book as a whole: type, decoration, and illustration were to be a unit, and production was to be carefully and skilfully handled. This is where the modern movement in printing begins, with the treatment of the book as an integral unit. The Vale Press books varied in subject-matter and included new works and older texts. One of its greatest achievements is the *Works of William Shakespeare* (1900–3), a 39-volume set that is often overlooked and can still be found very reasonably. The books were generally bound in decorative boards or white buckram, but special copies were issued in vellum with some

copies bound to commission with designs by Ricketts and T. Sturge Moore.

Lucien Pissarro's Eragny Press is also of interest, as he too cut his own illustrations directly on to the wood. Moving from France to London in about 1890, he became close friends with Ricketts and Shannon, and they encouraged each other in the use of original wood-engravings. The books are very French in feel, reproducing French texts (often classic children's tales such as Charles Perrault's *Deux contés de ma Mère L'Oye*, 1899), and volumes of verse by Christina Rossetti and John Keats. These were decorated with Pissarro's own wood-engravings, often printed in colours. With decorative initials and borders, use of gold and wood-engravings with an oriental look, the books are charming, light-hearted, and modern. The first was printed in 1894 and between then and 1914, 31 titles were issued. Every sheet produced by the Vale and Eragny presses was set and pulled by hand by the proprietor and the cost was high, so the editions were tiny (around 200 copies). The bibliographer Colin Franklin states, "These two presses, Vale and Eragny, stand together, private and self-contained, with an integrity which stretches even further than the great three, Kelmscott, Doves and Ashendene; for each was largely the work of one man from start to finish, including the engraving of decorations and illustrations."

The Vale and Eragny books were undoubtedly forward-looking, displaying an awareness of Art Nouveau and the importance of the aesthetic. In contrast, C.R. Ashbee founded the Essex House Press as part of the Guild of Handicrafts at Chipping Camden, Gloucestershire, in 1898 with the aim of continuing the historical traditions of William Morris. Charming though the books are, they are mostly of interest to collectors in relation to the Arts and Crafts Movement, which produced fine silver, furniture, and textiles.

Morris's revival of printing was very much in keeping with the Guild's beliefs and Ashbee produced a series of books in his style. Ashbee's statement of the Guild's aims is relevant to his books: "The Arts and Crafts movement began with the object of making useful things, of making them well and of making them beautiful; goodness and beauty were to the leaders of the movement synonymous terms." Ashbee bought two of the Albion printing presses Morris had used and several of the compositors and wood-engravers joined the press. Charles Whittingham's Caslon type was employed in several of the books. The books issued by the Press until its closure in 1909 ranged from Ashbee's own works and architectural books to *The Prayer Book of King Edward VII* and *The Essex House Song Book* (both 1903). One of its most successful series was its "Great Poems", 14 charming small books printed on vellum with illustrations coloured by hand and sometimes heightened with gold. The Guild operated a bindery run

4 Eragny Press. Jules Laforgue. *Moralités Legendaires.* 1897. Wood-engraved borders, initials and illustrations by Lucien Pissarro. Limited to 220 copies. **£400–600/$640–960**

5 Ashendene Press. Longus. *Les Amours Pastorales de Daphnis et Chloë.* 1933. Wood-engraved illustrations by Gwen Raverat, blue initials by Grail Hewitt. Limited to 290 copies. **£800–1,200/$1,280–1,920**. Also 20 on vellum.

6 Ashendene Press. *The Wisdom of Jesus, the Son of Sirach, commonly called Ecclesiasticus.* 1932. Initials in red, blue, and green by Grail Hewitt and others. Limited to 328 copies. **£1,000–1,500/$1,600–2,400**. Also 25 on vellum.

by Miss A. Powell which produced some fine bindings, many originated by Douglas Cockerell in his early days (see the next chapter).

Two other English presses that produced books before World War I are considered to be as great, or, by many, greater than the Kelmscott Press: the Ashendene and the Doves presses. The Ashendene Press was the personal enterprise of St John Hornby, a director of W.H. Smith, where part of his apprenticeship was spent in the printing-works. The first book, J. Hornby's *Journal*, was printed in 1895, and the first publications were printed entirely for St. John Hornby's own use in editions of 16 to 50 copies. The first title printed for sale was *Aucassin and Nicolette* (1900), in an edition of 40 copies, followed by a larger-scale edition (240 copies) of *I Fioretti* by St Francis of Assisi in 1901. These early pieces were produced at home in a summer-house and are fine examples of printing.

St John Hornby was a master craftsman in his own right: he could design and print beautiful books with no outside influence. One of the elements of a private press is that of the printer's choice, which can be made without deference to public taste, and this was present in all of the Ashendene books. St John Hornby was in the fortunate position of not needing to make a profit (unlike Pissarro, who had to live off his father, the painter Camille) and had

no financial restrictions. Apparently the Press eventually just about covered its costs, which was remarkable considering the scale of the books. These books ranged from the few small books printed in the early days (mostly personal pieces, now exceptionally rare) to large folio volumes of classical texts such as Dante's *Tutte le Opera* (1909), Cervantes' *Don Quixote* (1927–8), and *Thucydides* (1930), to the beautiful *The Wisdom of Jesus, the Son of Sirach, commonly called Ecclesiasticus* (1932), Thomas Malory's *The Nobel and Joyous Book entytled Le Morte d'Arthur* (1913), and Longus' *Les Amours Pastorales de Daphnis et Chloë* (1933).

The Ashendene Press books are completely unlike those issued by the earlier presses. St John Hornby's pages were simple, clean, and elegant. Initially using the Fell type lent him by Horace Hart of the Oxford University Press, he later employed two types designed for him by Emery Walker and Sydney Cockerell in 1902, the Subaico and Ptolemy types. Wood-engraved illustration was occasionally used, supplied by Gwen Raverat, Charles Gere, and others, but the decoration for which the Press is most renowned is its calligraphy. Initials were cut in wood by Eric Gill, his first book commission being the Ashendene Sir Thomas More's *Utopia* (1906), and others were supplied by hand or cut in wood and printed in coloured inks by Graily Hewitt, Ida Henstock, and Louise Powell. Dante's *Lo Inferno* (1902) was the first book from the Press to have initials supplied by hand, added by Graily Hewitt in coloured inks. The Ashendene Press was the longest surviving of these early presses, its last book being issued in 1935.

The Doves Press was formed in 1901 by T.J. Cobden-Sanderson and Emery Walker, and its clear, pure and restrained design can be seen to have a direct influence on modern book production. Extraordinarily, nearly all of its books were the same size, printed in the same format and type (adapted by Emery Walker from Jenson's Pliny). Some collectors may find this initially rather dull, but they are beautiful books to handle and to read. They appear to be the complete antithesis of both William Morris' medievalist approach and the Art Nouveau conception of a book as a work of decoration, not merely a neutral vehicle for the text, and yet it was the wider principles of both that lay behind Cobden-Sanderson's beliefs. Edward Johnston contributed the only decoration in the books, calligraphic initials cut in wood and printed in red, green, blue or gold, or in a few special books, added by hand. Another aspect that sets the Press apart is its partnership with the Doves Bindery. The books were issued in

SONNET I

FROM FAIREST CREATVRES WE DESIRE
INCREASE,
THAT THEREBY BEAVTIES ROSE MIGHT
NEVER DIE,
BVT AS THE RIPER SHOVLD BY TIME
DECEASE,
HIS TENDER HEIRE MIGHT BEARE HIS
MEMORY:
BVT THOV CONTRACTED TO THINE OWNE
BRIGHT EYES,
FEED'ST THY LIGHTS FLAME WITH SELFE
SVBSTANTIALL FEWELL,
MAKING A FAMINE WHERE ABOVNDANCE
LIES,
THY SELFE THY FOE, TO THY SWEET SELFE
TOO CRVELL:
THOV THAT ART NOW THE WORLDS
FRESH ORNAMENT,
AND ONLY HERAVLD TO THE GAVDY
SPRING,
WITHIN THINE OWNE BVD BVRIEST THY
CONTENT,
AND TENDER CHORLE MAKST WAST
IN NIGGARDING:
PITTY THE WORLD, OR ELSE THIS
GLVTTON BE,
TO EATE THE WORLDS DVE, BY THE GRAVE
AND THEE.

6

7 Doves Press. William Shakespeare. *Sonnets.* 1909. Three initials by Noel Rooke and Eric Gill after Edward Johnston. Limited to 265 copies, of which this is one of 15 on vellum.
£2,500–3,500/$4,000–5,600

standard bindings of limp vellum, or niger morocco with simple linear gilt tooling. The Bindery, operated under Cobden-Sanderson, who designed and made the early bindings but later simply drew the designs, also issued elaborate bindings to commission (see the next chapter). Emery Walker and Cobden-Sanderson quarrelled and parted ways in 1909 and the later books are the work of Cobden-Sanderson alone. The Doves Press books include plays by Shakespeare, works by Goethe, Ralph Waldo Emerson, Robert Browning, and John Ruskin, and its greatest achievement, *The English Bible*, published as five volumes (1903–5).

Oxford, Wales, and Waltham St Lawrence were the homes of the three most important presses operating in Britain during the two wars. The Shakespeare Head Press was set up in 1904 by A.H. Bullen with the aim of printing the complete works of Shakespeare in Stratford on Avon. This accomplished, he produced several other works before his death in 1920 when the press was bought by the Oxford bookseller and publisher Basil Blackwell. Bernard Newdigate was taken on as the designer and between 1921 and 1941 many fine works were produced, notably by Smollett, Defoe, Fielding, and the Brontës, as well as their three major works, Froissart, Spenser, and Chaucer. The Press also produced works on contemporary Gloucestershire craftsmen F.L. Griggs and Ernest Gimson. Characterized by clean, simple design, sometimes with

calligraphic ornamentation, the books are pleasant to read and handle today, although they are often overlooked by collectors. Perhaps not as well known, they can be harder to find than those from other presses.

Gwendolin and Margaret Davies, two unmarried sisters living in a grand mock-Tudor house in the wilds of Montgomeryshire, opened their home to artists and craftsmen so they could live and work without commercial pressures. Musical and literary festivals were an integral part of this life and in 1924 the first book was printed and bound at the Gregynog Press. The press was unique in that the binding was an integral part of each book and every title was issued in a specially bound edition as well as the finely bound ordinary edition. Its output included Welsh literature, poetry, fables, essays, religious texts, and love songs, as well as numerous ephemeral pieces for the festivals. The earliest books were small, simple productions, decorated with woodcut initials and headpieces by R.A. Maynard and Horace Bray, and comprised Welsh texts and the work of poets such as George Herbert and Edward Thomas.

The finest books were illustrated with wood-engravings by the best artists of the period, including David Jones, Blair Hughes-Stanton, and Agnes Miller Parker. The first of these was *Llyfr y pregeth-wr* (1927), illustrated with wood-engravings by David Jones. Blair Hughes-Stanton produced his first book for the Press,

8

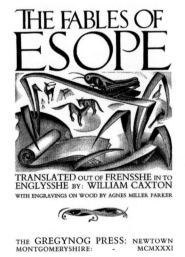

9

8 Shakespeare Head Press. Geoffrey Chaucer. *The Works.* 1928–9. Illustrations. Limited to 375 copies, of which this is one of 11 on vellum. **£7,000–9,000/$11,200–14,400**

9 Gregynog Press. Aesop. *Fables.* 1932. Wood-engraved illustrations by Agnes Miller Parker. Limited to 250 copies. **£2,000–3,000/$3,200–4,800**

10 Gregynog Press. *The Revelation of St. John the Divine.* 1933. Wood-engraved illustrations by Blair Hughes-Stanton. Limited to 250 copies on japon. **£1,000–1,500/$1,600–2,400**

10

Fine Printing and Typography

John Milton's *Comus*, in 1931, and in 1932 one of the masterpieces of the Press appeared, *Aesop's Fables*, with wood-engravings by Agnes Miller Parker. The books were set by hand, printed by machine, and featured the latest type-faces available from Monotype. This desire to use what was new and available, whether it was the best new type-faces or the best new artists, determined the quality of the books. Generally clean and simple, the text was often illuminated with coloured initials and sometimes refreshingly designed around the illustrations. It is the combination of these initials, wood-engraved illustrations and the simple but successful leather bindings of the ordinary editions and those designed, often by the artists, for the special editions, that makes these books particularly appealing to the collector.

The Golden Cockerel Press was the longest surviving press of the 20th century and produced the largest output: between 1921 and 1960 214 books were produced, with over 300 catalogues and prospectuses. There were three distinct periods of the Press; the earliest produced a few books that appear quite austere in comparison with the later productions. A.E. Coppard was a favoured author, and works by Thomas Browne, poems by Spenser, and translations of Latin works all appeared as simple,

unillustrated volumes bound in holland-backed boards. Harold Taylor, who had set up the Press, died in 1925 and Robert Gibbings took over. He ran the Press with his wife until 1933 and it was in these years that its most important productions appeared. From 1934 until 1960 Christopher Sandford took over and the Press became more of a publishing house producing fine books. Sandford designed the books and they were printed elsewhere, which kept their overheads low in troubled times.

From 1925 the Golden Cockerel books became distinctive through their use of the best wood-engravers, decorative bindings, and good paper and design. It was Robert Gibbings' relationship with Eric Gill and David Jones that pushed the Press to the forefront, and the books are an excellent way for the collector to acquire some of the best illustrated work of the 20th century. Its list of artists includes names such as Eric Gill, David Jones, John Nash, Gertrude Hermes, Eric Ravilious, John Buckland Wright, Blair Hughes-Stanton, Agnes Miller Parker, John Farleigh, Mark Severin, and Dorothea Braby. The most prolific illustrators were Robert Gibbings, Eric Gill, and John Buckland Wright.

From 1925 on, texts varied from religious to travel, mythical to contemporary, drama to cookery. Many of the books comprised early travel works reissued with new illustrations, such as Owen Chase's *The Wreck of the Whale-Ship Essex of Nantucket* (1935), or original pieces by T.E. Lawrence, St John Philby, and Gertrude Bell (including the latter's *The Arab War*, 1940). Editions were far larger than those from the earlier private presses, with 500 copies being quite a common print run, of which 50 would be specially bound. The books for which the Press is best known are those illustrated by David Jones and Eric Gill between 1925 and 1931. Jones provided wood-engravings for *The Chester Play of the Deluge* (1927) and *The Book of Jonah* (1926) and Gill illustrated and provided calligraphic initials for the masterpieces: Chaucer's *Troilus and Criseyde* (1927), *The Canterbury Tales* (1929–31), and *The Four Gospels* (1931). These three are the most expensive books, whereas other books can be found for quite modest sums. Gill's mastery of initials, decorative borders, and illustration, beautifully balanced with the text layout, is what makes them so impressive.

There are many other private presses from this period whose work warrants attention. Some names to look for include the Stanbrook Abbey Press, the Dropmore Press, the Cresset Press, and the Caradoc and Beaumont Presses.

11 Golden Cockerel Press. Geoffrey Chaucer. *The Canterbury Tales*. 4 volumes, 1929–31. Wood-engraved illustrations and borders by Eric Gill, initials in red, blue, and black. Limited to 485 copies. **£2,500–3,500/$4,000–5.600**. Also 15 on vellum.

Commercial Printing

The fine work produced by the private press movement encouraged commercial printers and publishers to adopt similar high standards. Periodicals began to appear on the subject, such as *The Imprint*, *Signature*, and *Fleuron*. Oliver Simon at the Curwen Press was producing fine commercial work, but it was Francis Meynell's Nonesuch Press that produced the best and most influential modern commercial work of this period. Founded in 1923, it was the first publishing house to use machines to produce "fine books". Meynell wished to reproduce the care and skill of the private press in a commercial environment, with "the set purpose of shaping the newest and most mechanical methods of production to the uses of fine book-printing. The Nonesuch method was to design its books to the last detail and to set specimen pages at its one-man 'laboratory press', sending these, or instructions based on them, for execution at any one of a dozen commercial printers." Although still limited, production was far greater and prices lower than those of the private presses, and the books were almost always oversubscribed before publication. This success led to other printers and publishers taking a new interest in the aesthetics of a book. Private press publications were never intended for the ordinary reader, indeed were often never read. Like William Pickering in the 19th century, Meynell wanted to produce attractive, inexpensive books meant for reading, but this time the public and trade were receptive and his influence was far-reaching. Geoffrey Keynes described Meynell in his introduction to the bibliography of the Press thus: "Artistic sensibility combined with practical skill to make him the most successful general book designer England has known."

Francis Meynell designed books using a variety of type-faces, while his wife Vera, with David Garnett, helped him choose and edit the texts. Between the publication of John Donne's *Love Poems* in 1923 and the last Nonesuch title in 1968, 140 books were issued. Publications include the great *Nonesuch Dickens*, 24 volumes with a further volume containing an original engraved plate for one of the illustrations (1937–8), the seven-volume *Works* of Shakespeare (1929–33), definitive editions of William Blake, editions of Dante, D.H. Lawrence, Isaac Walton, Homer, Darwin, Voltaire, Byron, and other works by John Donne. The printing was dispersed among several firms. Illustration was used, some of the most attractive appearing in the ten colour-stencilled books, of which several were stencilled at the Curwen Press: the first was Charles Perrault's *Mother Goose* (1925), and three were by E. McKnight Kauffer, *Anatomy of Melancholy* (1925), Benito *Cereno* (1926), and *Don Quixote* (1930). There were cheaper and unlimited series such as the Cygnets, for children, and "The Nonesuch Library" of prose, verse, lectures, and essays. In 1935 the *Nonesuch Century* was issued listing their first 100 books. These are generally the most sought-after titles today, although the attraction of the Press is that several of the smaller or more ephemeral books can still be

1 Golden Cockerel Press. *The Chester Play of the Deluge.* 1927. Wood-engraved illustrations by David Jones. Limited to 275 copies. **£600–800/$960–1,280**

2 Nonesuch Press. Bernard de Fontenelle. *A Plurality of Worlds.* 1929. Colour stencilled decorations by T.L. Poulton. Limited to 1,200 copies. **£50–70/$80–112**

3 Nonesuch Press. Richard Burton. *The Anatomy of Melancholy.* Two volumes, 1925. Illustrations by E. McKnight Kauffer. Limited to 790 copies. **£200–300/$320–480**

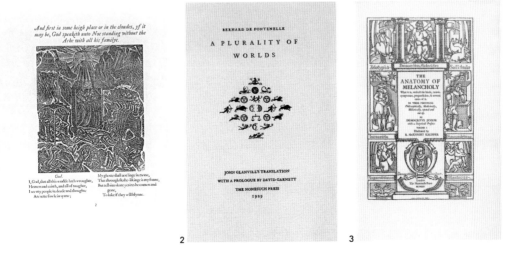

1

2

3

acquired quite cheaply. In 1936 Meynell sold the Press to the American George Macy, owner of the Limited Editions Club and Heritage Press, but continued as adviser and sometime designer until the Press closed. In 1981 the informative *A History of the Nonesuch Press* was published under the revived imprint by John Dreyfus.

In his early days Meynell had worked at his father's publishing firm, Burns & Oates, where he was trained by the great typographer Bernard Newdigate, and worked alongside one of the most influential typographers of the century: Stanley Morison. The two stimulated each other's interest in type-faces and ornament, and collaborated on several fine books at Burns & Oates and later at the Pelican Press. Morison's career is intricately bound up with the Monotype Corporation. In commercial printing, type-setting by hand had been superseded by mechanical setting on the American Linotype and Monotype machines (patented 1886 and 1887). The earliest types were simply copies of older type-faces. Morison and Meynell used the Monotype machines at the Pelican Press. After a period of upheaval in Morison's career he and Oliver Simon launched a journal of typography in 1922, *The Fleuron.* Simon edited numbers 1–4 and Morison 5–7. The same year Morison was appointed typographical adviser to the Monotype Corporation, where he devised a developmental plan of new type designs, education, and publicity. Monotype Garamond and Monotype Baskerville were two of the first types to be recut and were immediately successful. Morison commissioned Eric Gill to design the important Gill Sans

4 Stanley Morison. *Specimens of Monotype Times New Roman and its Related Series.* Lanston Monotype Corporation, circa 1935. Folding broadsheet. **£15–20/$24–32**

type and from the success of this in 1925 further new type was commissioned from a range of artists. He became adviser to the Cambridge University Press, designed the new type-face for *The Times* in 1932, became its typographical adviser and later editor of *The Times Literary Supplement* until his death in 1967. His classically based work has guided the most enlightened English and American printers and publishers ever since, and would make the basis for a fascinating collection. There are the books he designed or wrote (such as *The First Principles of Typography*, 1936, and *A Tally of Types*, 1953), volumes of *The Fleuron,* the printed ephemera and specimen sheets from the Monotype Corporation. There is a useful checklist of his writings by Tony Appleton.

Such a collection could be expanded to include Jan Tschichold, who worked on the Penguin books, and Berthold Wolpe who worked at Faber and Faber. These were the men who changed the face of European commercial printing and made good design and type-faces an integral part of modern book production. Working in the European tradition of Bauhaus, Dadaism, Futurism, De Stijl, and Constructivism, these typographers broke through the boundaries of that tradition. Herbert Spencer's excellent book *Pioneers of Modern Typography* is a good introduction to the New Typography formulated by Laszlo Moholy-Nagy and El Lissitsky and its influence throughout Europe and the US. Its more extreme theories were adhered to most closely on the Continent, but it undoubtedly influenced English and American typographers. As with Stanley Morison, one could look for books designed by these typographers or for their own writings.

American Printing

Although the best printing and book design during the first half of the 20th century is English, there have been some fine American typographers, and the private press has a long tradition in the US. Many of the early American presses were small and highly idiosyncratic.

Thomas B. Mosher of Portland, Maine, and Elbert Hubbard and the Roycrofters in Erie County produced books in the Arts and Crafts mould. Their books are interesting but slight, and do not command much interest or value today. More intriguing but little known is the Elston Press of New Rochelle. Its first book was *Sonnets from the Portuguese* (1900) and a further 15 appeared before 1902. Other small presses produced a variety of books, but the first of real interest is the Village Press founded in 1903 by Frederic W. Goudy, one of the greatest 20th-century American typographers. The few books they issued are worth seeking out: William Morris and Emery Walker's *Printing* (1903) is the first. The books were set by hand and bound by Goudy's wife, Bertha. Dard Hunter issued some fine books from his press in Ohio, many on paper-making, including *Primitive Papermaking* (1927) with specimens of papers inserted.

Much of the best American book design prior to 1950 was executed within commercial boundaries: Daniel B. Updike and the Merrymount Press; Bruce Rogers and the Riverside Press; George Macy and the Limited Editions Club; the Grabhorn Press; and William Edwin Rudge at the Mount Vernon Press in New York. Although both Rogers and Updike moved away from their early influences – William Morris and the Arts and Crafts Movement – their work remained retrospective. Updike achieved a reputation for outstanding typography and presswork, his most important book being *Printing Types* (1922). Rogers designed an edition of the *Holy Bible* for the Oxford University Press in 1935, which is considered one of the finest ever printed. A large volume, the typography was simple and clear with calligraphic opening initials and a recut Monotype Centaur type. By the end of the 1920s the influence of Rogers and Updike was spreading to other commercial printers. One of Rogers' greatest works was Stanley Morison's *Fra Luca de Pacioli of Borgo S. Sepolcro* (1933), printed at the University Press, Cambridge.

The Typophiles, an informal group who met and discussed their work in typography and printing in New York, began to issue a series of chapbooks in 1938 which forms a fine record of American printing. The first of these was *The Typophiles Whodunnit*.

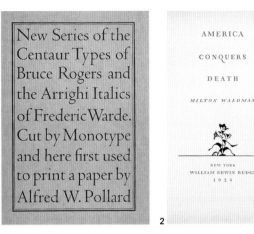

1 Bruce Rogers and Frederic Warde. A.W. Pollard. *New Series of the Centaur Types of Bruce Rogers and the Arrighi Italics of Frederic Warde Cut by Monotype*. 1929. **£15–20/$24–32**

2 William Edwin Rudge. Milton Waldman. *America Conquers Death*. New York, 1928. Limited to 500 copies. **£15–20/$24–32**

Limited Editions Club

The Limited Editions Club was set up by George Macy in 1929 with the aim of making the work of the best artists, printers, designers, and binders available to the public. Most importantly of all, the books were meant to be read. The first book was issued on 23 October, the day the American Stock Market collapsed, but as the economy fell, so membership grew, until the ceiling of 1,500 members was reached – membership ensured production was paid for in advance, and 1,500 was deemed the limit of each print-run. Texts included newly commissioned pieces as well as classic texts such as *Alice's Adventures in Wonderland*. The creators were often American, but also English and European. Two highlights most sought-after today are *Ulysses* illustrated by Matisse and *Lysistrata* illustrated by Picasso. The artists who worked on the books are diverse and include names such as Robert Motherwell, Henri Cartier-Bresson, Robert Mapplethorpe, Rockwell Kent, and Arthur Szyk. Designers included W.A. Dwiggins, Bruce Rogers, who worked on 12 of the books, and Francis Meynell of the Nonesuch Press, who designed 11. One of the most interesting works was *Great Expectations*, which had the "original" unhappy ending restored.

In 1956 Macy died and publications dwindled, to be revitalized upon new ownership in 1979. The Club is still producing fine books today. Most of the books can be acquired for very reasonable sums and make a fine introduction to the book arts of the 20th century.

Post-war Private Presses

The private press movement in both England and the US from the 1950s to the present day is inextricably linked with the practitioners of wood-engraving, lettering, and paper-making. Generally the books are issued in tiny editions and are designed either for distribution among friends or for limited sale. With a few exceptions, such as the Whittington and Rampant Lions, the presses are not full-time commercial operations.

In the US in Pennsylvania, Henry Morris experiments with books on paper-making and related subjects at his Bird and Bull Press. *The Bird and Bull Commonplace Book* (1971), for example, contains poems and light essays about paper-making, with specimens of various papers. John Fass, a fine typographer for the Harbor Press, produced extremely limited editions at his own Hammer Creek Press, including such esoteric works as *A Collection of Turtles* (1955), with illustrations by Fass, Valenti Angelo, and others. The Perishable Press in Wisconsin specializes in contemporary poetry, including Toby Olson's *Fishing: long poem* (1974), set by hand on paper made by the founders, Walter and Mary Hamady. The prolific wood-engraver Barry Moser has produced many fine books for his Pennyroyal Press, including *Alice's Adventures in Wonderland* (1982) and *The Adventures of Huckleberry Finn* (1985). Leonard Baskin's works are usually issued by his Gehenna Press, founded in 1942 in Northampton, Massachusetts. Working with wood-engravings and etchings, the artist and printer is one of the most important contemporary American illustrators. One of his major books is Ted Hughes' *Capriccio* (1990). Other presses worth watching out for include the Cheloniidae Press (Press of the Sea Turtle), the majority of whose books contain wood-engravings by Alan James Robinson, the Peter Pauper Press, and the Arion Press, which have published major work by Jim Dine including *The Apocalypse* (1982).

In England the most important presses from this period include the Whittington Press, the Rampant Lions Press, the Fleece Press, formed by the wood-engraver Simon Brett, the Gogmagog Press, established by Morris Cox in 1957 to print his own poetry, the Gwasg Gregynog, continuing the tradition of the Gregynog Press, and the Rocket Press. Will Carter, a fine calligrapher and letter-cutter, especially in stone and slate, formed the Rampant Lions Press around 1930, which in 1939 moved to Cambridge, its present home. Carter was joined by his son Sebastian in 1966. From 1960 on the Press printed several fine books for Douglas Cleverdon's Clover Hill Editions, including R.S. Thomas' *The Mountains*, illustrated by John Piper, and *The Story of Cupid and Pysche* (1974), the 43

hitherto unpublished illustrations by Burne-Jones engraved on wood, mostly by William Morris himself. Like all commercial private presses, jobbing printing is a necessity and their many fine examples of concert programmes, exhibition notices, and broadsides could form a good but inexpensive collection. The Press has printed the works of the wood-engravers George Mackley and Michael Rothenstein, John Piper's *India Love Poems* (1977), Christopher Fry's *Root and Sky* (1975), and works by Ted Hughes and Sylvia Plath, including *Earth Moon* (1975) and *Moortown Elegies* (1978).

The Whittington Press was founded in 1971 by John and Rosalind Randle, both initially working full-time in commercial publishing. Their first publication was Richard Kennedy's *A Boy at the Hogarth Press*, an account of the author's time working with Leonard and Virginia Woolf. Their range of books is huge, from grand, expensive volumes such as the reissue of William Nicholson's *An Alphabet* (1978), printed from the original woodblocks for the first time since the initial limited portfolio edition of 1898, to small, inexpensive children's books such as Juliet Caithness' *The Story of a Mouse of Immense Importance* (1973). The Randles worked closely with the wood-engraver Helmuth Weissenborn and his Acorn Press. He has become the most prolific illustrator of the Press and seven of his own Acorn Press books have been issued jointly with the Whittington. In its first decade 60 books were issued, all designed to be read and enjoyed but inspired by the Randles' love of fine printing, design, and illustration. They have won numerous prestigious awards.

Jonathan Stephenson set up the Rocket Press in 1981 in an old racing stable, with the aim of producing three or more books a year under his own imprint or for other publishers, but with high aesthetic appeal and good-quality letterpress text. Jonathan began printing while still at school; his first hardcover publication was for the Acorn Press *Shakespeare's Sonnets*, which was selected as one of the 30 best-produced books in 1982 and exhibited at the National Book League in 1983. It was Helmuth Weissenborn's last work. In England in the 1980s, there was a revival of interest in wood-engraving and this has created an environment in which the small private press can flourish.

There are numerous small presses operating today in England and the US. Membership of the Private Libraries Association, an international society of book collectors with an informative quarterly newsletter, will provide details of new private press books as they are issued, as well as furnishing access to useful and informative articles on the book world generally.

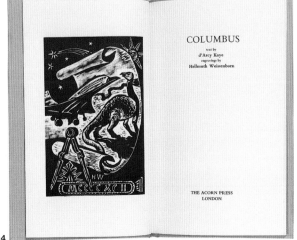

1 Perishable Press. Walter Hamady. *Travelli*. Mount Horeb. 1966.
Illustrations and typographical ephemera. Limited to 125 copies.
£600–800/$960–1,280

2 Chilmark Press. R.S. Thomas. *The Mountains*. New York, 1968.
Wood-engraved illustrations by Reynolds Stone after John Piper.
Limited to 240 copies. **£400–600/$640–960**

3 Old Stile Press. Willam Wordsworth. *Lines composed a few miles
above Tintern Abbey*. 2002. Illustrations from photograph by
N. McDowall. Limited to 150 copies. **£30–50/$48–80**

4 Acorn Press. D'Arcy Kaye. *Columbus*. 1978. Wood-engraved
illustrations by Helmuth Wiessenborn. Limited to 200 copies.
£20–30/$32–48

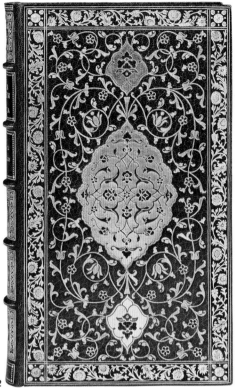

Binding

Joseph William Zaehnsdorf's *The Art of Bookbinding*, widely regarded as the first "modern" textbook on the art and craft of bookbinding, was published in 1880, and during the next ten years bookbinding underwent great and long-lasting changes, initiated in the main by T.J. Cobden-Sanderson. Joseph William Zaehnsdorf was the son of Joseph Zaehnsdorf, who in 1837 founded one of the oldest and longest surviving firms of craft bookbinders in London. The company merged with another distinguished firm, Sangorski & Sutcliffe, in 1988 to form SSZ Ltd, and today operates under the name of Sangorski & Sutcliffe.

Binding in the 19th century had flourished as a trade but the designs and techniques were still very traditional. The first change of approach came in the 1820s when the publisher William Pickering introduced the first cloth bindings, but these remained simple and unadorned until the latter part of the century. Collectors generally requested that their books be rebound in "retrospective" styles in the manner of the great early bibliophile Jean Grolier (16th century), or binders such as Samuel Mearne (17th century) or Roger Payne (18th century). The largest firms such as

Rivière and Zaehnsdorf were mostly concerned with such work and employed hundreds of people, each highly trained in one small aspect of the craft from which they did not deviate. Apprentices trained either as "forwarders" (those who did the structural work of the binding) or as "finishers" (those who undertook the decoration or tooling). In the largest firms there was a further sub-division of labour, and a book would go from the sewer to the forwarder, the edge-gilder, the headbander, the coverer, the finisher and finally to the assistant finisher, who would glue on the paper or cloth sides and paste down the endpapers. This system of apprenticeship and specialization ensured high standards throughout the flourishing trade. Standard styles were turned out, modified to fit the chosen book; rarely did the firms design their own tools or produce original designs. The materials were of the best quality but often cut very thin over heavy boards, the decoration executed with finely engraved tools, and the overall effect was elaborate. This sometimes resulted in designs that were gaudy and had little in keeping with the book itself.

In 1883, at the age of 43, T.J. Cobden-Sanderson, restless and lacking direction after practising for some

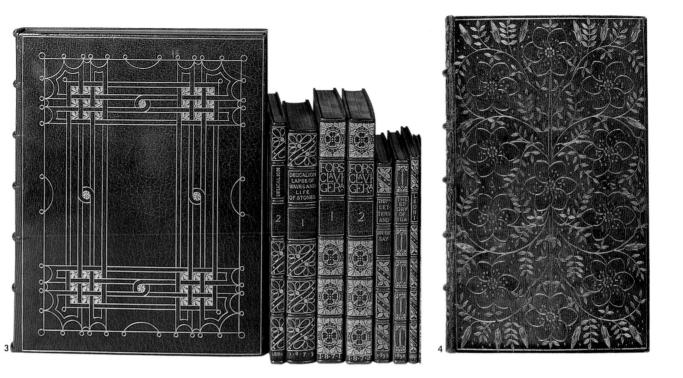

years at the Bar, took up the craft of bookbinding at the suggestion of William Morris' wife, Jane. He trained for six months at the bindery of Roger de Coverly, who himself had been apprenticed to Joseph Zaehnsdorf the elder, and six months later in 1884 set up on his own, carrying out all stages of each binding, except for the sewing, which he entrusted to his wife, Annie, and the edge-gilding, which was sent to the firm of Gwynn.

In 1893 he established the Doves Press, employed apprentices and ceased executing the bindings himself, simply creating designs for others to fashion until his death in 1922. From the beginning he was influenced by William Morris and the beliefs of the burgeoning Arts and Crafts Movement. His aim was to create fresh, non-derivative designs and to return to the basics of structure, rejecting many of the slack practices that had crept into the trade, such as the attachment of false raised bands to hollow backs made with low-quality waste paper. The task that he faced should not be underestimated. He was an intellectual trying to alter tried and trusted methods in a trade highly regulated and dominated by the apprentice system. "Non-trade" (i.e. non-apprenticed) binders

1 Zaehnsdorf. Edward Fitzgerald. *Rubaiyat of Omar Khayyam*. 1896. Olive-green morocco, covers elaborately gilt with floral and foliate decoration. **£500–700/$800–1,120**

2 Rivière. W.S. Gilbert. *The Bab Ballads*. Two volumes, 1869. Green morocco elaborately tooled in gilt with tan and crimson morocco floral onlays. **£4,000–6,000/$6,400–9,600**

3 Doves Bindery. John Ruskin. *The Works*. 47 volumes. 1862–99. Each bound in olive-green morocco tooled in gilt dated 19-CS-01 to 19-CS-07. **£12,000–16,000/$19,200–25,600**

4 Douglas Cockerell. *A Lamartine*. Graziella. Paris, 1888. Dark brown morocco with overall floral and foliate design tooled in gilt. **£600–800/$960–1,280**. One of the earliest bindings executed by Cockerell after joining Cobden-Sanderson at Hammersmith.

were regarded as amateurs by many, even as late as the middle of the 20th century, even though they were highly skilled and talented, and able to earn a living through their craft. T.J. Cobden-Sanderson wished to improve the forwarding of a book, but he also wanted to educate binders and encourage them to use the best materials possible, to design new patterns for tooling, and, where necessary, make their own tools (as he did). He believed the lettering should be beautiful and that careful attention should be paid to size, legibility, and spacing. Cobden-Sanderson's early designs were predominantly floral and leafy, clearly influenced by Morris. Morris himself had designed four floral tools for binding around 1870 which were used on a red morocco binding for a manuscript of *The Rubaiyat of Omar Khayyam* written and illuminated by him. These tools were subsequently lost. The bindings designed for the Doves Press books were some of the most modern to date, being simple and uncluttered, decorated with linear tooling, fine lettering, simple stylized floral tools (if any) and embracing the grain of the leather. Although Cobden-Sanderson had little impact on trade binding, he was the first "non-trade" binder and soon attracted many followers. This movement grew slowly, but steadily, throughout the 20th century and today the majority of hand-bookbinders are non-trade and his methods and principles are still followed.

Cobden-Sanderson employed Douglas Cockerell as his apprentice at the newly established Doves Bindery in 1893. After only four years he began teaching bookbinding at the newly formed Central School of Arts and Crafts. The following year, 1898, he set up on his own with two of his students, Francis Sangorski and George Sutcliffe, and in 1901 wrote the most popular bookbinding manual ever published, *Bookbinding and the Care of Books*, which remains in print today. He was director of the W.H. Smith bindery from 1905 to 1915 and in 1924 set up the Cockerell Bindery with his son Sydney, which continued in existence almost until the end of the 20th century. Douglas Cockerell's style is quite distinctive – Celtic-influenced, interlaced, and floral – and the W.H. Smith bindery books from this period, many to be found on Ashendene Press books, reflect this. Although doing little to encourage modern design, he was extremely influential and important in the transition of binding from the 19th century to the modern day by creating his own designs and tools, encouraging binders to create and not simply work with copies or pastiches of earlier designs, and in perpetuating and bringing to several new generations of binders the principles and methods of his teacher, Cobden-Sanderson.

Cobden-Sanderson gave a series of public lectures on bookbinding in 1888, 1889, and 1894. Women flocked to these lectures and amateur classes sprang up all over the country, the most important held at the Central School of Arts and Crafts. Sarah Prideaux had taken lessons in 1888 from Joseph Zaehnsdorf and from Gruel in Paris, and later gave lessons to women, the last of whom was Katharine Adams. She was the most competent of the women binding at this time; she also wrote several influential books, including *An Historical Sketch of Bookbinding* (1893) and *Modern Bookbinding* (1906). Her work was characterized

by simple borders and frames containing small dots or circles, with the occasional large floral tool. These were simple, elegant designs which complemented the fine leathers she used. She stopped binding in 1904.

In 1898 there was an exhibition of bindings executed by women at the bookseller Frank Karslake's shop in Charing Cross Road. The bindings were entered by many social unions, art guilds, and schools, and later that year these organizations were amalgamated into the Guild of Women-Binders. There was a male counterpart, the Hampstead Bindery, also established under the auspices of Frank Karslake. Both organizations were heavily influenced by the Art Nouveau movement sweeping Britain at the time with its ethics of decoration, and also by the interest shown in painting, embossing, and modelling leather. They were wound up around 1904.

The Art Nouveau movement and its emphasis on flowing, asymmetrical decoration began to influence the cloth bindings issued by several of the most enlightened publishers. The period from 1883 to the end of World War I saw some remarkable decorative commercial cloth bindings, often designed by the author or artist of the work and simply yet elegantly tooled in gilt. Publishers such as J.M. Dent, John Lane, and Blackie and Son commissioned these bindings, encouraged by the public reception of Art Nouveau, its oriental influences and reaction against the rigid symmetry and fussiness of Victorian design. Dante Gabriel Rossetti had been an early exponent of simple, elegant bindings in the 1860s with designs for his sister's *Goblin Market* (1862), but it was with the publication of Arthur Heygate MacMurdo's design for *Wren's City Churches* (1883) that Art Nouveau made its presence felt.

Laurence Housman designed fine bindings, usually gilt tooling on green cloth, for all his books, including *Goblin Market* (1893), and Aubrey Beardsley designed remarkable, fluid covers for his edition of Malory's *Le Morte d'Arthur* (1893–4), as well as for most of his other works. Charles Ricketts was a prolific designer both of commercial cloth bindings, such as Oscar Wilde's *The Sphinx* (1894), and of fine leather bindings for his Vale Press books. Thomas Sturge Moore also worked on designs for the Vale Press books and both he and Ricketts had a great influence on Sybil Pye, the first really modern craft binder.

Sybil Pye was entirely self-taught and began binding in 1906. Her early work was in the style of Ricketts and she used several of his tools before she progressed to fine panelled and inlaid abstract work, sometimes in vellum and one-colour leather, at other times using many different coloured leathers. Her work is often referred to as "Cubist", appearing at the time of Picasso's Cubist paintings, but was inspired by early Islamic bindings and architectural motifs. Sybil Pye was the forerunner of post-World War II

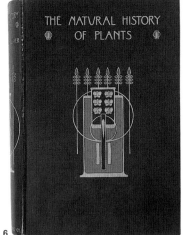

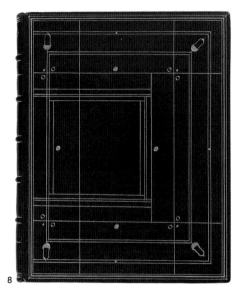

5 Hampstead Bindery. Thomas Campbell. *The Poetical Works.*
1837. Brown crushed morocco with coloured inlays and gilt tooling,
vellum liner gilt. **£1,000–1,500/$1,600–2,400**

6 Talwin Morris for Blackie & Son. F.W. Oliver. *The Natural History
of Plants.* Two volumes, 1904. Original blue cloth gilt. **£30–40/$48–64**

7 Sybil Pye. Alfred, Lord Tennyson. *Poems.* 1859. Illustrations by
Rossetti and others. Dark green morocco with abstract geometrical
design of onlaid coloured morocco tooled in gilt. 1949.
£2,000–3,000/$3,200–4,800

8 Charles Ricketts. Percy Bysshe Shelley. *Lyrical Poems.* 1898.
Contemporary red morocco gilt. **£4,000–6,000/$6,400–9,600**

9 Sangorski & Sutcliffe. James Thomson. *The Seasons.* 1842.
Pictorial onlaid and jewelled brown morocco, richly tooled in gilt.
£8,000–12,000/$12,800–19,200

10 Jessie M. King for Cedric Chivers. Thomas Lodge. *The Story
of Rosalynde.* 1902. Limited to 30 copies on japon. Contemporary
pictorial vellum decorated in ink and mother-of-pearl inlay by Jessie
M. King. **£4,000–6,000/$6,400–9,600**

expressive binding design, working in the manner of her great French contemporary, Pierre Legrain.

Her contemporary, Katharine Adams, set up on her own around the same time, having trained under Sarah Prideaux and Douglas Cockerell. Her first commission was from William Morris' wife Sarah, and she was encouraged by Emery Walker, C.H. St John Hornby, and Sydney Cockerell to bind for the most important collectors of books and manuscripts of the day, designing and cutting her own tools. Her work is noticeable for its delicacy and in particular her skill with pointille work, but it remains firmly rooted in the tradition of Cobden-Sanderson and Cockerell.

Francis Sangorski and George Sutcliffe had been apprenticed by their parents to rival binders before attending Douglas Cockerell's classes at the Central School of Arts and Crafts in 1897. In 1899 Douglas Cockerell offered them places in his bindery with Sutcliffe as finisher and Sangorski as forwarder, but was forced to make them redundant in 1901, whereupon they set up on their own. Skilled craftsmen and highly competitive, Sangorski & Sutcliffe gained a reputation for their lavish work, in particular for their use of coloured leathers, onlaid semi-precious stones and jewels, oriental motifs and highly elaborate gold tooling. Francis' brother Alberto and George's brother Alfred were renowned calligraphers and produced elaborate illuminated manuscripts for which Sangorski & Sutcliffe and, from 1912, Rivière executed bindings.

The first jewelled binding was commissioned in 1905 for a copy of *Epithalamion and Amoretti*. A census of these jewelled bindings executed between then and 1939 by Sangorski & Sutcliffe or their rivals Rivière was made by Miriam Wieder Elkind in 1975 (updated to 1985), which listed 105 such bindings. Sangorski & Sutcliffe were especially fascinated by the peacock and produced several jewelled peacock bindings, usually for *The Rubaiyat of Omar Khayyam*. The greatest of these bindings, known simply as the "Great Omar", was commissioned in 1912 by a wealthy American client and contained 1,050 jewels. Upon completion of the work the magnificent book was sent to the US on the *Titanic*. It went down with the ship and was never recovered. It is known today only by photographs and legend. A copy was made but that, too, was destroyed in World War II. A third copy was completed in 1989 and rests at the British Library. While the finest of these bindings on an illuminated manuscript by William Morris and Edward Burne-Jones may be worth £2 million, the collector can acquire a simple jewelled binding on an ordinary printed book for a few thousand pounds.

Elaborate decoration on bindings was often executed by women who were first and foremost artists. Leather modelling was often practised by the Guild of Women Binders, and Cedric Chivers of Bath also employed a number of women to do this. This firm is best known, however, for its series of painted "vellucent" bindings. The technique of painting under transparent vellum had been patented by Edwards of Halifax in 1785, but its popularity was short-lived. At the beginning of the 20th century Cedric Chivers revived the method, but instead of painting the underneath of the vellum, he painted the paper that lined the vellum. Several of the books were bound entirely in vellum, whereas others were bound in leather with painted vellum panels inlaid in the covers. The artist Jessie M. King designed and painted some of the finest bindings of these for Cedric Chivers.

Miss C.B. Currie was employed by the London bookselling firm of Sotheran to paint miniature watercolours to be inlaid in special leather bindings with elaborate gold-tooling executed by Rivière & Son. The first time the technique appears to have been used was in 1909 on an edition of G.C. Williamson's *Richard Cosway*. These bindings became known as "Cosway Bindings" and from 1912 until her death in 1940 the miniatures were usually attributed to Miss Currie. Those commissioned by Sotheran's and bearing a printed certificate are known as "Certified Cosway", while other examples bound by Riviere are known as "Cosway" bindings. Later examples commissioned by Bayntun & Rivière, formed when the Bath firm of Bayntun took over Rivière in 1939, and by Sangorski & Sutcliffe, are known as "Cosway style" bindings.

After World War I and the ensuing economic depression, hand-bookbinding went into a decline. Many of the practitioners had died or retired, and decorative commercial cloth binding was replaced by the decorative or pictorial dust jacket for which many of the best artists of the day provided designs (see Chapter 3). The vogue among collectors was for "original condition" and there were few commissions for rebinding. Books issued from the private presses tended to be bound in simple vellum, niger morocco or decorative boards. One exception to this was the Gregynog Press (see Chapter 4) whose bindery, run by George Fisher, was an integral part of the Press. George Fisher had trained as a finisher at the Central School of Arts and Crafts under Douglas Cockerell and was apprenticed to Rivière & Son. Attempting to set up on his own he was eventually employed, at the suggestion of Douglas Cockerell, to run the Gregynog Bindery in 1924. The Bindery had always produced fine bindings for the Press books but it was not until Fisher took over that the tradition of issuing a very small number of copies of each title in a special binding was established. Several of these bindings were designed by Fisher himself, but the best were by Blair Hughes-Stanton and William MacCance. When the Press closed in 1940 Fisher remained at the bindery for another four years, completing these special bindings.

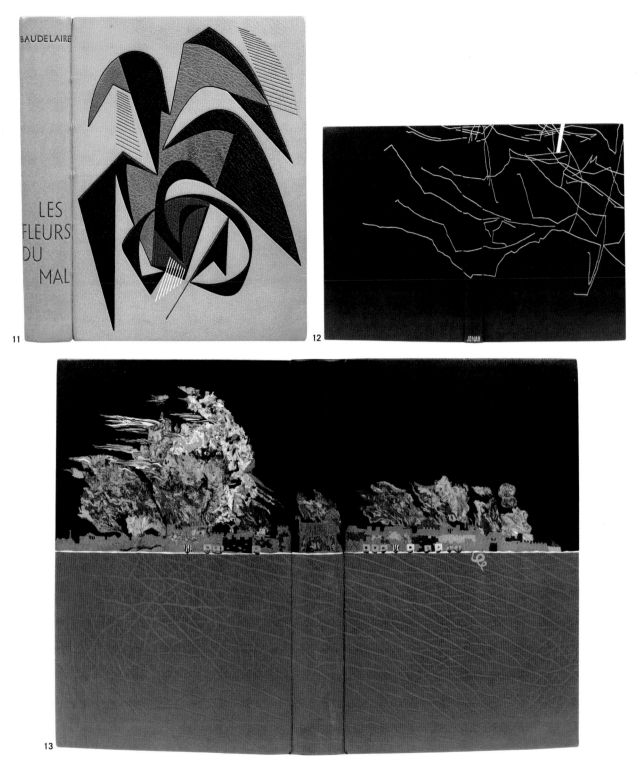

11   Edgar Mansfield. Charles Baudelaire. *Les Fleurs du Mal*. Paris, 1923. Illustrations by Raphael Drouart. Yellow goatskin, covers with abstract design of onlaid coloured goatskin tooled in blind, black, red, and white. 1959. **£5,000–7,000/$8,000–11,200**

12   Ivor Robinson. *The Book of Jonah*. Clover Hill, 1979. Wood-engraved illustrations by David Jones. Limited to 100 copies. Contemporary black goatskin with overall abstract design tooled

in gilt, with small white leather onlay on upper cover. **£2,000–3,000/ $3,200–4,800**

13   Philip Smith. Homer. *Homerou poiesis*. Munich, Bremer Press, 1923–1923. Two volumes. Limited to 615 copies. Contemporary morocco in shades of blue, with coloured and crushed morocco onlays depicting Troy in flames and Odysseus' travels at sea. **£20,000–30,000/$32,000–48,000**

Bookbinding in France during the 1920s and 1930s was reaching new heights of technique and artistry and eventually this began to reverberate throughout the English and American binding world. The hand-bound book was no longer a practical object but had become an artistic luxury. Pierre Legrain was undoubtedly the originator of contemporary binding design in that he was able to adapt his style to the book he was binding – Legrain's design consciously expressed the essence of the book. He died in 1929 after little more than ten years' intense creative activity, but his influence spread throughout France and the rest of the world.

Although he had had some impact on a few of the Gregynog Press designs, Pierre Legrain's expressive design, as opposed to pattern-making, did not achieve prominence in the education of binders until 1948, when Edgar Mansfield began teaching at the London School of Printing. Edgar Mansfield was born in 1907 and trained under William Matthews at the Central School of Arts and Crafts. He was first and foremost an artist and then a highly accomplished craftsman whose influence on contemporary binding should not be underestimated. He studied and solved problems of onlaying and inlaying leathers of varying shape, colour, and texture; he cut his own tools; he invented techniques whereby the grain of the leather was heightened; he worked with asymmetry and with pictorial designs that often incorporated lettering; he used continuous, intertwining lines and three-dimensional sculpted shapes; and he taught or influenced many of the most exciting contemporary binders working today. His aim was to bring "the philosophy and experience of a creative artist to the technique of the craft, and add one new dimension – the active interplay between expressive creative design, and potentially creative and expressive techniques and media". He was President of the Guild of Contemporary Bookbinders from 1955 until 1968 and taught at the London College of Printing until 1967. The Guild organized major exhibitions in the UK and throughout Europe and the USA, which attracted strong interest in the craft and modern design.

William Matthews, born in 1898, began his training at the age of 13 at the Central School of Arts and Crafts, setting up on his own in 1926. One of the greatest craftsmen of the 20th century, he trained several of the best contemporary binders, including Edgar Mansfield, Roger Powell, and Bernard Middleton. His gold tooling and lettering are particularly skilled, and just prior to his death in 1977 he was awarded the insignia of the City and Guilds Institute of London, the first time it had been awarded to a bookbinder.

His pupil Roger Powell, born in 1896, was also taught by Douglas Cockerell at the Central School, and he himself taught the craft at the Royal College of Art from 1943 to 1956. He was particularly interested in the structure of the book and he worked on the rebinding of many vellum manuscripts. Douglas Cockerell's son, Sydney, was also taught by his father and he too taught at the Royal College of Art. He wrote several books and undertook research into and development of marbled papers. He bound several fine works in vellum, working with the Glasgow-based calligrapher Joan Tebbutt. She would design the binding and carry out the lettering and black ink-work, and Cockerell would finish the gold tooling.

Elizabeth Greenhill, born in 1907, was one of the foremost women binders of the century. She was introduced to binding by Roger Powell's father, and studied in Paris with Pierre Legrain and in England with Douglas Cockerell and William Matthews. Initially working with restoration, she turned exclusively to designing fine bindings for commission and became President of the Designer Bookbinders.

Ivor Robinson, born in 1924, taught binding at the London College of Printing where he was greatly influenced by Edgar Mansfield and his ideas on binding as an expressive art. He was the first president of the Designer Bookbinders from 1968 until 1973 and one of the most important binders working in the latter part of the century.

One of the most original and accomplished of contemporary binders is C. Philip Smith, who was born in 1928 and studied under Roger Powell. Setting up on his own in 1961, he is renowned for experimenting with new techniques, structures, and feathered and tucked onlays, especially marbled inlaid leather. He is known particularly for his expressive bindings for J.R.R. Tolkien's *The Lord of the Rings*, notably his book walls comprising several copies of the same book. These book walls create a series of interlocking images: each book has its own individual design, and when the covers of the whole group are placed together in a display case, two further images are revealed.

The second half of the 20th century has seen a wealth of exciting bindings commissioned by collectors and bookdealers, and several societies have been set up to bring their work to the attention of the public. The most important is the Designer Bookbinders, who organize exhibitions and competitions, which is "devoted to the maintenance and improvement of standards in design and craft in bookbinding". Formed in 1968 as a result as internal change within the Guild of Contemporary Bookbinders, it continues to promote hand bookbinding. From 1991, its Fellows have been commissioned to bind the shortlisted Booker Prize novels for presentation to the authors. Other contemporary binders whose work is worth looking for are Sally Lou Smith, Michael Wilcox, Jeff Clements, James Brockman, Trevor Jones, and Jean Gunner.

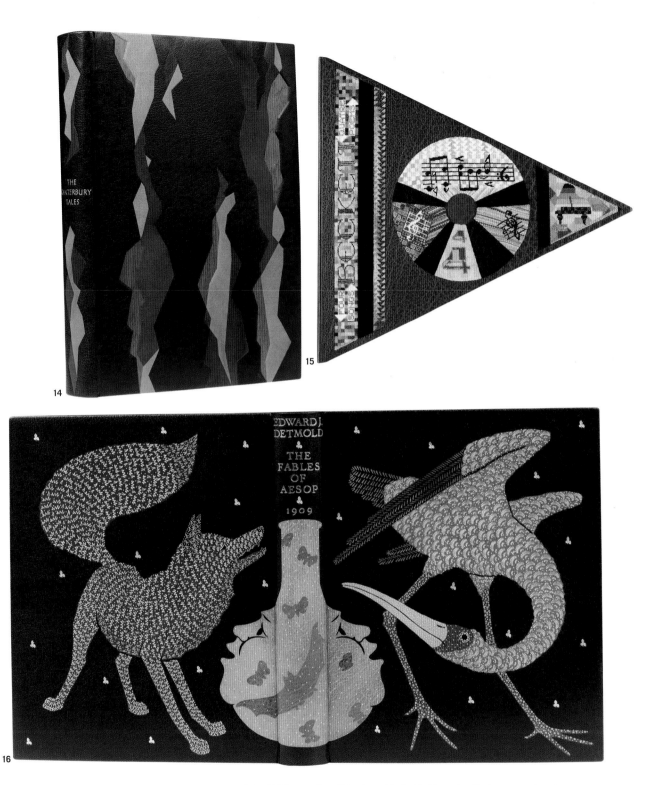

14 Sally Lou Smith. Geoffrey Chaucer. *The Canterbury Tales*. 1972. Etched plates by Elizabeth Frink. Limited to 200 copies. Contemporary black morocco over polished oak boards with geometric design of coloured morocco onlays incorporating the oak, tooled in gilt. **£25,000–30,000/$40,000–48,000**

15 Jill Tarlau and Antonio Perez Noriega. Samuel Beckett. *Quatre Poèmes*. New York, 1986. Etchings of musical notation after Bun-Ching Lam. Limited to 60 copies. Contemporary American binding of purple morocco with inlays of coloured morocco, veneer, and needlepoint. **£25,000–30,000/$40,000–48,000**

16 Michael Wilcox. Aesop. *The Fables of Aesop*. 1909. Coloured plates by Edward Detmold. Limited to 750 copies. Black morocco with large inlaid coloured morocco designs of a crane, fox, and a drinking vessel tooled in gilt. 1983. **£8,000–12,000/$12,800–19,200**

Glossary

Any specialized area of knowledge will have its own words and phrases which can mean little or nothing until explained. For the book-collector such words quickly pass into everyday terminology. Useful guides are John Carter's *ABC for Book Collectors* (7th edition, 1994), a personal view from one of the great book-trade names, still invaluable and widely used, even by those in the trade. Another guide is Jean Peters' *The Bookman's Glossary* (6th edition, 1983).

Cross references to other entries in the glossary are printed in SMALL CAPITAL LETTERS.

aquatint A process of engraving.

armorial Being stamped with the arms of a previous owner, usually a binding.

association copy Early ownership is associated with the author.

autograph Anything written in the hand of the author (see HOLOGRAPH).

bibliography 1. The history and scientific description of a book; 2. a list of books on a particular subject or by an author for further reading, arranged alphabetically, chronologically or by other means.

blank An unprinted LEAF forming part of the original book.

blind-tooled Decorative impression on book covers made without gold or colour.

browning Brown patches caused by damp reacting with acid in paper (see FOXING and SPOTTING).

calf A type of smooth, polished leather, made from the hide of a calf.

called for An indication of the completeness of a book according to a particular bibliographer, and not necessarily accepted alsewhere.

cancel Any part of a book substituted for what was originally printed, often the result of a printing error or, in the case of a "cancel title", a later edition with a new TITLE-PAGE inserted.

case, cased 1. A ready-made box for the protection of a book, a slipcase, or SOLANDER CASE; 2. a form of machined cloth binding made in quantity.

catchword A word printed in the bottom right-hand corner of a PAGE below the last line of text, which duplicates the first word over the page, used as a binder's aid.

chain lines Widely spaced lines, normally vertical, faintly visible in the texture of hand-made paper, resulting from the wire mesh in the papermaker's tray.

cloth Of binding: usually linen (buckram), silk or cotton, used from the 1820s.

collate 1. To check the physical completeness of a book; 2. to gather the SHEETS for binding.

collotype A photographic process of illustration, in use from the 1870s.

colophon A note at the end of the book giving details of printing, place, date etc.

commission A bookseller who buys at auction, or privately, on behalf of a customer, is "buying on commission" and will usually charge a fee of 10 per cent.

contemporary Of date: in terms of binding or colouring, this will mean within a decade, or more loosely a quarter of a century, from the date of publication.

corrigenda Corrections to the text noted on slips of paper inserted after publication (see ERRATA).

cropped Of margins: heavily trimmed, often with loss of text or illustration.

crushed Of MOROCCO: heavily pressed or rolled so there is no evidence of GRAIN.

deckle Of edges: rough and untrimmed edges of hand-made paper.

dentelles Decoration on bindings, a gilt border with a lacy pattern, usually on the inside edges of the leather where it is turned over the board.

device Trademark used by a printer or publisher on the TITLE PAGE or COLOPHON.

diced Of leather: stamped or ruled into a pattern of diamond squares.

disbound Books or pamphlets removed from a composite volume.

doublure Inside lining of a book made of leather or silk rather than paper.

drop title/dropped-head title Indicates no TITLE PAGE, the title being placed at the head of the first PAGE of text.

dry-point Form of ENGRAVING, with a more blurred outline than a normal engraving.

dust-jacket/wrapper Protective cover on modern books, used from the 1830s.

edition The total number of copies of a book printed from one setting of type.

endpaper The double LEAVES attached to the inside of the binding at the beginning and end. That pasted inside the cover is known as the paste-down and the other the free endpaper.

engraving A process of illustration (see Original Illustration Processes, pp.17–18).

errata Errors in the printing of a book noted on a separate slip of paper (see CORRIGENDA).

etching A process of illustration (see Original Illustration Processes, pp.17–18).

extra-illustrated Having additional illustrations inserted, often portraits or views.

facsimile An exact reproduction of an original LEAF or entire book.

fleuron A printer's ornament, originally flower-shaped.

footnote A descriptive note in a catalogue after the main BIBLIOGRAPHICAL entry.

fore-edge The front or outer edge of the PAGES of a book. Occasionally this will have a fore-edge painting: that is, a painting seen by fanning the pages, the edges of which are gilded after being painted.

format Size and shape of a book.

fount, font A set of type created to one design.

foxing Brown spots or stains in paper caused by metallic or chemical impurities (see BROWNING and SPOTTING).

frontispiece Illustration facing the TITLE PAGE.

gathering A single group of LEAVES formed by folding one SHEET of paper to the required size (see QUIRE).

gauffered GILT EDGES decorated by heated tools.

gilt edges (g.e.) The edges of a book decorated with gold leaf before binding (see TOP EDGE GILT).

grain Pattern on leather.

guard Strip of paper, or stub, which is pasted to the edge of a PLATE, or other LEAF printed separately, to ensure its secure insertion in the book.

half-title The LEAF before the TITLE PAGE, usually printed only with the book's title.

half-tone A form of illustration printed from an image photographed through a screen composed of small dots.

hand-coloured Watercolour added by hand to a printed illustration.

headband Silk band at the head and foot of the SPINE.

head-piece Decoration at the beginning of a chapter.

hinge The inside junction of the board with the back of the book (the SPINE).

historiated Of initials, capitals or borders: decoration of figures of men and animals added to manuscripts or early books.

holograph Entirely in the hand of the author; similar to AUTOGRAPH.

illuminated Decoration by hand in gold, silver, and colours, usually of flowers and similar designs; also printed books imitating the style.

impression The number of copies of a book printed at one time from one setting of type; a further impression could be printed from the same setting at a later date, and these would then be the first and second impressions of the first EDITION.

imprint The details of printing/publishing (name, place, and date) usually at the foot of the TITLE-PAGE. Where the printer is not the publisher the printer's details may appear elsewhere.

inlay Insertion of coloured leather into the main skin of the binding.

inscribed Added to by hand, usually indicating ownership or PRESENTATION. "Inscribed by the author" indicates the author has autographed the book.

issue Part of an EDITION, corrections or rearrangements to the text having been made.

Japanese vellum A type of glossy cream paper also known as japon, often used in the printing of de-luxe EDITIONs.

joint The outside junction of the board with the back of the book (the SPINE).

laid down Mounted on a stronger sheet of paper, usually an illustration or a damaged LEAF which has been removed.

laid paper Paper, made by machine or hand, exhibiting a pattern of crossed lines (see CHAIN LINES and WIRE LINES).

large-paper copy One of a small number of special copies of an EDITION printed on larger SHEETS of paper, generally producing wider margins.

leaf (leaves) The single piece of paper comprising two PAGES, one the front and one the back.

Levant Of MOROCCO: high-grade, loose-grained, and usually highly polished.

limited edition An EDITION limited to a stated number of copies.

limp A binding of VELLUM, leather or cloth not backed by boards.

line-block A process of photographically reproducing a drawing.

lithograph A form of illustration (see Original Illustration Processes, pp.17–18).

loose LEAVES or PLATES that are wholly or partly detached from the binding.

make-up The practice, now frowned upon, of making up or completing a book found to be lacking LEAVES or PLATES.

marbled Of paper: decorated by inserting the paper into a bath of water, on the surface of which are colours combed into a pattern.

misbound Having some LEAVES or PLATES bound in the wrong order.

morocco Tanned goatskin used for binding.

mottled An effect given to CALF by staining the leather with flecks of acid.

no date (n.d.) After further enquiry no date of publication can be found.

Niger Of MOROCCO: a soft skin with a variable GRAIN, naturally a buff colour.

not subject to return Used by auctioneers after a catalogue description to indicate that the book has not been COLLATED and could possibly be incomplete (see WITH ALL FAULTS).

offset Transfer of ink or discolouration from an illustration or text opposite.

original As published; for example, "original cloth".

out of series An unnumbered book in an EDITION which is otherwise limited and numbered.

page One side of a LEAF.

pagination Consecutive numbering of PAGES.

parchment The inner piece of the split skin of a sheep, prepared for use for writing, printing, and binding, an inferior VELLUM.

part One instalment of a book issued in instalments, popular in the 19th century.

perfect Complete as originally published.

photogravure A form of reproducing an illustration photographically from a relief-printed metal PLATE.

pigskin A type of leather: a rugged skin with a distinctive GRAIN not usually decorated.

pirated An EDITION published without permission of or payment to the author.

plate 1. A full-page illustration printed separately from the body of the text; 2. a metal or plastic cast of a typeset PAGE from which SHEETS are printed; 3. an engraved piece of metal for printing from.

plate mark The indented mark at the edge of an ENGRAVING left by the metal PLATE.

pochoir Colour added by hand to illustrations through STENCILs, used especially in France and

England in the 1920s and 1930s.

point Any distinguishing feature noted in a BIBLIOGRAPHY used in the identification of one ISSUE from another.

preliminaries All the LEAVES, blank or printed, before the main body of the text begins, including the TITLE PAGE and FRONTISPIECE.

presentation copy A book inscribed and presented, usually by the author, to someone else.

provenance The previous history and ownership of a particular book.

proof Advance or trial IMPRESSION of text or illustrations.

quarter-bound The SPINE is covered with leather of some kind; also described as "CALF-backed boards".

quire A group of LEAVES folded together before binding (see SIGNATURE, GATHERING).

rag paper Paper made from a pulp of rags.

rebacked The SPINE of a book has been replaced due to wear and tear, usually with a material similar to the original.

recto The front of a LEAF, that is, the right-hand page of an open book (see VERSO).

roan A thin, soft sheepskin used as a cheap substitute for MOROCCO.

roll Of binding: 1. a tool in the form of a wheel with a continuous or repeated design engraved on the edge; 2. the impression of this rolled design on the cover.

rubbed Indicating some wear to a binding, in particular the SPINE, JOINTS, corners or edges (collectively called the extremities).

rubricated Having headings to chapters or initial capital letters to paragraphs and elsewhere added in red, either printed or by hand.

runner One who sells books but has no stock, acting as a middleman between one dealer and another.

running head/title The title of a book or chapter printed at the top of each PAGE.

Russia A durable type of leather, with a rich, smooth finish, originally scented and often decorated (see DICED).

sheet The large piece of paper which when folded gives a GATHERING of folios.

signature The numbers and letters at the bottom of a PAGE indicating the correct sequence of binding. Sometimes each GATHERING is referred to as the signature.

solander case A type of protective box which will open up with at least one side falling flat.

sophisticated A polite way of indicating that a book has been doctored or MADE UP in some manner, such as with the insertion of a LEAF in FACSIMILE.

spine the back of the book joining the upper and lower covers.

spotting Brown spots in paper caused by impurites (see FOXING AND BROWNING).

sprinkled Of CALF and the edges of LEAVES: coloured with small specks.

sprung A book that has a weak SPINE and PAGES that are beginning to come loose.

state Of text and illustrations: indicating a variant form of a page resulting from alteration made during the printing process.

stencil Usually a thin sheet of metal or card from which a design has been cut out. The stencil is laid on the paper and colour applied, a different stencil being used for each colour.

stereotype A mould is taken of the original type-setting of a PAGE of text, cast in metal as one solid PLATE and used to print subsequent EDITIONS.

tall A book that has had the head and tail margins only lightly trimmed.

tipped-in Lightly attached at the inside or top edge, usually of a PLATE, or referring to the

addition of associated material such as an AUTOGRAPH letter.

title page The preliminary PAGE supplying details of title, author, date, and publisher.

top edge gilt (t.e.g.) The top edge of a book has been gilded, the other edges usually left UNCUT.

tree Of CALF: a decorative pattern, reminiscent of the trunk of a tree, caused by a chemical reaction, and usually highly polished.

typography The art and skill of designing printed matter, especially words.

unbound Never having had covers.

uncut Of paper: the rough edges have not been trimmed by the binder.

uniform Of books in sets: bound in the same style.

unopened The folded LEAVES of a book are still joined along the upper or outer edges.

unsophisticated Genuine and unrestored (see SOPHISTICATED).

variant A copy of a book which appears to differ from other copies in some manner.

vellum The degreased skin of a calf used for writing, printing, and binding.

verso The back of a LEAF, in other words, the left-hand PAGE of an open book (see RECTO).

vignette Small picture or design used as decoration on the TITLE PAGE or at the head or foot of a chapter or section.

volume The physical object; one book can comprise several volumes.

watermark Papermaker's trademark or date incorporated in the wire mesh of the tray, which becomes visible in the paper when held up to the light. Often used to determine the date of books with no printed date.

wire lines Of paper: the close-set lines that run at right-angles to the CHAIN LINES.

with all faults (w.a.f.) A warning sign signifying that even if a book is incomplete, the seller has no legal obligation to take it back once purchased (see NOT SUBJECT TO RETURN).

woodcut A form of illustration (see Original Illustration Processes, pp.17–18).

wood-engraving A form of illustration (see Original Illustration Processes, pp.17–18).

wove paper A form of paper used from about 1757 showing no lines, being made on a woven mesh of wires.

wrappers Paper covers of a book, which are plain, printed or marbled.

Further Reading

Many of the following books have been used as references for this guide. For each subject there will be many more specific bibliographies than it is possible to list here. A useful guide for earlier publications is T. Besterman's *A World Bibliography of Bibliographies*, Lausanne, 1965–6. Subscribers to www.worldbookdealers.com can access a comprehensive range of bibliographies. Some of the books listed are in print, others have been reprinted, but the majority will have to be acquired second-hand. Auction catalogues and bookseller's catalogues will often list appropriate works of reference.

Price Guides

American Book Prices Current, Washington, prices compiled from auctions, available as a CD-ROM

Joseph Connolly, *Collecting Modern First Editions*, 1988

Crispin Jackson, *Collecting Children's Books*, 2001

R.B. Russell, *Guide to First Edition Prices, 2002–2003*, 2001, prices compiled from booksellers' catalogues

Journals

Antiquarian Book Review, monthly

Antiques Trade Gazette, book pages, weekly

The Book and Magazine Collector, monthly

The Book Collector, quarterly

General Introduction

Nicholas Barker, *Treasures of the British Library*, 1988

Philippa Bernard, ed. *Antiquarian Books: a companion for booksellers, librarians and collectors*, 1994

John Carter, *Taste and Technique in Book Collecting*, 3rd impression, 1970

John Carter and Percy Muir, *Printing and the Mind of Man*, 2nd revised edition, 1983

Jean Peters, ed. *Collectible Books: some new paths*, New York, 1979

Catherine Porter, *Miller's Collecting Books*, 1998

O.F. Snelling, *Rare Books and Rarer People*, 1982

Alan Thomas, *Great Books and Book Collectors*, 1975

Grant Uden, *Understanding Book Collecting*, 2nd edition, 1995

Bibliographical Aids and Glossaries

Fredson Bowles, *Principles of Bibliographical Description*, 1994

John Carter, *ABC for Book Collectors*, 7th edition, 1994

Philip Gaskell, *An Introduction to Bibliography*, 1972

Jean Peters, *The Bookman's Glossary*, 6th edition, 1983

English and American Literature

Sylvia Beach, *Shakespeare and Company*, New York, 1956

Malcolm Bradbury, *The Modern British Novel, 1878–2001*, 2001

Jacob Blanck, *A Bibliography of American*

Literature, New Haven, 1955–1983, 7 volumes

Carmen Callil and Colm Toibin, *The Modern Library: the 200 best novels in English since 1950*, 2000

Cyril Connolly, *100 Key Books of the Modern Movement from England, France and America, 1880–1950*, 1986

Joan Crane, *Robert Frost: a descriptive catalogue*, Charlottesville, 1974

Margaret Drabble, ed., *Oxford Companion to English Literature*, new edition,1985

Leon Edel and Dan H. Laurence, *A Bibliography of Henry James*, 1961

R. Federman and J. Fletcher, *Samuel Beckett, his Works and his Critics*, Berkeley, 1970

Audre Hanneman, *Ernest Hemmingway*, Princeton, 1967

Donald Gallup, *T.S. Eliot: a bibliography*, New York, 1969

Donald Gallup, *Ezra Pound: a bibliography*, New York, 1969

Adrian H. Goldstone and John R. Payne, *John Steinbeck: a bibliographical catalogue of the Adrian H. Goldstone Collection*, Austin, n.d.

Richard Lancelyn Green and John Michael Gibson, *A Bibliography of A. Conan Doyle*, 1983

Andre Hanneman, *Ernest Hemingway: a comprehensive bibliography*, Princeton, 1967–1975

James D. Hart, ed., *Oxford Companion to American Literature*, 4th edition, New York, 1965

John Hayward, *English Poetry*, 1950

B.J. Kirkpatrick, *E.M. Forster*, 1965

B.J. Kirkpatrick, *A Bibliography of Virginia Woolf*, 3rd edition, 1989

John S. Van E. Kohn, *First Books by American Authors, 1765–1964; More First Books by American Authors, 1727–1971*, Seven Gables Bookshop, 1965–1972

Stanley J. Kunitz and Howard Haycraft, eds, *Twentieth Century Authors*, New York, 1942–1955

Linton R. Massey, *William Faulkner*, Virginia, 1968

Eileen McIlvaine, et al. *P.G. Wodehouse: a comprehensive bibliography and checklist*, New York, 1990

Colonel W.F. Prideaux, *A Bibliography of the Works of Robert Louis Stevenson*, 1917

Richard Little Purdy, *Thomas Hardy: a bibliographical study*, 2nd edition, 1979

Ellery Queen [Fred Dannay and Manny Lee], *Queen's Quorum: a history of the detective-crime short story as revealed by the 125 most important books published in*

this field, 1845–1967, New York, 1969

David A. Randall, ed., *Science Fiction and Fantasy*, Bloomington, 1975

W. Roberts, *A Bibliography of D.H. Lawrence*, 1963

Keith Sagar and Stephen Tabor, *Ted Hughes: a bibliography, 1946–1980*, 1983

Andrew Sanders, *The Short Oxford History of English Literature*, 2nd edition, 2000

John Slocum and Herbert Cahoon, *A Bibliography of James Joyce*, New Haven, 1953

James McG. Stewart, *Rudyard Kipling: a bibliographical catalogue*, Toronto, 1959

R.A. Wobbe, *Graham Greene: a bibliography and guide to research*, New York, 1979

Children's Books

Jacob Blanck, *Peter Parley to Penrod*, New York, 1956

Tessa Chester and J. Irene Whalley, *A History of Children's Book Illustration*, 1988

Wayne G. Hammond and Douglas A. Anderson, *J.R.R. Tolkien: a descriptive bibliography*, 1993

Peter Hanff and Douglas Greene, *Bibliography Oziana: a concise bibliographical checklist of the Oz books*, New York, 1969

Anne Stevenson Hobbs and Joyce Irene Whalley, *Beatrix Potter: the V&A collection*, 2nd edition, 1988

Leslie Linder, *A History of the Writings of Beatrix Potter*, 1971

Gertrude C.E. Masse, *A Bibliography of First Editions of Books Illustrated by Walter Crane*, 1923

Iona and Peter Opie, *The Classic Fairy Tales*, 1974

Thomas Schuster and Rodney Engen, *Printed Kate Greenaway: a catalogue raisonné*, 1986

Victor Watson, ed., *The Cambridge Guide to Children's Books in English*, 2001

Sidney Herbert Williams, Falconer Madan, Roger Lancelyn Green and Denis Crutch, *The Lewis Carroll Handbook*, new edition, 1979

Illustrated Books

David Bland, *The Illustration of Books*, 2nd edition, 1953; *A History of Book Illustration*, 1969

Albert Garrett, *British Wood Engraving of the 20th Century*, 1980

Eleanor M. Garvey and Philip Hofer, *The Artist and the Book, 1860–1960*, New York, 1982

Pat Gilmour, *Artists at Curwen*, 1977

Edward Hodnett, *Five Centuries of Book Illustration*, 1988

Alan Horne, *The Dictionary of 20th Century British Book Illustrators*, 1994

Simon Houfe, *The Dictionary of British Book*

Illustrators and Caricaturists, 1800–1914, 1978

Ann Conolly Hughey, *Edmund Dulac: his book illustrations*, Maryland, 1995

Mark Samuels Lasner, *A Selective Checklist of the Published Work of Aubrey Beardsley*, Boston, 1995

John Lewis, *The 20th Century Book*, 2nd edition, 1984

Richard Riall, *A New Bibliography of Arthur Rackham*, 1994

Christopher Skelton, *The Engravings of Eric Gill*, 1983

Fine Printing and Typography

Cock-a-Hoop: a bibliography of the Golden Cockerel Press, January 1950–1961, December 1962

Tony Appleton, *The Writings of Stanley Morison*, 1976

Alan Bartram, *Five Hundred Years of Book Design*, 2001

John Dreyfus, *A History of the Nonesuch Press*, 1981

Colin Franklin, *The Private Presses*, 1990

Bibliography of the Golden Cockerel Press, 1921–1949, 1975

Dorothy Harrop, *A History of the Gregynog Press*, 1980

C.H.St.J. Hornby, *Ashendene Press, Bibliography*, 1935

Giovanni Mardersteig, *The Officina Bodoni, Verona*, 1980

Ruari McLean, *Typography*, 1980

Linda Parry, ed., *William Morris*, 2nd edition, 1996

William S. Peterson, *A Bibliography of the Kelmscott Press*, 1984

Will Ransom, *Private Presses and their Books*, New York, 1929

Herbert Spencer, *Pioneers of Modern Typography*, 3rd edition, 1990

Binding

Frank Broomhead, *The Zaehnsdorfs*, 1986

Bernadett Callery and Elizabeth Mosimann, eds, *The Tradition of Fine Bookbinding in the Twentieth Century*, Pittsburgh, 1979

Mirjam Foot, *The History of Decorated Bookbindings in England*, 1992

Edgar Mansfield, *Modern Design in Bookbinding*, 1966

Bernard Middleton, *A History of English Craft Bookbinding Techniques*, 1988

Marian Tidcombe, *The Doves Bindery*, 1991; *The Bookbindings of T.J. Cobden-Sanderson*, 1984; *Women Bookbinders, 1880–1920*, 1996

Useful Addresses

Most reputable booksellers will be a member of one of their national associations: the main ones are listed below. For other countries contact ILAB, who will provide details of the relevant association. Each association will have a code of rules to determine the conduct of its members.

The Antiquarian Booksellers' Association (ABA). Sackville House, 40 Piccadilly, London W1J 0DR. www.ABAinternational.com. The association publishes an annual handbook containing a glossary and all members have to abide by the "ABA Code of Good Practice" which is printed in the handbook.
Provincial Booksellers' Fairs Association (PBFA). The Old Coach House, 16 Melbourn Street, Royston, Herts SG8 7BZ. www.pbfa.org.
Antiquarian Booksellers' Association of America (ABAA). 20 West 44th Street, New York, NY 10036-6604, USA. www.abaa.org.
International League of Antiquarian Booksellers (ILAB). Secretary: Helen R. Kahn, P.O. Box 323, Victoria Station, Montreal, Quebec H3Z 2VB, Canada.

Private Libraries Association. Ravelston, South View Road, Pinner, Middlesex HA5 3YD. International society of book-collectors which publishes a quarterly journal.

Multi-dealer web-sites

Advanced Book Exchange www.abebooks.com
Biblion www.biblion.com
Bibliopoly www.bibliopoly.com
Bookfinder www.bookfinder.com
World Book Dealers www.worldbookdealers.com

Auction web-sites

Ebay www.ebay.com
Sothebys www.sothebys.com
Christie's www.christies.com
ICollector www.icollector.com
Bonhams www.bonhams.com
Swann Galleries www.swanngalleries.com

Index

Acknowledgments

The book would not have been possible without the help of Sotheby's, who gave us permission to use photographs from their archives, and in particular of my colleagues Peter Selley, Dr Philip W. Errington, and Wayne Williams.

Also, thank you to Ken Adlard, Kim Ridge, and Natasha Porter-Ridge.

Picture Credits

The following kindly lent books from their stock for photography or allowed us to use photographs from their archives: Christie's, Bertram Rota Ltd, Peter Harrington Antiquarian Bookseller, Maggs Bros Ltd, Henry Sotheran, and Nigel Williams Rare Books.

Key: t top b bottom c centre r right l left OPG Octopus Publishing Group

Sotheby's Back cover l, c & r The Arthur Rackham pictures are reproduced with the kind permission of his family, 1, 3, 7r, 8l & r, 11t, ct & cb, 21tl & bl, 22, 23 Private Collection, 24tl, tr, c, bl & br © Estate of Eric Ravilious 2003. All Rights Reserved, DACS, 25tl, tc, tr & bc, 26l, c & r, 27l & r, 28l, 29l & r, 33l & c, 34l, c & r, 37t, cl, cr, bl The dust jacket was designed by Evelyn Waugh and is reproduced by permission of PFD, on behalf of The Estate of Laura Waugh & br, 39l, c & r, 45l, 47cr, bl & br, 48tl, 51tl, tr & cl, 54l, c & r, 57tl & cl, 58cr & br, 64l & r, 65t, 66c, 73tl, cl & c, 74br, 75t & c, 76l & r, 77t, 78l & c, 79t, c & b, 80tl & tr, 81r, 82l & r The Arthur Rackham pictures are reproduced with the kind permission of his family, 83tl, bl, c & r, 84l & r, 85l, c & r, 86l & r, 87tl, tr, c & b, 89tl, 90tr, 92c The Arthur Rackham pictures are reproduced with the kind permission of his family, 93t & b, 94l, c & r, 95l, c Illustration by Pauline Baynes taken from The Last Battle by C S Lewis © C S Lewis Pte Ltd 1956 & r jacket art by Pauline Baynes © C S Lewis Pte Ltd. Illustrations reprinted by permission, 96l, c & r, 101tl, c, cr & bl, 102t, c & bl, 103l & r, 104t Christmas Morning by William Nicholson from The Velveteen Rabbit by Margery Williams (William Heinemann 1922)© Elizabeth Banks & c, 106br, 108t Maxfield Parrish (R)/ Licensed by ASAP and VAGA, New York/DACS, London 2003, 110r, 111b, 114r, 115r, 116r, 116l & 117t, c & b The Arthur Rackham pictures are reproduced with the kind permission of his family & r, 118t, c & b, 119t, c & b, 120l & c, 121l Barmaid from London Types by William Nicholson (William Heinemann, 1898)© Elizabeth Banks & r, 122l & r, 123t & b, 125tl & tr © ADAGP, Paris and DACS, London 2003, 126r © Estate of Eric Ravilious 2003. All Rights Reserved, DACS, 127l & c, 129tl & tr © Estate of Rex Whistler 2003. All Rights reserved, DACS, 131t, c & b, 132, 133l & r, 135t, c © Estate of Gwen Raverat 2003. All Rights Reserved, DACS & b, 136, 137l, c & r, 138, 139l & r, 144l & r, 145l & r, 147tl, tc, tr, cl, cr & b, 149tr & b, 151tl, tr & b; **Christie's Images** 5, 6, 7l, 9t & b, 11b, 24bc, 28c & r, 30l, 31t & b, 35t & b, 38l, c & r, 40t & b, 41l, c & r, 43cr & b, 51bl & br, 52t & b, 57cr & tr, 58 cl & bl, 63b, 65b, 66l, 71cl, 77b, 84c, 91tl, tr, bl & br Line illustrations by E H Shepard copyright under the Berne Convention/reproduced by kind permission of Curtis Brown Ltd, London, 109c & b, 112t; **OPG/Ken Adlard** Front Cover, 13, 15t, c & b, 17tl, tr, cr, bl & br, 18t, ct, cb & b, 25bl & 63l Samuel French & br, 32l & r, 33r, 43tl, tr & cl, 44l, tr & br, 45c & r, 47tl, tc, tr & cl, 48tr & bl, 51c & cr, 53t & c, 55t, c & b, 57b, 58tl, tc & tr © The Stein Estate, 61tl, tr, cl, cr, bl & br, 63tc, tr, c & cr, 66r, 67l, c & r, 68l, c, r & b, 69l, c & r, 71tl, tc, tr, c, cr & b, 73tc, tr, c & br, 74t, cl, cr & bl, 75bl & br, 78r, 80bl & br, 81l & c, 86c, 89tr, bl & br Express Newspapers, 90cr, bl & br, 92t & b, 97l, c & r, 98t, c & b, 99tl, tr, c & b reproduced by kind permission of Enid Blyton Ltd (a Chorion Company), 101tr, cl & br, 104b The Estate of Edward Bawden, 105t, c & b, 106tl, tr, cl, crt, crb, & bl, 108c & b, 109t, 110l & c, 111t & c, 112b, 113l & r Haunted House © Jan Pie?kowski 1979 (Heinemann)114l, 115l, 116c, 120r, 121c, 122 c, 125cl & cr cover illustration by William Nicholson from Moss and Feather by W H Davies (Ariel Poems 1928)© Elizabeth Banks & b, 126l & c The Estate of Edward Bawden, 127r, 129cl © Courtesy of the artist's estate/Bridgeman Art Library, cr Reproduced by permission of The Henry Moore Foundation, bl & br, 130l, c & r, 139c, 140, 141l & r, 143t, cl, cr & b; **OPG/Time Ridley/Nigel Williams Rare Books** 48 cl; **OPG/Steve Tanner** 48br & 53b; **OPG/Ian Booth/Maggs Bros Ltd** 48cr; **Nigel Williams Rare Books** 21cr; **Peter Harrington Antiquarian Bookseller** 30r; **Maggs Bros Ltd** 149tl

Mitchell Beazley would like to thank the following publishers who have kindly given permission to publish copyright images:

Andersen Press Ltd 106tl Saving Sinbad! by Michael Foreman; **Andre Deutsch Ltd** 63cr Shrivings by Peter Shaffer; **Barefoot Books** 84l The Gigantic Turnip, illustrations © Niamh Sharkey (Barefoot Books 1998); **Bloomsbury Publications Plc** Reproduction permitted courtesy of Bloomsbury Publications Plc 23 Illustration © Thomas Taylor, 27r, 55t, 61tr, 96l & r Illustrations © Thomas Taylor & c Illustration © Cliff Wright; **Constable & Robinson Ltd** 57cl, 73tl & 78l; **Egmont Books Ltd** 89tl & 105b; **Faber & Faber** 25tl & tr, 43tl, tr & cl, 47tr & bl, 55c,

67c, 68c, r & b, 69c, 71tr & cr, 106bl, 125cr & br, 127l & r & 129tl; **Golden Cockerel Press Ltd** 24tr, 121r, 122c, 123t & b, 138 & 139l Courtesy of The Golden Cockerel Press Ltd; **Donald M Grant Publisher Inc** 110c Henry Eichner; **The Gregynog Press & The National Library of Wales** Images courtesy of The Gregynog Press & The National Library of Wales 122l, 137c & r; **Hachette Livre** 90cr; **Hamlyn** 73cl, 76l & r, 97c & 101cl; **Harcourt Inc** 57b copyright 1949 and renewed 1977 by Eudora Welty, reproduced by permission of Harcourt Brace & 51cl; **HarperCollins Publishers Inc** 90br, 110r & 112t; **HarperCollins Publishers Ltd** Reprinted by permission of HarperCollins Ltd back cover l & 79b © Agatha Christie 1937, 54c © Patrick O'Brian 1970, 55b © Frank McCourt 1996, 61bl © Arundhati Roy 1997, 79c © Agatha Christie 1938, 90l © Michael Bond 1979, 94c © Alan Garner 1965, 95l © J R R Tolkien 1937, 95c & r © C S Lewis 1952 & 102bl © Roald Dahl 1973; **Hodder & Stoughton Ltd** Reproduced by permission of Hodder & Stoughton Limited 74bl The Tailor of Panama by John le Carré, 92t Peter and Wendy by J M Barrie & b Peter Pan and Wendy by J M Barrie, 99tl Five Get Into Trouble by Enid Blyton & c Shock for the Secret Seven by Enid Blyton, 118t Stories by Hans Andersen & c Fairy Book illustrated by Edmund Dulac & 119t Hansel and Gretel by J L C and W C Grimm; **Houghton Mifflin** Reprinted by permission of Houghton Mifflin 30r cover from The Portrait of a Lady by Henry James (Boston: Houghton Mifflin, 1881) & 81c cover from The Old Patagonian Express by Paul Theroux (Boston: Houghton Mifflin 1979). All rights reserved; **Kingfisher Publications plc** Back cover r, 101br, 116l & 119c; **Macmillan Ltd** 58bl, 61cl & 78c, images reproduced by permission of **Macmillan Children's Books** 21r & 86r covers from The Jungle Book 1894 & The Second Jungle Book 1895 by Rudyard Kipling illustrated by J Lockwood Kipling 99b cover from The Island of Adventure by Enid Blyton 1944 illustrated by Stuart Tresilian, 114l cover from Goblin Market by Christina Rossetti 1893 illustrated by Laurence Housman & 119b illustration by Edward Detmold from Jungle Book by Rudyard Kipling 1903; **W W Norton & Company Inc** 58tl & 63tr; **The Old Stile Press** 143cr; **The Orion Publishing Group** 47cr, 67l, 74br, 80br, 94r, 115r, 117t, 122r & 131cl; **Oxford University Press** 98t & c & 104c; **The Penguin Group (UK)** 34c, 48bl, 61br, 63c, 73c, 106crb (Viking) © Janet & Allan Ahlberg 1987 & tr (Hamish Hamilton) © Raymond Briggs 1978 & 127c (Puffin) © Harold Curwen 1948; **Random House Group Ltd** 6, 7l, 8l, 11t & ct, 24c, 25bc, 26c & r, 27l, 31t, 32l & r, 33l, c & r, 37cl & br, 43cr, 44l, tr & br, 45l, c & r, 47tl, tc, cl & br, 48tl & br, 54l & r, 58cl, cr & br, 61tl & cl, 63tc, 64r, 69l, 71c & b, 73tr, 74t, cl & cr, 75t, c, bl & br, 79t, 80bl, 81r, 82r, 83tl, 86l © Alan Aldridge & c, 89tr, 97l, 103r, 106cl & crt, 112b, 115l, 116c & r, 117c & b, 120c, 121l, 129br © Bill Brandt, 130c © Mervyn Peake & 131t Illustration © Ralph Steadman. Used by permission of The Random House Group Ltd; **Random House Inc** Used by permission of Doubleday, Dell Publishing, Alfred A Knopf or Random House Children's Books, all imprints of Random House Inc 41l cover of The Sound and the Fury by William Faulkner published by Random House Inc © 1929, renewed 1957 by William Faulkner, 53t Alfred A Knopf, c cover of The Firm by John Grisham, Dell Publishing & b cover of Hell's Angels by Hunter S Thompson published by Random House Inc © 1966, renewed 1967 by Hunter S Thompson, 66r Alfred A Knopf, 73br cover of Pet Sematary by Stephen King, Doubleday, 77b & 78r Alfred A Knopf,102t & c, 106tr from The Snowman by Raymond Briggs © 1978 by Raymond Briggs, Random House Children's Books, 109t from How The Grinch Stole Christmas! By Dr. Seuss, © by Dr Seuss Enterprises, L P 1938, renewed 1965. Random House Children's Books, c from The 500 Hats of Bartholomew Cubbins by Dr Seuss, © by Dr Seuss Enterprises, L P 1938, renewed 1965. Random House Children's Books & b from And To Think That I Saw It On Mulberry Street by Dr Seuss, TM & © by Dr Seuss Enterprises, L P 1937, renewed 1965 Random House Children's Books; **Scholastic UK Ltd** All Rights Reserved. Reproduced by permission of Scholastic UK Ltd 25br & 105t; **Simon & Schuster Inc** Reprinted with the permission of Scribner (an imprint of Simon & Schuster Adult Publishing Group), Simon & Schuster Books for Young Readers (an imprint of Simon & Schuster Children's Books) or Simon & Schuster Inc 24cb & 40t cover for The Great Gatsby by F Scott Fitzgerald (New York: Scribner 1925), 39c cover for A Farewell to Arms by Ernest Hemingway (New York: Scribner 1929) Scribner & r cover from For Whom the Bell Tolls by Ernest Hemingway (New York: Scribner 1940), 40b cover for Tender is the Night by F Scott Fitzgerald (New York: Scribner 1934) 41r, 51tl cover for Catch 22 by Joseph Heller (New York: Simon & Schuster 1961) Simon & Schuster Adult Publishing Group, 85r © Brian Froud, 105c from Eloise in Paris by Kay Thompson, illustrated by Hilary Knight. Copyright 1957 Kay Thompson, copyright renewed © 1995 Kay Thompson, Simon & Schuster Books for Young Readers & 108t; **The Viking Press** 41c & 52t; **Thames and Hudson** 131b; **Walker Books Ltd** 106br cover illustration © 1990 Nicola Bayley taken from The Mousehole Cat written by Antonia Barber. Reproduced by permission of Walker Books Ltd London; **Frederick Warne & Co** 87tl © Frederick Warne & Co 1901, 87tr © Frederick Warne & Co 1902, 87c © Frederick Warne & Co 1907, 87b © Frederick Warne & Co 1911. All reproduced by permission of Frederick Warne & Co.